TOU[...]G THE [...]D

JOURNEYS IN THE NATURAL WORLD

BRIAN JACKMAN

BRUCE COLEMAN

First published in 2003 by
Bruce Coleman
16 Chiltern Business Village
Arundel Road
Uxbridge, UB8 2SN

Distributed by
NHBS Ltd
2–4 Wills Road
Totnes
Devon TQ9 5XN

British Library Cataloguing-in-Publication Data
A catalogue record for this book is available from the British Library.

ISBN 1 872842 04 6

Typeface used: Palatino.

Edited and designed by
D & N Publishing
Lambourn Woodlands, Hungerford, Berkshire.

Printed and bound in Great Britain by JW Arrowsmith Ltd, Bristol.

DEDICATION

For my grandchildren, Luca and Jude – the next generation.

How often have you taxed yourself with long journeys before sunrise and in the twilight? Do not despair, even though the search be long.

Translation of an inscription on an 18th-century ceremonial horn, Lamu, Kenya.

CONTENTS

CONTENTS

ACKNOWLEDGEMENTS

My greatest debt of gratitude goes to the distinguished list of national newspaper and magazine travel editors who have kindly allowed me to use the essays reproduced in this book. The essays span the years between 1988 and 2002 (please see the list below for details), and have not been updated since they first appeared.

Many people have supported me during that time, and none more so than Christine Walker at the *Sunday Times*, whose unstinting encouragement has been inspirational. At the *Daily Telegraph* and *Sunday Telegraph* I would like to thank Gill Charlton and also Graham Boynton, her successor, who shares my passion for Africa. My sincere thanks also go to Cath Urquhart at *The Times*, Charlie Burgess at the *Guardian*, Sarah Miller, editor of *Condé Nast Traveller*, and Bridget Swann at *Dorset* magazine.

First in line for thanks to those who made this book possible is Bruce Coleman, my publisher, who dreamed up the idea and had the faith to make it work. I am also grateful to David Price-Goodfellow and Susi Bailey for their editing skills, and to Mike Unwin for his evocative illustrations. And, as always, my thanks also go to Mike Shaw, my literary agent at Curtis Brown, and Jonathan Pegg, his assistant, for their constant support and encouragement.

One of the joys of having worked for so many years as a travel writer is meeting a host of wonderfully talented and warm-hearted people who have given me not only their friendship but also more hospitality than I can ever repay. This is especially true in Africa, where my list of friends reads like a *Who's Who* of the good and great in the world of game wardens, safari guides, scientists and wildlife photographers.

For golden days in Kenya with the lions of the Masai Mara I would like to thank Jonathan and Angie Scott, as well as Jock Anderson of East African Wildlife Safaris, who was in at the start of it all. Aris Grammaticus of Governor's Camps was also there at the beginning, and has given me more hot-air balloon safaris than I

ACKNOWLEDGEMENTS

deserve. Other indefatigable Kenyan hosts, helpers and safari companions over the years are Iain and Oria Douglas-Hamilton, Julian and Jane McKeand, Stephano and Liz Cheli, Calvin Cottar, Ron and Pauline Beaton, Ian Craig, Kuki Gallmann, Giulio Bertolli, Richard Leakey, Herbie Paul and family, and Jake Grieves-Cook.

One of my most valued Kenyan friends is the photographer David Coulson, with whom I travelled to the Skeleton Coast and the Namib Desert. In Botswana I would like to single out Ralph Bousfield for introducing me to the magic of the Makgadikgadi Pans at Jack's Camp, and Mike Penman for a thrilling first taste of the Okavango Delta. Nor can I mention Okavango without thanking Randall Jay Moore (and Abu the elephant!) for the ultimate safari – on elephant-back through the delta. In Tanzania, Mike and Gisela Leach have always been generous hosts at Ngare Sero Lodge, their idyllic home at the foot of Mount Meru. The same is true of Paul Oliver, at Oliver's Camp in Tarangire National Park, Aadje Geertsema at Ndutu Lodge in the Serengeti, Margaret Kullander at Gibb's Farm and Alan Elliott in Zimbabwe, whose former safari company, Touch the Wild, provided the inspiration for the title of this book.

Everywhere in Africa I have always received the most tremendous support from the travel industry. In particular, I would like to thank Primrose Stobbs at Abercrombie & Kent, Chris McIntyre at Sunvil Africa, Bill Adams at Safari Consultants, Nick Van Gruisen at Worldwide Journeys and Will Jones at Journeys by Design. Other companies that have indulged my love of Africa with characteristic generosity include Cazenove & Loyd, Wilderness Safaris and Orient-Express in Botswana, and CC Africa in South Africa. And, of course, I could never have set foot in the bush without the means of getting there – unfailingly provided by British Airways, South African Airways, Air Namibia, Air Botswana and Airkenya. The same goes for all those safari drivers, lodge managers, cooks and camp staff who made me feel so much at home wherever I happened to be.

Generosity and hospitality are qualities I have encountered not only in Africa but all over the world. So many people have helped to arrange my trips that I fear I may not have the space to mention them all. But I must thank the following individuals: Maurice Mullay for my visit to Shetland; Mac and Tracy Mace for my stay on Bryher in the Isles of Scilly; and Christopher 'Swanny' Swann, skipper of the *Marguerite Explorer*, for a memorable week cruising in the Hebrides. Further afield, my thanks are due to Ann Scott, who sent me to Madeira; Kader Chelbi for enabling me to visit Kerkennah; Paul Chatenoud,

[7]

owner of the Green Door (the greatest little B&B in Donegal); and Julia Spence and Linda Hearn of Inntravel for organizing countless walks into the loveliest corners of Europe.

I must also acknowledge the help of national tourist offices, especially those of France, Spain and Ireland (Bord Fáilte). Their staff have always been hugely supportive, and have never failed to be both efficient and friendly to a fault.

But, of course, even the most glamorous assignment can be a lonely business without good travelling companions. Here I would like to thank the following friends and colleagues: fellow travel writer Robin Neillands, for dreaming up the idea of walking over the Pyrenees to celebrate our fiftieth birthdays; Clive Boursnell, the gifted photographer who accompanied me in Extremadura and East Germany; Hugh and Jane Arbuthnott of the Walking Safari Company who led me through their favourite corner of Andalucia; Andy Tucker of Naturetrek, who drove me around the Cévennes; Gerard Gorman, the birdman of Budapest, who showed me the cranes of the Hortobágy; Ali and Moira Ross, for having the patience to try to improve my skiing skills; Christopher Wilmot-Sitwell of Cazenove & Loyd Expediciones and Guilherme Rondon, the owner of Barra Mansa, for a memorable stay in the Pantanal; Tom Winter – Crocodile Dundee in all but name – for his dry wit and bush-wise skills in Australia's Kakadu National Park; John Kipling and the crew of the *Searcher* for the privilege of watching the grey whales of Baja California; and Jeffrey Rayner and Captain Gerhardt Lickfett, the enigmatic skipper of the *Star Clipper*, for the pleasures of sailing in a tall ship. Finally, my most heartfelt thanks of all to Annabelle, my wife, my perfect travelling companion.

I am truly indebted to those national newspapers and magazines that have so generously given permission for the essays to be reproduced in this book. Below is a list of where each and every one originally appeared:

Island Fever
England – The Isles of Scilly: *Sunday Times*, 21 May 1989.
Scotland – Islands of the Simmer Dim: *Sunday Times*, 26 June 1988.
Scotland – Orkney: *Sunday Times*, 8 June 1986.
Zanzibar – Mnemba: *Sunday Times*, 28 April 2002.
Kenya – Lamu: *Times Magazine*, 8 January 1994.
The Galápagos: *The Times*, 1 January 2000.

Tunisia – Kerkennah: *Sunday Times*, 3 November 1990.
Madeira and the Islas Desertas: *Sunday Telegraph*, 7 November 1993.

European Trails
The Pyrenees – Across the Great Divide: *Sunday Times Magazine*, 28 June 1987.
Spain – A Land as Hard as Oak: *Sunday Times Magazine*, 27 January 1991.
Spain – Picos de Europa: *Sunday Times*, 5 March 2000.
Spain: Andalucía: *Sunday Times*, 17 May 1992.
France – Islands of Silence: *Daily Telegraph*, 17 February 2001.
France – The Bastides of Aveyron: *Guardian*, 25 June 1994.
Ireland – The Final Frontier: *Sunday Times*, 26 August 2001.
East Germany – Over the Wall: *Sunday Times Magazine*, 20 May 1990.
Hungary – The Cranes of Hortobágy: *Sunday Times*, 14 September 1997.
The Swiss Alps – A Brush with Euphoria: *Sunday Times Magazine*, 1 October 1989.

On Safari
Botswana – Jack's Camp: *Daily Telegraph*, 7 September 1997.
Botswana – The Lions of Savuti: *Daily Telegraph*, 21 November 1998.
Botswana – Abu's Camp: *Condé Nast Traveller*, September 2001.
Kenya – The Masai Mara: *Roaring at the Dawn*, Swan Hill Press, 1995.
Kenya – Laikipia: *The Times*, 27 January 2001.
Kenya – Back from the Dead: *Sunday Times*, 12 December 1989.
Kenya – Elsa's Kopje: *Condé Nast Traveller*, February 2000.
Kenya – Reclaiming the Last Frontier: *Daily Telegraph*, 16 September 2000.
Tanzania – The Serengeti: *The Times*, 16 May 1992.
Zimbabwe – The Matobo Hills: *Sunday Times*, 8 January 1995.
Namibia – Journey to the Coast of the Dead: *Sunday Times Magazine*, January 1991.

Sea Time
The Caribbean – All I Ask is a Tall Ship: *Times Weekend Review*, 1 October 1992.
Kenya – Giants at the End of the Line: *Sunday Times*, 21 January 1990.
Scotland – The Hebrides: *Daily Telegraph*, 31 December 1994.
Mexico – Grey Whales of the Baja: *Sunday Times*, 23 September 1990.

ACKNOWLEDGEMENTS

Distant Horizons
India – The Tigers of Kanha: *Sunday Times*, 13 March 1988.
Australia – Kakadu: *Sunday Times*, 17 July 1988.
Morocco – The Land Where Spring is Born: *Daily Telegraph*, 2 December 2000.
Brazil – The Pantanal: *Sunday Times*, 17 February 2002.
Belize – Britain's Lost Empire of the Sun: *Daily Telegraph*, 17 July 1993.
Turkey – A Lycian Rhapsody: *Sunday Telegraph*, 29 March 1998.
Turkey – Cappadocia: *Sunday Telegraph*, 14 February 1999.

Home Ground
Cornwall – West Penwith: *Daily Telegraph*, 28 June 1997.
Devon – Tarka Country: *Sunday Times Magazine*, 5 July 1987.
Gloucestershire – Slimbridge: *The Countryside in Winter*, Century Hutchinson, 1985.
My Dorset: *Dorset*, October 1999.

INTRODUCTION

All the best journeys begin with a map. It is at once the most invaluable and the most evocative travel document ever devised. When I was a boy growing up in the anonymous streets of suburban Surrey, maps were the tangible evidence of the wider horizons I could not see. They were an escape route, passports of the mind, able to transport me to places I had read about and longed to visit, yet which seemed as remote to me then as the dark side of the moon. Even now, my old school atlas (dated 1940, and with most of the globe a rich colonial pink) still falls open at Africa. There it lies, that huge, dusty continent, shaped like an elephant's ear, scattered with the names that echoed in my imagination like talking drums. But today I can look at it as familiar territory, having followed its elephant paths and game trails from Kenya to the Cape.

My travelling life began, modestly enough, with family holidays in Cornwall. In Ewell, where I grew up, the nearest stretch of seaside was the Sussex coast between Eastbourne and Worthing, and that is where most of my school friends went. But my father, who worked for what was then the Southern Railway, used to be given privilege tickets that enabled us to travel further afield; and so to Cornwall we went every summer, the most longed-for treat of the year. In those days, in the late 1930s and the war years of the 1940s, Cornwall was a decidedly upmarket destination, and I adored our visits to Polzeath and St Ives. It was the start of a love affair that has remained with me to this day, and there is not a year of my life in which I have not crossed the Tamar for at least a week or two.

Not until I was 15 did I go abroad for the first time, and even then it was only as far as Paris with my Uncle Fred and Peter, his son, who shared my abiding interest in the natural world and is now a distinguished Fellow of the Royal Society after spending a lifetime studying Darwin's finches in the Galápagos. Paris was a revelation. It was not just Notre-Dame cathedral and the grand boulevards; here was a whole new way of living, made manifest by the (to me) novel smells of garlic and Gauloises cigarettes, croissants for break-fast, pavement cafés and my first taste of real coffee.

My first independent trip abroad came about seven years later. By then I had completed my two years' national service as an able sea-man in the Royal Navy, and set of again with my cousin Peter, only this time without my Uncle Fred to chaperone us. For reasons I can-not remember, we had chosen to go to the Costa Brava. Maybe the name – the Wild Coast – intrigued us. Anyway, we travelled down by train to Figueres in Catalunya (Catalonia), and then by bus to Roses on the coast.

That bus ride was the start of another lifelong love affair – this time with Spain. We were crammed in among a crowd of country folk going back to their homes on the coast. Many of the women were dressed in black, as if for a funeral, but wore huge smiles and sat with giant wicker baskets filled with bread and air-dried ham and ripe apricots, which they pressed upon us. The men, mean-while, passed around leather wineskins, squirting the contents in ruby streams at arm's length into their open mouths. Somewhere at the back of the bus a guitarist began to play, and we drove on down to Roses beneath the roadside plane trees to the raucous singing and clap-clap-clap of those joyful and warm-hearted people.

Of course, this was a Costa Brava as yet hardly touched by the great post-war travel boom and, during our stay in Roses, we met only one other Englishman. Roses was still a true fishing village, its coastline uncluttered, and we sunbathed and swam from its deserted coves and chased swallowtail butterflies over its thyme-scented headlands. Much later, during the 1970s, I went back, but the Roses I knew had been buried under a concrete tsunami of urban development.

By this stage I had joined the *Sunday Times* after an undistin-guished career that had begun as a Fleet Street messenger boy. From this lowly post I had moved on to become a copy-writer with Poly Travel, churning out purple prose for their holiday brochures, and it was at this time that I met the man who would change my life. His name was Ted Appleton and he worked in the accounts department, but at the same time, I discovered, he also wrote travel articles for women's magazines. One day he told me that he was about to go to Italy for a week. 'On holiday?' I asked innocently. 'Not exactly,' he replied. 'It's a kind of working holiday.' He explained how he was being sent there by *Woman's Own*, who wanted him to write some-thing for their travel pages. 'You mean they give you a free trip just to write an article?' I said. 'It's even better than that,' he replied. 'I get paid for writing the story.' I listened incredulously, and decided right then that that was what I wanted to do.

Achieving my ambition took rather longer, including a seven-year stint with the British Tourist Authority, but in 1970 I made it and became the lowest-paid journalist on the staff of the *Sunday Times*. I did not care about the money. With luck, that would improve. What mattered was that under Harold Evans, its great campaigning editor, the *Sunday Times* had become the most exciting newspaper in Britain and its travel pages were second to none.

Somehow I survived my baptism into the frantic world of Fleet Street – largely because I was so fortunate in my choice of sympathetic colleagues. Among those who used to sub-edit my copy was Ian Jack, now editor of *Granta*, who once famously complained to me that he was merely the middle seven letters of my name. How lucky I was to learn the tricks of the trade from him and others, including Philip Clarke, for whom I had the privilege of working when he was editor of the *Sunday Times Magazine*. At that time my fiercest critic – and staunchest friend – was my colleague Richard Girling, who later became best man at my wedding. He once introduced me with the words: 'This is Brian Jackman; he is licensed to use adjectives.' Praise indeed coming from the journalist who was voted Specialist Writer of the Year at the UK Press Awards for 2002.

And so, for the next 20 years, the *Sunday Times* became my ticket to travel the world. There were no limits; I went everywhere, from the Falkland Islands to Everest Base Camp. I still retain a copy of an expenses form I submitted to the paper's accounts department, claiming 'to hiring an elephant' in Kanha National Park in India. But I had to wait four years before I was finally allowed to travel to the one continent above all others that I longed to see. In May 1974 I was invited on a press trip to Kenya, where Hilton Hotels had opened a new safari lodge close to Tsavo National Park.

I knew I was going to like Kenya even before I went, having grown up on a diet of big-game hunting books brought home from the local library by my father, who never even got as far as Calais but was an inveterate armchair traveller. But nothing I had read could have prepared me for the impact of the African bush at first hand. Greedily I drank it all in: the chorus of doves that greet the dawn; the cheerful Kenyans and their husky Swahili voices; the smell of the earth after rain; and the never-to-be-forgotten sight of a herd of elephants, the same colour as Tsavo's red laterite dust, crossing the road in front of our Land-Rover.

When the press trip came to an end I pleaded to stay on, and found someone who was prepared to fly me by light aircraft down to the Masai Mara National Reserve. The rainy season was just ending and the high plains were as green as Ireland. The wildebeest were still down in the Serengeti and would not arrive until July; but I saw and heard my first lion and knew I would return. And return I did. Now, looking back over all the nights I have spent under canvas in the African bush, it pleases me to think that they add up to more than two years of my life.

Looking back, I can see now that what also helped me to survive in the cut-throat world of Fleet Street was my passion for wildlife and wild places. So, while others went to New York or the Caribbean, I took off into the Okavango Delta or the high Pyrénées. In ecological terms I had found a niche and was able to make it my own.

When I began my career in journalism, travel to long-haul destinations such as East Africa was still confined to the well-heeled. But then came the package-holiday revolution and the jumbo jet. Together they did for travel what paperbacks did for English literature, and the world began to shrink until there was nowhere, from Amazonia to Antarctica, that could not be visited on a fortnight's trip from London Heathrow. But increasingly, as mass tourism spread around the Mediterranean and beyond, I found myself heading on foot into the quieter corners of Europe. In Spain I sought solitude in the mountains. In midmost France I found myself walking through dreamy valleys whose kingfisher rivers and old-fashioned hay meadows conjured up the lost world of my childhood with poignant intensity.

Today, these lands of lost content are beyond price. As pristine landscapes everywhere become harder to find, they need to be cherished as never before. But how? I have come to believe that responsible eco-tourism is often the only human activity that can ensure the survival of the world's natural resources by exploiting them in a sustainable, non-consumptive way. There is a saying in Africa – 'If it pays, it stays' – meaning that wildlife and wild places have a much better chance of survival if they are shown to have an ecomomic value whose benefits outweigh other forms of land use.

If the essays collected here have a single theme it is this: despite all the changes that continue to threaten our planet, it is still a beautiful world, and one worth fighting to preserve.

Brian Jackman
West Milton, Dorset

ISLAND
FEVER

ENGLAND – THE ISLES OF SCILLY

One day in spring, when the Isles of Scilly were the warmest place in Britain, I walked over the white-sand causeway from St Agnes to Gugh. The sun shone from a cloudless sky and I sat on a rock and listened to the first cuckoo calling across a blissful silence of gorse and granite. The sea was an intense Aegean blue, shot through with sharp emerald gleams where sand lay beneath the shallows and with the deep indigo of submerged reefs and kelp beds. Near by, on a beach as soft as talc, the last of the winter storms had flung up the bleached bones of a seal, which lay now in the marram grass, together with a scattering of mauve mussel shells, dried seaweed and odd bits of driftwood. A pair of oystercatchers with coral-red beaks were piping at the tide's edge. Otherwise the only footprints in the sand were mine.

Forget the Maldives, the Seychelles, the Grenadines. The Isles of Scilly are only 45km from Land's End, but they lie out in the Gulf Stream where frosts are rare and sunfish bask in summer. There are no snakes, no mosquitoes, no muggers. Take the helicopter from Penzance and you can be there in 20 minutes.

Heathrow it isn't. You touch down in a daisy field, as effortlessly as a gull on a roof, and step out into a luminous, sea-girt world that looks like the Cornwall of 60 years ago. Breathe deep. The salty Scillonian air will rot a car in three years, but it is wonderfully pure and a joy to inhale – distilled over 3,000km of ocean by Atlantic breezes that bring unusual and exotic birds to the islands: nighthawks and magnolia warblers from America, hoopoes and golden orioles from southern Europe.

Out of the wind, the climate is kind. While the rest of Britain shivers in the grip of winter, the Scillonians are busy in their pocket-sized bulb fields, cutting daffodils for the London market. By springtime, parts of the islands are as luxuriant as the Mediterranean. Palm trees sprout from cottage gardens, bees drone among giant azure spires of echiums from the Canaries. On St Mary's I saw a blue field, like a Picasso painting: a solid carpet of Spanish blue-bells. Other fields are bright with Bermuda buttercups and whistling jacks – wild red gladioli from Africa once grown commercially but now gone native, rooted among the more familiar West Country wildflowers.

When my roving days are over, this is where I, too, should like to put down my roots, in a small granite house, snug under the sea wind, with a garden full of daffodils and a view of the bluest sea this side of the Caribbean. On Bryher I met a man who has done just that. Mac Mace is a professional diver from Nottingham who has successfully transplanted himself on this, the smallest of Scilly's five inhabited islands, where he and Tracy, his wife, run a guesthouse. The sea begins at his garden gate. From his lounge he can point out the sites of 22 shipwrecks. Indoors is a brass signal cannon retrieved from the wreck of Admiral Sir Cloudesley Shovell's flagship, HMS *Association*. 'Possibly the last gun she fired before she struck on the Gilstone Ledge on a stormy October night in 1707,' says Mace.

'She was a 96-gun ship of the line and she was carrying the Queen's plate, 10 chests of Sir Cloudesley's own and great riches of the grandees of Spain. Now she's lying in a 30m-deep valley, scattered across a seabed of cottage-size boulders. You can see the snouts of her cannons, but the gold and silver coin and other arte-facts have dribbled down between the rocks. Getting at them is more like mining than diving.'

Yet, little by little, the *Association* is yielding up her treasure: English silver coins welded together by centuries of corrosion; Portuguese gold pieces as bright as the day they were minted. Last year Mace found an apricot stone, which he almost persuaded to germinate, and, most poignant of all, a seaman's gold ring inscribed with the words: 'In thy breast my heart does rest.'

On a sunny day the waters around Bryher are idyllic, a maze of ledges and gull-haunted islets threaded by glittering turquoise channels. One such stretch has the most beautiful name in all Scilly: the Garden of Maiden Bower. But how different it is in a big winter storm, when Hell Bay seethes like scalded milk and the roaring seas break clean over the outlying rock castles of Mincarlo.

Mac Mace knows well the unimaginable power of the sea. Once he dived on the ill-fated tanker *Torrey Canyon*, wrecked on the Seven Stones reef in 1967. 'She's huge, an 11-storey hull of solid iron,' he says. 'Yet the sea has shoved her along the bottom for more than 100m since she went down.'

He is equally knowledgeable about Bryher, knows every inch of its 120ha of yellow gorse and Iron Age cairns. 'Look,' he cries, sinking to his knees to identify a blue pinhead in the grass. It turns out to be a rare miniature violet, which, he says, grows only here and on Jersey.

'People come to Bryher and ask us what there is to do, and we tell them there's nothing. That's the joy of it, that and a sense of man having lived here for 3,000 years.'

On Bryher, as elsewhere in the Scillies, such joys are synonymous with peace and tranquillity. Even on St Mary's, where locals complain about the island's 300 cars, traffic has a minimal presence. Boats are far more important, and every morning a stream of launches sets out from St Mary's Quay to deposit visitors on the off-islands for the day. The finest beaches are on St Martin's, and at certain times of the year, when the tide runs out and the sea-light pours across the shining sands, you can walk barefoot to Tresco, more than a kilometre away, without ever wading more than knee-deep.

In April 1989 a new hotel opened on St Martin's, a rare event in the Scillies, and one that inevitably aroused a degree of acrimony among the island's 80 inhabitants. Yet, as a visitor, I can only say that its modest slate and granite proportions sit happily on the shores of Tean Sound, no more conspicuous than a row of coastguard cottages, and I know of no other hotel in Britain, and few elsewhere, with lovelier seascape views.

Tresco, most popular of the off-islands, is a private paradise owned by the Dorrien-Smith family, whose eccentric ancestor, Augustus 'Emperor' Smith, created the subtropical gardens of Tresco Abbey more than a century ago. The Scillies are renowned for their mild winters, but in January 1987 the unthinkable happened when the inhabitants of Tresco awoke to find everything buried under 15cm of snow. For the abbey gardens it was a disaster. It was so cold that the sap froze in the trees and many tender plants were lost. Even today the windbreak hedges of high pittosporum stand grey and stricken around the bulb fields. But at Tresco Abbey the gardens have made a miraculous recovery and remain among the wonders of Britain. This is a closed world of rock roses and goldfinch song, drowsy and sun-warmed, steeped in the incense of Monterey pines, its granite terraces overwhelmed by cascades of pink mesembryanthemums and Madeira geraniums.

Here, too, is Tresco's extraordinary Valhalla of shipwreck figureheads. Gilded and ghostly white, they fly out of the shadows as if they were still cleaving the wild Atlantic. There are golden lions, blue dolphins, a Highland chieftain and a Puritan maid. But the loveliest and most enigmatic by far is a brown-eyed wench with a comb in her hair – the Spanish Lady – salvaged from a mystery vessel dashed upon the Scilly Rocks.

Back in Hugh Town, I bought a wreck chart of the Scillies produced by Roland Morris of Penzance, every inch of it littered with the names of dead ships: barques and brigantines, East Indiamen and ships of the line, clippers bound to Falmouth for orders, Dutch galliots, French crabbers, proud schooners and humble steam trawlers. It is a chilling document, a roll-call of the deep, listing the hundreds of ships lost and men drowned in these islands over the centuries. But it is also a vivid testimonial to the romance of sea travel, a geography and history lesson all in one.

It lists cargoes of fustic and indigo, tea from Foochow, coal from Cardiff, and each terse entry tells a story. 'The ship *Polinarus*, on passage from Demerara to London with rum and sugar, lost with all hands, 1848... the SS *Schiller*, wrecked on the Retarrier Ledges with the loss of more than 300 lives... the *Louise Hannah* from Lisbon to her home port of Poole with oranges and wine, lost off Annet, all hands lost, 1839.' And listen to the names of the rocks that sent them to the bottom: Tearing Ledge, the Hellweathers, Great Wingletang, the Gunners, the Beast and the infamous Gilstone.

> *Who sank the Association?*
> *I, said the Gilstone,*
> *She sank like a millstone.'*

Next day I went out to the Western Rocks to visit some of those unrepentant old murderers. The boat rose and fell among the hills of blue water. Shell-bursts of spray blossomed against the Haycocks, too far away to hear, and the Bishop Rock lighthouse stood pencil-slim on its solitary pinnacle like an admonishing finger. What courage it must have taken to live there, marooned among those fearsome deeps, knowing that the first lighthouse to be built on the Bishop was washed away in a storm.

Puffins whirred from beneath our bows, and grey seals with sleek mottled bodies and wistful eyes slipped into the water as we nosed among the reefs of Rosevean and Melledgan. Even on a calm day the sea is never still. The tide sucks constantly at the barnacled granite, swilling around the teeth and tusks of those grim ledges to subside with a sinister gasp, like the last breath of a drowning sailor. You think of all the fine ships that have come to grief here, and the sunless silence of the kelp forests below, and pray the weather holds.

On my last morning, as cloudless as the first, I rented a bike in Hugh Town and went freewheeling down the empty lanes to the sea. The day stretched before me and I felt as carefree as a child. Where the road ended, I left the bike among the bluebells, knowing nobody would steal it, and set out along the coast path to Porth Hellick. The coconut scent of the gorse rolled in thick yellow tides across the clifftops. The sea lay glassy calm. Out on the horizon, beyond Great Arthur, the faint smudge of a ship caught my eye. I stared at it through my binoculars in disbelief. It was a ghost ship, a dream from the past: a great square-rigger under full sail.

That evening she lay at anchor in St Mary's Road. She was the *Belem*, a French sail-training ship homeward bound for Nantes. But for me, her masts and shrouds deep-etched against the dying golden light, she was a haunting echo from a century ago, when these perilous waters were the crossroads of the world and the swift, six-oared Scillonian pilot gigs – *Shah, Bonnet, Golden Eagle* – rowed out between the Western Rocks to guide the tall ships safely home.

SCOTLAND – ISLANDS OF THE SIMMER DIM

A mist as cold as a Viking ghost lay on the sea. There was no sign of Sumburgh Head, the first landfall after leaving Aberdeen. The Isle of Mousa was a vanishing shadow passed to port as we slid into Bressay Sound with a posse of kittiwakes in our slipstream and fulmars skimming beneath our bows. Even before I could see Shetland the damp air held the promise of land close by – a smell compounded of fish, kelp, peat and rain – guiding us into Lerwick harbour.

The 300km overnight voyage from Aberdeen to Lerwick is the longest ferry crossing in Britain. You sail at 6pm on the P&O ferry *St Clair* – known affectionately to Shetlanders as the 'Blue Canoe' – and dock at 8am next morning. God knows what the Vikings thought of their North Sea voyages, with nothing but a salt sheep's head to gnaw on, but the Blue Canoe offers three-course dinners and soft beds in comfortable cabins and, if the weather is kind, the bare hills behind Fladdabister framed in the porthole at breakfast time.

The long passage north underlines the remoteness of Shetland. In Lerwick you are closer to the Arctic Circle than to London, nearer to Bergen than Aberdeen. Spiritually and physically, the islands remain tied to their Scandinavian past. Shetland place-names sound as if they might have been carved in runes, half Norseman's saga, half *Lord of the Rings*. Where else in Britain could you find the Haa of Stova, Dragon Ness, the Geo of Vigon, the Sneckan and the Slithers?

Now, as then, Shetlanders live in the eye of the wind, cast up on holms and skerries among the long arms of the sea, in stone houses stuck fast like limpets to the shores, or in lonely crofts rooted among wet rushy fields and iris marshes. In their faces and their voices is the echo of their Viking forefathers, as distinctive as the curving prows of their traditional wooden rowing boats, the yoals and sixareens that lie so snugly at rest in their nousts above high-water mark.

Five centuries of Scottish culture have washed over Shetland since the Danes gave the islands away as a wedding dowry, but old loyalties die hard. In the 17th century the infamous Earl Patrick ruled in Scalloway. He built a castle there and bonded its stones with blood and mortar as he tried to sweep away the old Viking laws and rights of *scathold*, or common grazing. Today the earl's lair lies open to the sky, and modern Shetlanders have even taken to flaunting their own flag – a white upright cross on a sea-blue background. In midsummer the cliffs are bright with sea pinks and campion. Lochsides and meadow bottoms glitter with a king's ransom in marsh marigolds, and orchids flower by the roadsides. This is the time of the 'simmer dim', when it never really gets dark, when you can still read the *Sunday Times* at midnight and only a few brief hours of eerie twilight separate the long northern days. These are the days when the air sparkles and the green holms lie becalmed in a sea of Caribbean blue. But nobody comes here to lie in the sun, not when the islanders have 30 different words to describe the subtleties of Shetland rain.

Shetland is for those who put a price on solitude, and who value the silence of empty hills and bays above the torrid pleasures of the south. Some come to fish – to spin for sea trout in the voes or hunt giant skate and halibut in the churning deeps beyond Bard Head. Some come to dive on the Shetland wrecks – on the Dutch East Indiaman *De Liefde*, lost on the Out Skerries in 1711, or the 'Silver Ship' *Wendela*, wrecked off Fetlar in 1745.

A hundred islands, 18 inhabited and all of them haunted by a brooding sense of time long past. On Mousa stands a Pictish broch – the finest in Britain – a drystone tower, squat and kiln-shaped, dripping with history. You can read in the *Orkneyinga Saga* how it was besieged in AD1153, when an eloping Viking and his love took refuge in its walls. Nobody lives there now, but on calm nights the midsummer dusk comes alive with the flickering, bat-like shapes of the storm petrels that nest between its stones.

On South Mainland near Sumburgh is the great archaeological showcase of Jarlshof. Here, too, lived the Iron Age broch builders, eaters of limpets, who huddled like puffins in round stone houses under the turf until the Vikings drove them out and built their own settlements among the ruins.

Further up the coast, between Fitful Head and Scalloway, I left the main road and walked out along a tombolo, a narrow causeway of moon-white sand between two green bays, to St Ninian's Isle. In

1957 a schoolboy scratching among the ruins of St Ninian's Church had dug up a hoard of Pictish silver. Now its only treasures are gold lichens on the rocks, and the silver shining sea.

Like most Shetland beaches the sands of St Ninian were deserted except for seals and oystercatchers. I searched the shore for otter tracks but, instead of the distinctive five-toed prints, found only jellyfish washed up by the tide. Later, with the late Bobby Tulloch, I had better luck. Tulloch was a Shetlander born and bred, who could trace his parentage back to the 16th century and had an unsurpassed knowledge of local wildlife. For 21 years he was warden of Shetland for the Royal Society for the Protection of Birds and, when I met him, he was still living on the island of Yell, only 6km from the house where he was born.

The mist that had blanketed Lerwick on my arrival had gone in the night. The sun shone. The air was sharp and clear, opening up immense vistas of sea and hills and islands, great fleets of holms and skerries reaching away to the remote Ramna Stacks off the northernmost tip of Mainland. On the ferry to Yell I stood in the bows and watched grey seals bobbing in the swirling tide. Puffins and black guillemots – known here as tysties – flew fast and low over the water, and Arctic terns were diving for sand eels.

At Mid Yell Voe we set off in Tulloch's boat, the *Starna*. We were looking for otters but on the way we stopped to watch salmon being fed in huge floating cages. Salmon farming had become big business in Shetland – second only to North Sea oil – and there was hardly a voe or inlet that did not have its fish pens. The salmon are weaned in fresh water, introduced to the sea pens as smolts and cropped 18 months later, when they usually weigh 5kg. Two men were shovelling food into the cages. As the pellets fell through the netting the pens came alive with surging shadows. The fish fed in a frenzy, lunging and turning with silver gleams as if someone beneath the surface was swinging and hacking with a broadsword.

We left the voe and headed for Hascosay, an untenanted island between Yell and Fetlar. Its 300ha were home to at least 30 otters, said Tulloch, and we looked for them along the Bow of Hascosay between Taingar and the Point of the Gunnald, where the turf breaks away in low peaty hummocks by the shore, creating ideal holts and hiding places for these elusive animals.

Otters like to feed when the tide is flowing and fish emerge from their hiding places. The conditions were perfect, but we could see only seals and razorbills. Then, as we headed into the lee of Burra

Ness, I caught a quick glimpse of a flat brown head, the flick of a tapered tail as whatever it was dived, leaving scarcely a ripple. Moments later it reappeared, a fierce whiskered face framed in sharp focus in my binoculars. 'Otter,' said Tulloch. 'A young dog. He'll be hunting for lumpsuckers and butterfish in the kelp forests.'

For 15 minutes we watched him swimming and diving. Then he came ashore, romped up the beach, rolled in the shingle, lay on his back and licked himself dry until his fur – sleek as a seal's when he emerged from the water – had dried itself in punkish spikes. We left him an hour later, sleeping behind a rock, and chugged on to Fetlar for a picnic on the beach. Fetlar is famous for its snowy owls, found nowhere else in Britain. Three years earlier I had come here and been lucky enough to see one of these magnificent birds, a true Arctic hunter with round yellow eyes, its plumage the colours of ice and rock. But today we had neither the time nor the transport to reach the hillsides where the owls could be found.

Instead, we made our way back to the Sound of Yell, where mergansers were swimming under the cliffs of the rock stack known as the Greybearded Man. Tulloch throttled down the engine and we nosed into the wet mouths of caves and chasms where the water lay deep and clear under our keel and the sunlight slanted down into a darkness of kelp. Above us, every ledge held its pair of nesting fulmars, and all around us the tide sloshed and gurgled against the barnacled rocks from which seals watched with soft brown eyes.

In the days that followed, Tulloch introduced me to the rain-goose and the bonxie – Shetland names for the red-throated diver and the great skua. The divers nest on desolate lochans, sitting tight among the pink-flowering spikes of bogbeans. The skuas breed on the moors of Unst, Britain's most northerly island, robbing gannets and dive-bombing anyone who walks too close to their nests.

The skuas were spectacular. So, too, were the gannets, kittiwakes, shags and puffins that share the teeming cliffs of Herma Ness. But of all these northern wonders there was nothing to match the first sight of a wild Shetland otter.

SCOTLAND – ORKNEY

I am a southerner with the sun in my bones. Not for me the endless weeks of drenching rain, the grey winds and bleak northern winters. But in summer, when blue skies return to Orkney and daylight lingers until midnight, there is a magic here, profound contentment and peace beyond price.

Among the 67 isles of Orkney you can find space and solitude on a scale undreamed of in Britain's deep south. Last summer I spent a few days there travelling by boat among the seal skerries and seabird cliffs until London seemed as remote and improbable as the dark side of the moon.

In Kirkwall's red-sandstone cathedral an organist was playing the psalm preludes of Herbert Howells. The great chords crashed out in the gloom, strong enough to rattle the bones of the martyred Earl Magnus Erlandson, axed to death and walled up in a pillar here nearly 900 years ago.

The cathedral is still the most dominant building in Kirkwall. It is an odd little town, turned in upon itself, as if trying to shut out the searching winds that set the fishing boats rocking at their moorings. Its step-gabled houses stand end on to narrow paved streets never meant for modern traffic, still dreaming of the days when Orkney lay at the centre of world affairs.

In 1914 the main anchorage of the Royal Navy was here at Scapa Flow, the great natural harbour that is the cold grey heart of Orkney. The *Hampshire* sailed from here in a summer storm in 1916, only to strike a mine off Marwick Head and go down with the loss of some 900 men, including Lord Kitchener. In that same year the British Fleet steamed out from Orkney, bound for Jutland. The battle that followed was inconclusive, but when the war was over the Kaiser's Grand Fleet was interned in Scapa Flow. There the might of Germany – 11 battleships, five battle-cruisers, eight cruisers and 50 destroyers – lay until 21 June 1919, when, on the orders of Rear-Admiral Ludwig von Reuter, the fleet was sent to the bottom. Most have since been salvaged for scrap, but some, including the 25,000-tonne battleship *Konig*, are still there.

Porpoises were leaping in the Flow when I sailed to Hoy on the local car ferry. Most of Orkney is a lowland vista of glittering bogs and rolling moors. Only Hoy is highland, and its sombre summits draw the eye. Here, north of Rackwick at St John's Head, are the highest cliffs in Britain, falling sheer to the sea more than 335m below.

I followed the path as far as the Old Man of Hoy, a sea-girt finger of red sandstone the height of St Paul's Cathedral. Until 1966 it had never been climbed, but then a three-man team led by Chris Bonnington made it to the top. Yet even then the Old Man's days were numbered. Already the topmost 15m are teetering and one day wind and weather will reduce him to a headless stump.

Back on Mainland, the largest island in the archipelago, I spent an enjoyable day's sightseeing, taking in three of the great set pieces of prehistoric Britain: the Ring of Brodgar, Maes Howe burial mound and the Stone Age village of Skara Brae. To the south-east of Maes Howe, below the hills of Orphir, a hen harrier was hunting in a valley thick with the purple spikes of the beautiful northern marsh orchid. Orkney is altogether a good place for birds. The Royal Society for the Protection of Birds is now the biggest landowner in the islands and binoculars are almost de rigueur for visitors.

In spring and summer the seabird cliffs of Marwick Head on Mainland and the Noup on Westray are packed with breeding colonies of auks and kittiwakes. The sound is deafening, the hen-house reek of their guano-spattered tenements almost overwhelming. On Papa Westray, where the last great auk in Britain was killed in 1813, the RSPB now has a reserve at the north end of the island. With the resident summer warden I walked over turf starred with the tiny mauve flowers of the rare Scottish primrose to see Britain's largest breeding colony of Arctic terns. Every year some 4,500 pairs nest on Papa Westray, and woe betide anyone who strays into their domain.

The warden never went without a hat, he told me. 'Bonxies only buffet you,' he said, 'but Arctic terns draw blood.' As he spoke, a 'dread' of terns rose from the ground, filling the air with harsh chittering screams as a marauding skua swung past us. Often, said the warden, he had watched these hefty predators zoom in to snatch a sitting tern with hardly a pause, or decapitate an oystercatcher and then neatly scoop out its insides. The Vikings must have loved them.

Even Papa Westray, one of Orkney's most remote islands, is easy to visit on a day trip aboard the ferry that transports passengers to the out-islands, and the voyage alone is worth the fare. North from Kirkwall past Thieves Holm and Shapinsay the horizon is filled with flotillas of islands. Then you head home in the 'grimlins', the Viking twilight that lasts until midnight on a golden June evening, the sea lying calm in Westray Firth and the long day dying behind Rousay like the going down of a great fire.

ZANZIBAR – MNEMBA

It was on Manda Island in northern Kenya that the first true bare-foot luxury lodge took root. That was 30 years ago, when Bruno Brighetti, a former composer and musician, opened the Blue Safari Club. 'I built it as a place of refuge,' he says. 'A place for the poets of the sea and the wind.' Other exclusive hideaways followed, building on Brighetti's success. Nobody realized it at the time, but slowly, from beneath their high-peaked, *makuti*-thatch roofs, a uniquely African architectural style was emerging: a novel blend of bushveld baroque and Arab-Swahili coastal culture that has now spread south all the way down to Mozambique.

Unlike conventional resort hotels, these back-to-nature lodges are thoroughly eco-friendly and ingenious in their use of local materials. Fashioned out of driftwood, palm fronds and mangrove poles, they live and breathe with the spirit of Africa. But even more important than their style is their barefoot-beach-lodge ethos. As the name suggests, these are places where there's no need to dress up or watch the clock. Instead, just kick off your shoes and drop out into a world ruled only by the lap of the tides and the swing of a hammock.

Don't expect sophistication. This is Crusoe territory, where you sleep in a room open to the sea winds and the beach begins at your veranda. Nightlife? Forget it – unless you include the tiptoe dance of ghost crabs caught in the glow of a beach barbecue. But – and this is the whole point – essential luxuries remain: king-size beds, a fan to keep you cool at night, and seafood that even Rick Stein would drool over.

If you are looking for the ultimate among these Indian Ocean hideaways, then Mnemba is the place, a privately owned atoll off the north-eastern tip of Zanzibar. Once it had nothing but a well, used by local fishermen who believed its waters were drawn from the very heart of Africa. Today it is one of the most sought-after holiday spots in the world – the crème de la coconut-crème.

Getting there involves a 15-minute speedboat ride from a beach where fishermen are busily unloading the day's catch from their outriggers, and then a wet landing. 'Welcome to our swimming pool,' says the boatman as I wade ashore to be welcomed with a glass of cold tea and African honey. 'And there,' he says, pointing to the deep purple shadows of submerged coral gardens, 'is our house reef.'

The sand is almost too hot to walk on, but the gift of shade is only a few steps away. Under the casuarina trees are 10 beachfront cottages with hand-woven Zanzibari palm-frond floors and king-size beds as soft as sleep. There are no doors or windows, but privacy is absolute as each cottage is hidden in its own green tunnel of screwpines.

Barefoot-casual is the Mnemba dress code. For dinner – that morning's catch of kingfish, say, with a pineapple salsa, and a lemon-grass brulée for dessert – a *kikoi* (a colourful Swahili cotton wrap-around) is perfectly acceptable. You'll find one laid out beside your bed, together with a straw hat and a guide to the 300 fish species that swarm around Mnemba's reefs. At all times, indolence rules. On your private veranda you can while away the hours playing *bao*, the world's oldest board game, on a slab of carved ebony with seeds as counters. And every cottage has its own beach bed, primitive but supremely comfortable, with a soft white mattress and palm-frond awning. It's an ideal spot to perfect the art of *pumzika* – the Swahili word for snoozing.

The atoll itself is tiny – you can stroll around it in 20 minutes. But it is encircled by 15km of virgin coral reefs, and at low tide the receding water exposes an infinity of lukewarm pools and wave-ribbed sands, where you feel you could walk forever and still not reach the horizon. With its huge skies and noisy flocks of wading birds, it reminded me of the north Norfolk coast – except that the sands are powdered coral and the sea temperature is a blissful 28°C.

The tidelines are strewn with treasures of the deep: mottled cowries, strange starfish and the pink-satin carapaces of ghost crabs. The light flung back by the burning sands is dazzling, intensifying the colours of the sea. Across the lagoon, a long thin line of white marks where the waves are breaking on the outermost reefs. Beyond it, sharp against the blue, are fishing dhows, whose shark's-fin sails have graced these waters since the time of Sinbad. And beyond them is nothing but a toppling wall of storm clouds coming down with the warm *kaskazi* trade wind.

When the heat becomes too much to bear, it's time to cool off with goggles and flippers. Just off the beach, shoals of fish are circling the house reef, rising and falling among the corals in a slow-motion ballet. Butterfly fish – their lips permanently pursed as if about to blow a kiss – glide past in stately golden convoys. Every species is a miracle of colour and design. There are angelfish with humbug stripes, Moorish idols like crescent moons, and parrotfish browsing on the corals with an audible crunch.

Everywhere at Mnemba, above and below the surface, there is life. At night, green turtles haul themselves ashore to lay their eggs in the sand. One morning, immersed in a book, I looked up to see a suni – an antelope no bigger than a hare – staring at me across my veranda.

By now, Mnemba had me hooked. Almost against my will, I could feel its insidious lethargy taking hold. Not for me the activities on offer: diving, kayaking, windsurfing, deep-sea angling. Instead, I lolled and strolled, and the white band where I had worn my discarded wristwatch became as brown as the rest of me.

Lying in bed at night, I could hear the dull roar of the sea breaking on the reefs as the waves ran before the *kaskazi*, and from much closer came the wash of wavelets as they collapsed on the beach and fell back with a gasp, like the untroubled breathing of a sleeper. A few more days of this, I decided, and I could end up in thrall to the barefoot life for ever.

KENYA – LAMU

On the flight up from Nairobi, the plane's shadow skimmed across a land as red as Mars, an endless sea of bush rolling north to Somalia. But at last the desert gave way to the Tana River delta and, soon after, the low-lying islands of the Lamu archipelago. We landed on Manda Island, on a grass strip hacked out of the bush. Stepping out into the fierce heat of northern Kenya was like walking into a giant blow-dryer. Here, on the scorching rim of Africa, was a wooden jetty and, at its end, a sailing dhow called *Pepo*, meaning 'Wind'. In the stern, too tired to lift his hand, the dhow captain nudged the tiller with his bare foot and steered us out into the blue channel between Manda and Lamu.

Soon, Lamu town appeared across the tideway, a low-profile waterfront of coconut palms, dhow masts and flat-roofed Arab houses. Then, from around the curving channel, there came the sugar-white gleam of the minaret at Shela, 2.5km beyond the town, where I stepped ashore to the friendliest welcome in Kenya. All around the boat, small boys were diving into the clear water. On the jetty, barefoot villagers with bright *kikois* wrapped around their lean shanks waited to carry my bags to the hotel. '*Jambo! Karibu!*', they cried. 'Hello! Welcome!' Swahili is a gentle language. Every word ends in a vowel, and on Lamu you will hear not the kitchen Swahili of up-country Kenya but the real thing. Even to my untutored ear I could make out every syllable.

The Peponi Inn at Shela is one of the great landfalls of Africa, an oasis of coolness between the sandhills and the sea. Its name means 'Where the Wind Blows', and its position on the shore is designed to catch every last whisper of the monsoon breezes. Now it was February and the *kaskazi*, the north-east trade wind, was pouring through the hotel gardens, heavy with the sweet scent of frangipani. From the terrace, where the black snouts of ancient cannons still point across the channel, I watched two fishing dhows drift past the sands of Ras Kitau, their sails sharp-etched against the blue water.

I was given Room 18, cool and simple as a cave, with high, beamed ceilings and a broad-bladed brass fan stirring the air. Outside, stone steps led from the veranda to the beach. From the start, I knew I was going to like it here. By day, bee-eaters called from the Nandi flame-trees. At night, bats fluttered through the lamplit dusk. For supper there was crab bisque, grilled snapper drenched in lime juice, and a delicious dessert of sliced mango and home-made sorbet.

From the Peponi a leisurely boat trip is the only way into Lamu town. Life on Lamu is languid, laid-back, easy-going. Even the names of the old wooden sailing dhows rocking at their moorings reflect its mood of contented indolence: *Furaha* (Happiness); *Malaika* (Angel). The town itself is an exotic marriage of two worlds, Africa and Arabia: a labyrinth of mosques, coffee-shops and peeling houses threaded by the narrowest of alleys. Even in the main street, the Usita wa Mui, there is scarcely room for two donkey carts to pass. The rest of the streets have no names, but the various *mitaa*, or town wards, are known by evocative titles such as Pangahari (Sharpen your Sword) and Mwana Mshamu (the Syrian's Daughter).

Other relics of earlier times can be seen in the town museum, including Lamu's famous brass *siwa*, a 2m-long ceremonial horn made in about 1700 and inscribed: 'How often have you taxed yourself with journeys before sunrise and in the twilight... Don't despair, even though the search be long.' Side by side with this mighty relic is the great ivory *siwa* from Pate Island. Together, they rank among the finest art treasures in Africa.

Historic it may be, but in truth Lamu is a raddled old town. Caught up in its web of airless alleys, with their open drains and leprous walls, you may well find yourself gasping for the ocean winds of Shela. Yet there is no denying its raffish charm. In the market square, outside the 19th-century fort that served as a prison in British colonial times, old men dressed in traditional long cotton *kanzus* and embroidered skullcaps known as *kofias* lounge on benches playing *bao*, an ancient board game of baffling complexity. At dusk, when the coffee-sellers emerge with their conical brass pots, veiled women flit down the streets in their black *buibuis*. It is almost as if the 20th century had never arrived. There is no television, no sound of aircraft overhead, no traffic. The only vehicles on the entire island are a couple of old Land-Rovers belonging to the district commissioner. For everyone else, life moves no faster than the dhow.

Even before the birth of Islam, Arab dhows were voyaging down the coast of the unknown continent they called the Land of Zinj. The hardy seafarers began to trade with the islanders of the Lamu archipelago, and as they intermarried with the local Bantu people they gave rise to a whole new culture, called *Sawahil* after their word for coasts. Until the 1970s the dhow trade was Lamu's lifeblood. Every winter the great ocean-going dhows of Arabia came down from the Persian Gulf, along with Red Sea *sambuks*, double-ended *booms* from Kuwait and Iran, and scimitar-prowed *zarooks* from the Yemen, running before the *kaskazi*. Then, laden with all the romantic cargoes of Africa – ivory and rhino horn, amber, shark fins, turtle shells and mangrove poles – they would wait until the end of March for the northbound *kusi* to blow them home.

Habu Shiri, a retired dhow captain, remembered those days. I found him sitting under a tree on the waterfront, mending a sail with his fisherman friend, Hassani Mzee. 'Many times I have crossed the Indian Ocean,' said the old man with a faraway look in his eye. 'From Zanzibar to India, going with the south wind, it would take us 30 days. Now that trade is ended. The big dhows stopped coming more than 20 years ago.'

Today it is the tourist trade that keeps Lamu's economy afloat. Most of the fish Hassani catches are sold to the local hotels, but he is happy. 'We are pleased to see the tourists,' he said. 'Without them, there would be many poor people in Lamu, and many sad hearts.' Like most of the small inshore fishing dhows to be seen along the waterfront, Hassani's boat is a *jahazi*, built to a traditional local style, with a straight bow, wine-glass transom and coconut matting strung along the gunwales to keep out the spray. Nowadays, many *jahazis* have diesel engines as well as sails, but at Matondoni, a creekside village a few kilometres outside Lamu town, the hulls are still built as they always were, with adze and bow-drill, and with no blueprint but the shipwright's unerring eye.

The woodworker's art is also much in evidence in Lamu town, in backstreet furniture shops where elaborate hand-carved chests are made, and in the wealth of ornate wooden doorways, which open to reveal tantalizing glimpses of hidden courtyards. The finest of these Swahili houses date from the 18th century, Lamu's golden age, and are built of coral-limestone blocks, often three storeys high, with steps leading to a thatched rooftop eyrie where it is pleasant to sit at sundown.

In recent years Lamu has become home to a colourful coterie of individualists: misfits, drifters and romantics, refugees from the outside world, for whom the island's remoteness makes it a perfect hideaway. One of its most legendary denizens was the late Bunny Allen, last of Kenya's old-time white hunters and still very much alive when I met him in 1994. Sitting barefoot on the roof of the rambling, Arab-style house he had built 30 years earlier, Allen was a ghost from Karen Blixen's Africa, a gypsy with a ring in his ear and a string of leopards' teeth around his neck, who remembered the days when every thicket held a rhino and elephants with 50kg tusks still roamed the savannahs. As a young man he had hunted with Denys Finch Hatton and Karen Blixen. 'Ah, that Blixen gel,' he sighed. 'Delicate as Chinese porcelain.'

'Mind you,' he added with a wicked chuckle, 'I always preferred Dresden myself. You know, rosebuds popping out all over the place.'

As a professional hunter Allen had escorted all kinds of celebrities on safari, including Ava Gardner. Even when I met him, when he was in his mid-eighties, his hooded eyes were sharp and clear, and you could see why women adored him. But Kenya had changed, leaving him beached in Lamu. Like the dhow fleets and the disappearing rhino, he belonged to the past, a part of that vanishing Africa in which it seemed that the game would go on for ever.

Back in Shela after lunch, I walked out along the deserted beach that stretches for 13km beside the Indian Ocean. Cowrie shells littered the tide's edge. The sand was soft underfoot. The sea was warm, and I floated on my back, watching weaver birds in a flowering acacia. Later, I took a *jahazi* across to Ras Kitau and ordered a beer at the solitary bar. Here on Manda, I was told, elephants sometimes still left their giant footprints in the sand, and even lions had been known to swim across from the mainland.

The sun slid down across the bay and we sailed home. The barefoot crew were expert seamen. Swiftly, they hauled taut the bleached canvas sail until the boom bent like a bow and the boat flew before the wind, its wooden prow cleaving the green sea like a dolphin. By now Lamu's insidious lethargy had begun to work on me. I put away my watch, cast aside my shorts and took to wearing a *kikoi*, even at dinner. I padded barefoot to the beach, swam more slowly, slept more deeply. If I was not careful, I thought, I could end up like Bunny Allen, ensnared by island life for ever.

THE GALAPAGOS

Sitting on the beach on Hood Island, something both absurd and wonderful happened to me. A mockingbird perched on the end of my binoculars. It could happen only in the Galápagos, one of the few places on earth where wild creatures have no fear of humans. Stepping ashore on Plaza Sur Island I had to pick my way between recumbent sea lions that were using the jetty as a sunbed. On Seymour Island I strolled through a breeding colony of boobies (tropical gannets), which completely ignored me as they concentrated on their courtship rituals, marking time on their sky-blue feet.

The reason for this extraordinary display of trust is rooted in the history of the Galápagos and their sheer remoteness. The islands – 13 big ones, half a dozen little ones and more than 100 rocks and islets – lie on the Equator, 1,000km off the Ecuador coast in the boundless Pacific. Here, far from humans and other terrestrial predators, life evolved in an age of innocence that lasted until the chance discovery of the Galápagos in the 16th century, when a ship carrying the Bishop of Panama was blown off course in 1535.

Those first Spanish voyagers called them the Islas Encantadas, or Enchanted Isles, but in reality they are desert islands, arid mounds of volcanic cinders strewn across 130,000sq km of ocean. In the 17th century they became a lair for English buccaneers, who named the islands after their captains and their kings. Then came the American whaling fleets, which not only hunted the sperm whales to near extinction but also carried off the Galápagos giant tortoises in their tens of thousands. Stowed in the holds, the tortoises could be kept alive for up to a year – a perfect way to store fresh meat in the days before refrigeration. The buccaneers and whalers were also responsible for introducing swarms of alien animals – rats, dogs, cats, pigs, goats – which are still causing untold harm to the islands' unique ecosystems. Yet the wildlife appears as tame as ever, to the delight of the 60,000 tourists who visit the Galápagos every year.

Ecuador may be a poor country but no one can doubt its desire to protect the islands. Today, 97 per cent of the archipelago is a national park, yet huge problems must still be overcome if it is to remain among the world's great conservation flagships.

Recent years have seen a massive immigration from the mainland, of people seeking a better life in the Enchanted Isles. When the park was created in 1959 there were just 400 people living in Puerto Ayora, the largest town in the Galápagos. Now there are 8,000 – a situation that last year forced Ecuador to pass a law restricting immigration to the islands. Outside the towns, alien animals continue to ravage the islands. Santiago Island alone is infested with 100,000 goats. A further 80,000 are steadily eating their way into one of the last giant-tortoise strongholds on Isabela, and there is always the risk of other unwelcome species turning up. The latest arrival is a wasp with a very nasty sting; it hitched a ride from the mainland on a shipment of fruit in 1988 and is now widespread.

Most serious of all has been the destruction of marine life by illegal fishing. For at least two decades, foreign boats equipped with miles of baited hooks have been plundering these rich waters. For the poachers, anything of value has been fair game, from sharks' fins to sea-lion penises. And with 70,000sq km of ocean to protect, the national park's lone patrol boat and a couple of Ecuadorian navy vessels have been powerless to stop them.

In the early 1990s fishermen stumbled on a lucrative new market for *pepinos de mar* (sea cucumbers), a highly prized delicacy in the Far East. When the Ecuadorian government banned the trade in 1994, feelings ran high in the islands. In the so-called 'Pepino War' that followed, a national park warden was shot and fishermen even threatened to kill Lonesome George, the islands' most famous giant tortoise. Since then, life has settled down again, and in March 1999 fishermen and conservationists agreed on a compromise which, it is hoped, will satisfy both sides.

The only way to see the islands is from a cruise boat, with shore excursions led by a naturalist-guide. There are more than 100 such vessels operating in the islands, some big enough to carry 90 passengers, others with room for no more than a handful. The boat I chose was the *Beagle III*, a 22m motor cruiser with space for 10 passengers and a crew of six, including Luis Rodriguez, our English-speaking guide. Named after the ship in which Charles Darwin made his famous voyage to the Galápagos in 1835, *Beagle III* is herself a classic example of evolution, from scientific research vessel to comfortable cruise boat. She was built in England for the Charles Darwin Research Station in 1969 and is one of the few family-run boats in the islands, owned by Augusto Cruz, a native Galápagueño, and Georgina, his British wife.

With the red, blue and gold Ecuadorian flag fluttering in the breeze and a bunch of bananas strung up astern to ripen in the sun, we set off on the first leg of our voyage, to Seymour Island. For the next seven days *Beagle III* became my home, a never-to-be-forgotten week during which I put away my watch and lived barefoot like a buccaneer, but in far greater comfort. There were hot showers and a soft bunk, and wonderful meals eaten under the quarterdeck's shady awning, of home-made soups followed by grilled fish or lobster, served with salad, rice and red beans.

Every day we swam and snorkelled, floating above shoals of yellow-tailed surgeon fish and puffer fish stippled with guinea-fowl spots. We watched schools of black eagle rays glide past like squadrons of Stealth bombers, and one morning, swimming around the Devil's Crown – a spectacular drowned volcano off the coast of Floreana – we saw our first shark, a sinister shadow lurking in the blue. But in the Galápagos, it seems, even sharks exhibit a benign attitude towards humans. Best of all was the day we spent dancing with sea wolves, or rather, swimming with sea lions. In Spanish sea lions are called *lobos de mar*, and now here we were, partners in a slow minuet whose rhythms only they could hear as they circled around us, rising and falling through the sunlit water.

On Seymour Island we followed marked trails through thickets of prickly pear cactus, balancing like tightrope walkers as we hopped from one volcanic boulder to the next. Frigate birds soared overhead on switchblade wings, the males with throat sacs like red balloons, and the smell of guano filled the air with its acrid henhouse reek. Out on the horizon I could see the distinctive volcanic silhouette of Daphne Major, the tiny island on which my cousin, Peter Grant, has spent the best part of 20 years studying Darwin's finches. These drab little birds, 13 species in all, are descended from one common ancestor and are confusingly similar in appearance.

'Only God and Peter Grant can identify all Darwin's finches' is a popular saying among the tour guides. But each finch has a different beak for coping with a different food, and Darwin saw them as a textbook example of evolution through natural selection. In Darwin's day the accepted wisdom was that the Act of Creation had taken place on 23 October 4004BC, a date conjured up by Bishop

Ussher in the 17th century. But what Darwin discovered during his five weeks in the Galápagos was enough to blow the Bishop's beliefs out of the water.

My cousin's painstaking research has revealed how this remarkable adapt-or-die process is still going on. Yet while Darwin's finches may still be taking shape on nature's drawing-board, I could not imagine evolution improving on the waved albatrosses we saw on Hood Island at Punta Suarez, where the ocean swell pounds the cliffs with gasping force. Masters of the air with a 2.5m wingspan, the albatrosses rode the wind with matchless grace above the boiling surf.

Every island has something special. On Plaza Sur we were greeted by the honking territorial calls of the 250kg beachmasters, the top guns of sea-lion society. Above the shoreline, metre-long land iguanas with peeling skins and punkish hackles were munching at the prickly pears as we headed for the Men's Club, a patch of volcanic clifftop polished smooth by generations of bachelor sea lions.

On Floreana we waded ashore clutching postcards to drop into the island's unique postbox – a wooden barrel on a pole. The original barrel was placed here by a British whaler captain in 1793 and the system is still working. The idea is simple. You leave your own unstamped cards and take those you find inside to post when you get home. Times vary. 'From four days to two years,' said Luis. But ours arrived in a week.

Even in Puerto Ayora, wildlife abounds. Pelicans perch on the harbourside rooftops and marine iguanas – the world's only seagoing lizards – bask on the slipways, spitting salt from their nostrils as you walk past. Puerto Ayora is also the only place where you are guaranteed to see the Galápagos giant tortoises, the bathtub-sized creatures that roamed the islands in their tens of thousands before humans arrived. Here at the Charles Darwin Research Station, tortoises are raised in captivity until they are big enough to resist attacks by dogs and rats, then repatriated to their home islands. In the station's incubation rooms, tortoise eggs are kept warm with hairdryers. 'It's far more reliable than high technology,' said Luis. 'A sophisticated incubator might take days to repair if it broke down, and the eggs would have perished. But if a hairdryer fails you simply plug in a new one.'

Only on Bartolomé Island did we encounter anything remotely like a tourist honeypot. This is where cruise boats anchor while visitors snorkel in the lee of Pinnacle Rock or climb to the island's cindery summit for a frigate-bird's view of Sullivan Bay. Bartolomé's burnt-out landscape was, said US astronaut Buzz Aldrin when he came here, more like the surface of the moon than any other place on earth he had seen. But Sombrero Chino, a tiny island named after its resembance to a Chinese hat, we had all to ourselves. Only boats with fewer than a dozen passengers such as ours are allowed to anchor here and we made the most of it, swimming in an emerald-clear channel with only turtles and penguins for company.

Some conservationists blame tourism for contributing to the problems that have afflicted the Galápagos in recent years. But having been a part of it for a week, I now truly believe that eco-tourism is the only hope for their survival. On arrival at Baltra airport every visitor must pay a national park entry fee of US$100, and I was hugely impressed with the responsible way in which shore excursions are conducted. So long as the tourist dollars keep pouring in, I see no reason why these unique islands should not continue to be a showcase for evolution through the next millennium.

TUNISIA – KERKENNAH

One of Tunisia's more profitable sidelines is the baking of clay pots for the squid fishermen of Kerkennah. The inhabitants of these flat, sandy islands have devised a novel method of fishing. No bait is required, no hooks or nets, only a string of clay pots in which the night-loving squid can hide by day. From October until the following summer, long lines of pots – they look like miniature Greek amphorae – are staked out in the vast area of shallows surrounding Kerkennah. With luck, when they are hauled up next day, each pot will hold a resident squid.

With the Japanese willing to pay handsomely for a daily catch of perhaps 100kg of squid, the Kerkennis have never had it so good. El Attaya, where 500 fishermen and their families live at the northern end of the islands, is being rebuilt, and although the new houses conform to the flat-roofed, single-storey cubist tradition of North Africa, they now bristle with TV aerials, status symbols of Kerkennah's booming economy. Tourism, too, has arrived, although it has barely scratched the surface. Every morning at Sidi Youssef the ferry from Sfax disgorges a fresh load of passengers – mostly sun-starved Europeans lured by the promise of warm seas and lonely beaches. But the sands of Kerkennah extend for miles – more than enough to absorb ten times as many visitors as find their way to this sleepy Tunisian archipelago.

The isles of Kerkennah are true desert islands: a 40km strip of sand and palm groves, cut adrift from the rest of Tunisia and cast away into the Mediterranean. There, 25km offshore, they have come to rest in a limpid world of sand shoals and shallow bays – oases in the sea. Nowhere does the land rise above 3m, and the rest is barely high enough to keep the palms and fig trees dry-shod.

In earlier times the islands were a nest of pirates and a place of banishment for adulterous women. 'To Kerkennah!' was the Tunisian equivalent of telling someone to go to hell. But a growing band of British visitors will tell you it is closer to paradise. Even in

October the days are still deliciously warm, with temperatures over 20°C and nights pleasant enough that you can to sit outside in a light sweater. The same is true in April, and if all you want is somewhere quiet under the sun, there is no other low-season destination within three hours of Gatwick that can outshine Kerkennah.

From Sidi Youssef a single dusty road disappears into the date palms, then strikes out across the salt marsh between Gharbi and Chergui, the main islands. Accommodation is a toss-up between a couple of two-star hotels, the Grand and the Farhat, both within strolling distance of each other on Chergui, the biggest island. Each has its devotees. The Farhat is a pleasing Tunisian pastiche of whitewashed archways and rooftop patios; the Grand has oleander gardens behind it and the beach in front. Both serve fresh local fish, bread and olives served with *harissa*, that fiery Tunisian dip with a kick like Semtex, and, according to season, grapes, dates and watermelons.

I stayed at the Grand in a room with a balcony overlooking the beach and blue-painted shutters that concertinaed open to frame a perfect view of the sea between two date palms. At night the voice of the sea crept in, and I went to sleep with the sound of the tide lapping in my ears and woke to a flood of luminous light almost too bright to bear as the sun rose over the palms. For the next few days I enjoyed a born-again childhood, paddling in gin-clear seas that never seemed to rise above my waist no matter how far out I waded.

On my first evening in Kerkennah when the moon came up at dusk, I had watched two old men, trousers rolled above their knees, hunched like herons in the water. They were fishing for soles, which bury themselves in the sand at night, flushing them out with their bare toes and spearing them with barbed metal rods. Now, in the dazzling sunlight, I, too, felt the sudden wriggle of a flatfish beneath my foot and watched it shimmy across the seabed to bury itself in a new hiding place with only its goggle eyes raised above the sand. At every step, shoals of small silver fish glanced away. There were strange shells, exquisite sea anemones, and startled squid no bigger than my fist, which vanished in a smokescreen of black ink.

Along many parts of the coast, curious palisades extend for miles into the sea, like half-drowned hedgerows. The Kerkennah soil may be poor and sandy, but the islanders have made gardens of their fertile sea, dividing its shallows into submarine fields with long lines of palm fronds. The fronds are stuck into the sandy bottom, forming impenetrable walls that funnel passing shoals of fish into the waiting nets or wicker traps – a method of fishing known as *charfia*. In summer, when the waters are still and clear, the fishermen put to sea to harvest sponges, which they locate by peering down through the water with a glass-bottomed box and then pull up with a long, hooked pole. It is not difficult to find a fisherman who will take you out for a few dinars, and the Grand Hotel lays on regular trips throughout the season.

One day we took a painted boat, a blue and white felucca with peeling decks and a lateen sail, and two fishermen who poled us out into deeper water, floating over meadows of sea grass and the upturned mouths of giant abalone shells. When at last a breeze sprang up and the sail hung full-bellied from its slender boom, we drifted down the coast to a deserted bay where the palms curved away into a luminous distance so blurred with heat that it was hard to tell where the sea ended and the sky began.

The crew waded ashore with a bag of charcoal and lit a fire to bar-becue fresh mullet on the beach. While we waited for the fish to cook, some of our party played rounders on the sands, watched by a solitary horse tethered to a rotting hulk. Others sunbathed or hunted for shells, while one couple just sat in the water, engrossed in a serious debate about self-esteem.

There was something strange, almost surreal, about that indolent place. When the tide fell back it exposed miles of salt-smelling sand-flats that lay wet and glittering in the sharp sea-light. Under those huge skies, bounded by level horizons, it might have been East Anglia but for the stranded feluccas and their slanting masts.

MADEIRA AND THE ISLAS DESERTAS

Floating on my back in the clifftop swimming pool at Reid's Hotel in Funchal, I could just make out the tops of high hills rolling away into the mountainous heart of Madeira. Mountainous is a good word for Madeira. From the sunless floor of the Atlantic abyss to the 1,861m summit of Pico Ruivo, the whole island is really one gigantic mountain, 6km high.

Everywhere on Madeira, life inclines to the vertical, and nowhere is there a better example of the islanders' total disregard for the concept of vertigo than on the high mountain walk from Pico do Arieiro to Pico Ruivo. If you are reasonably fit you should manage it easily in three-and-a-half hours – in terms of stamina there are far tougher stretches on the Pennine Way. However, what this walk demands – and what I was totally unprepared for – is a head for heights and the ice-cold nerves of a mountain goat.

The staff from Reid's Hotel had brought a picnic. Hampers were unpacked on a stone table hacked out of the mountainside. Out came chicken legs, salad, melon, cheese and fruit juice. But the sight of the path had taken away my appetite. It stretched before me like a nightmare, the most famous walk in Madeira: a stone tightrope suspended between solemn, broken-toothed peaks; a skywalker's highway, teetering along the ridges with nothing but clouds on either side. Forcing myself to peer over the edge, I could see the great cliffs falling away into unimaginable depths, to the safe, green world of laurel forests and terraced fields far below.

To be fair, it is a proper footpath, a metre wide, and was built in the late 1960s with stone steps and solid paving to replace the original shepherds' path. Some stretches even have protective wire railings held in place by iron stanchions, although these are not to be trusted, and in several places they have been swept away by landslides and rock falls.

The mountains looked as if they had been incinerated. Ahead loomed the rusty lava pinnacles of the Pico das Torres, Madeira's second-highest mountain, with the path clinging perilously to its precipitous flanks. In some places, flights of stone steps vanished into the mist. Elsewhere, just when it seemed that there could be no way forward, the path plunged into a tunnel through the cliffs.

Leading the way was Dr Frank Zino, an eminent local naturalist, mountain-wise and nimble-footed. He was born on the island but is more English than the English. At one time he worked as company doctor for the BBC in London, before returning home to become a GP in Funchal. It was Dr Zino who pointed out the wildflowers sprouting from every cliff and crevice: white saxifrage, wild geraniums, fleshy leaved aeoniums and the giant purple spires of echiums, known here as the 'pride of Madeira'.

Gangs of swifts went scything past. Above, a buzzard sailed on the updraughts. 'Up there,' said Dr Zino, pointing to a narrow balcony of grass marooned among the crags, 'is the breeding ground of Europe's rarest seabird, the gadfly petrel.' The Madeirans call it the *freira* (the nun) because of its soft grey, black and white plumage. For years the birds were thought to have become extinct. Then, in 1969, Dr Zino's father rediscovered them. Now it is thought that up to 20 pairs breed on the island.

At last the precipices were behind us and we toiled on through a forest of giant heather, 6m tall, until we reached the rest house below the summit of Pico Ruivo. Here, from the highest point on the island, we watched the sun set over a sea of cloud, then fell ravenously upon a supper of *espetades* – Portuguese-style kebabs cooked over an open fire on a spit of bay laurel, whose pungence impregnated the meat with its delicious flavour.

Next morning we were joined by Michael Blundy, whose family own Reid's Hotel, and Manuel, a forest guard dressed in khaki, who was going to lead us down an unmarked shepherds' path to the valley 300m below. We started in bright sunlight, but as we descended, zigzagging steeply through hanging gardens of ferns and orchids, the clouds closed in. The damp air smelled of bracken and marjoram, and out of the mist came the sound of goat bells and the sinister hiss of mountain streams falling into the unseen void beneath our feet.

In three hours we reached the evergreen cloud forests of the Laurisilva, the world's largest tract of laurel forest, its ancient trees bearded with moss and lichen. By now, with the mist swirling even more thickly, it was as gloomy as an English November day. And then suddenly we were out of the cloud. Our trial by vertigo was over. Below lay a sunlit path – blissfully horizontal – which would lead us back to civilization along the Levada do Caldeirão Verde, one of the 2,000km of aqueducts that carry water from the mountains to irrigate the terraced fields below.

At the end of it all Michael Blundy summed up our walk with typical British understatement. It had been, he said, 'on the strenuous side of strenuous'. But if I had thought that Pico Ruivo was no picnic, it was nothing to what lay ahead.

The next day I set off from Funchal harbour with Dr Zino to visit the Islas Desertas, a group of three islands whose blue iceberg silhouettes lay nearly 30km away on the south-eastern horizon. The Desertas are the wildest islands in the Atlantic. The barren summits of a drowned mountain range, they have been protected since 1990 as part of the Parque Natural de Madeira. Although the public cannot stay overnight on the islands, a day trip makes a fascinating contrast to the botanical paradise of Madeira.

For our journey Dr Zino had commandeered an ancient, 15m gaff-rigged ketch called the *Boa Tarde* (Good Afternoon), normally used to ferry men and provisions to the guards' house on Deserta Grande, the main island. Ahead lay a four-hour voyage. The force-six winds whipped up white horses all around us, and as soon as we left the shelter of the Bay of Funchal the boat began to wallow in the 2m swell.

As we drew nearer I could make out the islands more clearly, their jagged walls of volcanic rock separated by narrow, treacherous channels. Together they made a daunting picture. The northernmost of the three Desertas is the Ilheu Chao, a low, flat island, 1,852m long. At one end is a sea stack known as Sail Rock, which in certain conditions looks like an old square-rigger under full canvas. To the south rose the dark, hogbacked cliffs of Bugio. But we were making for Deserta Grande and the guards' house at Doca, where a gigantic landslide had fanned out into the sea to create a natural breakwater.

As its name suggests, Deserta Grande is the biggest island, 13km long, with savage cliffs soaring sheer from the Atlantic. Scrambling ashore onto a beach of volcanic boulders, I felt as if I had just arrived on Mars. We had dropped anchor as the sun was setting. Now, its dying rays ignited the red crags 350m above us to create a scene of utter desolation.

From the late 15th century, all three islands were owned by descendants of João Concalves Zarco, Madeira's discoverer and first governor. Long ago, houses stood here, with a chapel, threshing floors and dew ponds to collect water; but the last permanent inhabitants left in 1802 after a giant waterspout stripped away what meagre grazing had existed. Unbelievably, there is a path to the top of Deserta Grande, scarier than anything encountered on Pico Ruivo. In the old days, lookouts kept watch here for passing whales, using white sheets to signal to the whaling ships offshore. Now, apart from rabbits, feral goats and a large black spider whose bite is said to be lethal, the summit is devoid of life.

Later we sailed to Bugio. The sea threw up steep, confused waves that ran at us from every direction, causing our boat to roll alarmingly. All along the base of the cliffs the swell was surging into the wet black mouths of caves whose depths are a refuge for the endangered monk seal, an animal so rare that only 300 are left in the world. On Madeira, the monk seal is known as *o lobo marinho* (the sea wolf) and between 12 and 20 of these mysterious creatures live in the Desertas. With binoculars I peered into the sea-wolf's lair, but in vain. If the seals were at home they were sensibly keeping a low profile.

In late afternoon the wind picked up again. For the last time we raised anchor and ran for home. Behind us, the sawtooth summits of Deserta Grande were tearing great holes in the clouds. Dolphins plunged around our bows, and Cory's shearwaters skimmed like boomerangs down the long blue troughs of the waves. There was no shelter from the driving spray, but the sun was in our faces and at the end of the voyage, like a vision of heaven, was the promise of a hot bath and the soft white beds of Reid's Hotel.

EUROPEAN
TRAILS

THE PYRENEES – ACROSS THE GREAT DIVIDE

Sometimes, on a fine summer's day when the plains of Haute Languedoc and Gascogne are quivering in the heat, you can see what appears to be the vague outline of an immense cloudbank lying along the southern horizon. Only when you are close enough to pick out the gleam of high glaciers and snowfields do you realize that you are looking at the Pyrénées.

For centuries the Pyrénées have acted as a natural barrier, cutting off Spain from the rest of Europe. The Moors called them El Hadjiz – the Barricade – the great wall between the dusty brown African landscapes of Iberia and the green fields of France, 435km of jagged peaks and crests running from the Bay of Biscay to the Mediterranean.

The Romans used the few high passes as imperial trade routes, linking the cities of Caesar Augustus (Zaragoza) and Burdiglia (Bordeaux). Medieval pilgrims following the road to Compostela toiled over the Col de Somport on their way to the shrine of St James the Moor-slayer. Sometimes a battle would wash around the foothills, but for the most part the Pyrénées kept aloof from the mainstream of history. Only occasionally, as in AD778 when the Basques butchered Charlemagne's rearguard in the Col de Roncesvalles, did the sounds of war disturb the mountains' ancient silence. And so they remained well into the 20th century, lonely and untrodden except by shepherds and hunters, a refuge for bandits, a stronghold for smugglers and a favourite wartime escape route used by the Resistance for helping RAF pilots to leave Nazi-occupied France.

Even today, despite the rash of new ski resorts, the inevitable desecration of pylons and power lines and the modern roads that now traverse the high cols or tunnel their way through the impassable rock, the Pyrénées have preserved their sense of apartness. Compared to the Alps they remain oddly ignored. Few writers have been drawn to them other than Belloc and Freya Stark, who found them 'wilder than the Alps, lapped around with forests rather than pastures – stretches of uninhabited lands – more like Asia'.

Certainly the Pyrenean forests – the highest in Europe – are one of the glories of the region, with dense canopies of beech and resinous pinewoods climbing to a height of 2,500m before giving way to bare rock. On the French side, Bigorre, midway along the massif, is the region of the High Pyrénées, with Vignemale (3,298m) as its loftiest peak. The most beautiful stretch is preserved as the Parc National des Pyrénées, which contains over 230 mountain tarns and extends along the frontier for more than 100km.

The best place for exploring Bigorre is Luz-St Sauveur, an attractive little town with a fortified church and an excellent visitor centre for the national park, which begins about 20km up the valley beyond the mountain village of Gavarnie. Here, as elsewhere in the region, the Bigourdains are fond of drinking champagne laced with a tot of armagnac. This deadly concoction goes by the name of the *pousse rapière* – the sword-thrust. They also make a rib-sticking soup, *la garbure*, which consists mostly of cabbage and potatoes with odd scraps of pork thrown in for good measure.

On the way into Gavarnie stands a roadside statue to Count Henri Roussel, an eccentric 19th-century mountaineer who climbed Vignemale 33 times and built caves in the rocks where he entertained his guests at extravagent candlelit dinners in full evening dress. Above the village looms the Cirque de Gavarnie, the greatest natural wonder of the French Pyrénées: a gigantic bowl set beneath the awesome crests of Marbore, its curtain walls of twisted strata capped with glaciers and plumed with cascades that plunge for hundreds of metres into the shadows below.

From Gavarnie you can follow the red and white paint splashes that mark the long-distance mountain trails of the *grandes randonnées*, twisting and turning on their laborious ascent to the Refuge de la Brèche, perched at 2,587m on the edge of the Cirque de Gavarnie. But this is serious walking and you need to be fit and fully equipped.

On the Spanish side of the Pyrénées the scenery is even more dramatic. Here lies the valley of Ordesa, Spain's answer to the Grand Canyon and a strong contender for the most beautiful national park in Europe. Its lower depths are an earthly paradise of fathomless beechwoods filled with the sound of the Río Arazas as it leaps and crashes down the valley on its way to the scorching plains of Aragón. Its upper limits are the sky-high rimrocks of the canyon walls, weathered into fantastic shapes, with huge prows and pinnacles and brooding citadels of tawny limestone that turn to gold in the evening light. To drive there from France involves an epic journey over the Puerto del Pourtalé and then down through Sallent-de-Gállego – a good 100km from Luz-St Sauveur. Or there is a radical alternative. If you are reasonably fit, don't mind camping and have a head for heights, you can walk. In good weather you can do it in three days – a superb high-altitude hike *sans frontières* – and no one will ask to see your passport where you cross the border at a height of nearly 3,000m.

I made the trip with three friends, starting out on the Spanish side and finishing up in France at Gavarnie. We set off from Torla, the mountain village that stands at the entrance to the Parque Nacional de Ordesa, confronted by the towering rock walls of Mondarruego (2,828m). The first few kilometres were easy and we passed many visitors who had come to Torla to explore the canyon's lower reaches, wandering through the woods from one waterfall to the next. But soon the path began to climb more steeply until at last it emerged above the tree-line in a different world of high-mountain pastures where gentians bloomed and the air tasted sharper. Here we camped (illegally, we later discovered), in the great amphitheatre of the Circo de Soaso, whose headwalls close in around this classic U-shaped glacial valley.

Next morning there was frost on the tents, but long before midday we were walking in shirtsleeves again. Even at this altitude, more than 2,000m above sea-level, we saw lizards, autumn crocuses and butterflies basking in the sun.

All this high country is the home of eagles and vultures, most notably the lammergeyer, or bearded vulture. In Spanish this enormous raptor is known as *quebrantahuesos* – the bone-breaker – due to its unique feeding habit of dropping animal carcasses on the rocks to get at the marrow. Spain is now the bone-breaker's last European stronghold, and even here fewer than 80 pairs survive, most of them in the High Pyrénées of Alto-Aragón. Here, too, in the remotest valleys, the brown bear lingers like a legend, although few are seen. But the isard, the Pyrenean version of the chamois, are common everywhere, picking their way across perilous ledges with no regard for the void beneath.

At first there had seemed to be no way out of the Circo de Soaso. We watched braver souls heading off through a defile in the direction of *Las Clavijas* – a set of iron pegs hammered into the cliffs by a 19th-century ibex hunter – but they called for the nerves of a tightrope walker. Then we spotted the faintest trace of a path zigzagging up precipitous aprons of scree to a crag where hands as well as feet were needed to gain the easier slopes above.

That night we stayed at the Goriz Mountain Refuge, dining cheaply and well on rabbit stew and sharing a three-tiered dormitory with 70 snoring Spaniards. The room was warm, but the air was thick enough to cut with a cheesewire and we were glad to be on our way again in the morning.

Now the last of the limestone pastures lay behind us. We toiled on past lonely tarns covered with a skin of ice, into a lunar wasteland of frost-shattered rock. Above us, glaciers glinted against the sky as we passed beneath Monte Perdido – the Lost Mountain. Somewhere a raven grunted, and its guttural voice was taken up in the silence and flung, echoing, from crag to crag. Ahead rose the savage summits that run like watchtowers along the spine of Europe's wildest frontier – the triple peaks of Marbore, the crooked gables of El Tallon. And in between, like a missing tooth, was a gap in the intervening crest of 100m cliffs called the Brèche de Roland.

Roland was the paladin killed by the Basques as he fought to secure the safe withdrawal of Charlemagne's forces across the Pyrénées. His death at Roncesvalles (nowhere near the Brèche de Roland) became the stuff of legend. The Basques became Saracens, and Roland a giant with a magic sword, Durandel. With his dying strength, Roland struck the mountain, trying in vain to break his sword so that it would not fall into the hands of his enemies; the result was the Brèche de Roland, the natural gateway for mountain walkers passing between Spain and France.

Mountains are sacred places and sometimes they give rise to profound thoughts. I remembered that I had undertaken this walk as a rite of passage, a kind of mid-life challenge to celebrate the passing of my fiftieth birthday. Now, standing in the portals of the Brèche, one foot in Spain and the other in France, it occurred to me that I was poised on the roof of my life.

Behind me lay the ground I had covered, and all the mountains of Spain fading away in five distinct ranges (one for each decade, I thought), to the infinity of the horizon. Ahead to the north lay the mountains of France, hazy and indistinct in the September sunshine. Somewhere down there, beyond the snowfields that sloped around this wide upper lip of the Cirque de Gavarnie, was the promise of dinner, a hot bath and clean sheets in Luz-St Sauveur.

It was growing colder. I took one last look back into the golden haze of Spain, then turned and walked down through the snow to begin the rest of my life.

SPAIN – A LAND AS HARD AS OAK

Above Plasencia the road to Ávila climbed between steep terraced hillsides of olives, figs and cherries. In spring, when the cherry orchards are in flower, these hillsides are incomparable. But now it was October and the leaves were changing colour. Under the trees, men were pruning and sawing, burning the old wood, and the autumn smoke rose like incense through the branches. I asked one of the men how many cherry trees he owned. 'Twenty,' he said, rubbing the sawdust from the teeth of his saw with calloused hands. 'Beautiful, are they not? But you must look after them. You must love them like you love your mother.'

Lower down in the silent valley a young man with a stubbled chin and denim jacket was ploughing behind a brown mare. He clucked at the horse, coaxing her past a smouldering bonfire of dead wood. '*Oiga!* Do you hear me? Go on,' he said softly, urging the mare forward. She was six years old and very gentle, he said.

The sun had vanished behind the clouds. A depression was moving in, shrouding the hills in drizzle, but still the autumn colours of the cherry trees gave out their lantern glow as if lit from within. The blossom came in March or April, said the ploughman, depending on the severity of the winter, and was a sight to behold.

Above the village of Jerte there came a sound as old as Spain: the brassy clank of cowbells. Men on horseback with lapping capes and wooden stirrups were driving their cattle down from the high summer pastures, as they had done for centuries. Higher up the valley the sound of bells rang out again. This time it was a flock of goats, herded by men on foot with their dogs. They flowed past in their thousands, like a river, holding up the traffic as they pattered along in the rain. They had come from Ávila over the Puerto de Tornavacas – the Pass where the Cows Turn. Now they were heading for the *invernaderos*, the winter pastures around Trujillo in Extremadura, and still had another week's march to go.

Extremadura is literally the land beyond. For the nomadic herdsmen of the *transhumancia*, driving their animals for hundreds of kilometres from the summer grazing grounds of Old Castile, Extremadura was the end of a long hard journey. Nobody knows how long this great pastoral migration has been going on. Some say it began in the fifth century with the Visigoths. In time, traditional drove roads, *cañadas*, were established – a web of grassy highways, some of them 75m wide, spanning the country between the mountains and the plains.

Today the *transhumancia* is withering away. The young men no longer want to pursue the lonely life of the shepherds. Developers and farmers are stealing huge tracts of the old greenways, and much of the migration is now by truck or train. Soon, perhaps, the last shepherd will set out on the last journey over the lavender-smelling hills, and a whole way of life will pass away. But for now, and a few years yet, the flocks still come over the high passes, and the lean, gaunt men in brown cloaks that reach down to their boots stride into Extremadura.

Hard, austere, slow to change. In many ways this wild, western province remains the one least touched by the 21st century. It is the most conservative, the purest, the most intensely Spanish. Fierce black fighting bulls roam the vast estates whose owners can trace their pedigrees right back to the wars of the Reconquest against the Moors. In summer the white storks build their nests on every church tower, even in the heart of Cáceres. And the Black Virgin of Guadalupe still draws the devout to her monastery in the mountains, where Columbus prayed before setting out to find America.

Above all, Extremadura remains a land of trees, of the *encina*, or holm-oak – an evergreen oak whose upper branches are lopped every four years to make charcoal – and of the cork oak, whose wrinkled bark is stripped every ninth year to leave the trunks a rich terracotta red, as if they had just been painted. A French nobleman writing in the 18th century noted that Spain was so heavily wooded that a squirrel might run from the Pyrénées to the Mediterranean without ever touching ground. While that is certainly no longer true, much of Extremadura remains well wooded, with cattle and sheep grazing under widely spaced oaks. Even today you can still find landscapes that look much as they must have done to Wellington's soldiers in the Peninsula Wars. And the *dehesa*, as this Arcadian wood-pasture is called, is strictly protected.

In the remoteness of the *dehesa*, old customs cling on, old legends persist, of sacred oaks, Moorish treasures. In many country districts there is still a tradition of folk medicine, dispensed by a *curandero*, or white witch. If a child is sick, people still say, 'The moon has taken him.'

South of Plasencia I came into a country of stony hills where red kites wheeled in the wind and olive trees turned to silver in the brilliant air. The land was hot and yellow, like Africa, with the same sense of space and distance, reaching out to the bony carcasses of distant mountain ranges. I crossed the Río Tajo (Tagus) and found a signpost that said 'Portugal 68km', and after a few more kilometres I reached Garovillas. It was midday and the town's narrow streets were deserted. I strolled around the cobbled plaza, walled in by 18th-century houses whose upper storeys formed a cool arcade, propped up on lurching granite pillars. One of the walls had been defaced by graffiti, including a scribbled drawing of a fighting bull. An old lady saw me looking at it and tut-tutted her displeasure. '*Que barbaridad*,' she said. 'Do the young do such things in England?'

Near by, in a cavernous bar, old men with oaken faces and cloth caps were watching a quiz show on television. Someone had just won a car to delirious applause. Framed photographs on the walls showed scenes from the town's annual *encierro*, or running of the bulls, with a man lying badly gored.

After Garrovillas I rejoined the main road, which follows the line of the Ruta de la Plata, the silver highway of the Phoenician traders, running the length of Spain from Gijón to Sevilla. By the time I reached Zafra it was almost dusk and the starlings were roosting in the palm trees. The *parador* was closed for repairs but the three-star Huerta Honda next door was very comfortable and its restaurant, Barbacana, was the best in town.

Zafra is the southernmost of the white towns of Extremadura. In its narrow streets and cobbled plazas, among its fountains and wrought-iron balconies, the influence of Andalucía, less than 30km away, is very strong. Zafra was named by the Moors, but Mérida, some 50km to the north, was once called Augusta Emerita, the capital of Roman Lusitania. It was built in 25BC as a place of retirement in which veterans of the V and X Legions could see out their days, and much of their city has survived, including the magnificent Roman theatre and a famous bridge. Two thousand years ago its 60 granite arches echoed to the measured tread of Roman soldiers; today they are still in use, carrying traffic for nearly a kilometre across the Río Guadiana.

In Mérida I met a pig farmer. His name was Mariano Señoron Rubio and he waxed lyrical about the charcoal-grey pigs of

Extremadura, which are turned out in November to fatten on the acorns of the evergreen oaks. 'I love my pigs,' he said. 'They have such strong sensibilities. Did you know that when piglets finish suckling they go and kiss their mothers?'

Most of the 3,000 pigs on his farm would end up as *jamon serrano*, those glorious golden haunches that hang by their trotters from the beams of every bar in Spain. Every year, Rubio told me, the Spaniards ate 26 million such hams, shaved into delicious translucent slices. 'Making ham is an art,' he said. 'That's why it costs so much. It's a food for lords.'

It was in Mérida, too, that I met Miguel Angel Bedate, a painter widely known in Spain for his pictures of Extremadura. With his shoulder-length hair and gaunt El Greco features he made a truly bohemian figure, wandering the countryside in search of subjects to paint: charcoal-burners, bullfighters and, above all, the evergreen oaks so characteristic of the region.

'Extremadura for me is light and colour,' he said. 'There's a long-held belief that there is nothing here but emptiness and desolation. I want to break the mould and paint the contentment.'

I went with him to see a reservoir the Romans had built at Cornalvo, a blue lake in the profound silence of the *dehesa*, where each oak stood in its own dark pool of shade. 'I have very deep feelings for these old trees,' he said. A storm had passed a week ago and the banks of the reservoir, bare all summer, were now covered with mauve drifts of autumn crocuses.

Afterwards we drove a short distance and then walked into a magical tract of primeval Mediterranean woodland. With its spreading oaks and glades of bracken it was not unlike the New Forest, but the air was heavy with the scent of cistus, the hot aromatic smell of the south, and an eagle owl, a bird the Spanish call *el gran duque*, flew off under the trees like a huge moth. Extremadura is a birdwatcher's heaven. Here live not only eagle owls and red kites, but azure-winged magpies and imperial eagles. In Monfrague, a national park renowned for its rare black storks and vulture colonies, I watched a goshawk snatch a magpie and dash off with it through the cork oaks, leaving a trail of drifting feathers.

There are still lynx in this wild land, and while I was in Monfrague reports came in that wolves had just killed 48 sheep in the Sierra de San Pedro near the Portuguese border. Nowadays the wolf is a protected species and farmers receive generous compensation for the loss of their stock, but hunting is a national sport, and at weekends the autumn countryside echoes to the sound of Spaniards blazing away at partridge, hare and wild boar. Like the British, the Spanish have shooting in their blood. After all, as Jan Morris wrote in her excellent book, *Spain*, war for the Spaniards is a vocation. They live in a land littered with castles. Even their language, which gave the world the word guerrilla, has the staccato clatter of machine-gun fire. And, of course, it was Extremadura that produced the conquistadores, those rapacious soldier-adventurers who fought their way from California to Chile to seize the New World. Among them was Francisco Pizarro, the butcher of Peru, whose triumphant statue, sword in hand, visor flung back, sits astride his warhorse in the main square of his home town, Trujillo. Pizarro was 50 when he killed the Inca, Atahuallpa, and conquered Peru. The writer HV Morton described him and his men as 'the first American gangsters', beating Al Capone by 400 years.

Approaching Trujillo on the road from Cáceres, the first impression is of a hill town reminiscent of those in Tuscany, with tall towers and slender cypresses bristling against the sky. I climbed a flight of granite steps and came at last to the castle of the Moors, haunted by jackdaws. Beneath the ramparts, beyond the towers and rooftops of the little town, stony fields ran out into a landscape laid bare by wind and sun, where Pizarro and his three brothers had worked as swineherds before they set off for Peru.

Down in the square the cracked bells of St Martin's rang out, striking the hour with a sound like a battleaxe beating on a Moorish shield. The wind rose. A storm was coming. Threads of rain hid the sharp outlines of the far sierras and apocalyptic shafts of light fell across the yellowing sheepwalks where the flocks of the *transhumancia* would spend the winter. Here, and at the Shrine of Guadalupe, and in the medieval streets of Cáceres, the sense of the past is overpowering, as if Pizarro and his fellow conquistadores had decamped only a month or so ago, marching out into the darkening plain.

From Trujillo I made my way back to Plasencia again, with the Sierra de Gredos on the eastern horizon. The road climbed steeply now, clinging to the sides of the Garganta de los Buitres (the Gorge of the Vultures) until at last it levelled out at the Puerto de Honduras, the highest pass in Extremadura, 1,430m above sea-level. This was Dartmoor writ large, a land of open hills scattered with granite boulders, but below I could see the Ambroz valley and beyond, more hills and valleys rolling westward into Portugal.

In Hervás, the medieval village that lies at the heart of the Ambroz valley, I met an 80-year-old goatherd dressed in jeans and carpet slippers. 'When I was a young man I fought in the war,' he told me proudly. 'The civil war?' I asked him. 'Of course,' he said. 'The Spanish war,' as if there had been no others.

In the 18th-century convent church, a tortured Christ weeps tears of blood beneath a crown of thorns. But Hervás is best known for its old Jewish quarter: a maze of backstreets with names such as the Calle de la Sinagoga, some so narrow that I was hardly able to squeeze through without rubbing both shoulders against the walls. The Jews arrived in the 15th century, hoping to avoid the terror of the Inquisition in this remote corner of Spain. Today their descendants still gather in the Taberna Judia, a local bar with the Star of David set in cobbles in the floor.

South-east of Hervás, in the foothills of the Sierra de Gredos, lay more of that beautiful park-like country where black bulls wandered under the trees and sweet chestnuts grew by the roadsides. There were granite knolls and groves of oaks with twisted limbs, and damp leaves underfoot, smelling of England. Through it all runs the Vera valley, with its woods of oak and chestnut, its tumbling trout streams and fertile terraces. It was here that the Emperor Charles V came in 1556, dragging his gout-ridden body to the monastery at Yuste.

In the 16th century Charles was the most powerful ruler on earth. Don Carlos, by the Grace of God King of Castile, León, Aragón, Sicily, Jerusalem, Navarra, Granada, Jaén, Valencia, Galicia, Mallorca, West and East Indies... the list of his kingdoms goes on forever. It was during his reign that the conquistadores Pizarro and Cortés added Peru and Mexico to his overseas' possessions.

But in 1566, world-weary and racked with pain, the ageing emperor decided to return to Spain and end his days in Extremadura. He was exhausted when he arrived at Laredo on the Bay of Biscay, having come all the way by sea from Germany. From Laredo he travelled south as far as Tornavacas and, from there, he was carried over the mountains to Jarandilla in a single day, reclining in a curious leather-bound box-chair, like an old sea-chest, which can still be seen in the monastery at Yuste, where he died two years later. Inside the monastery, in a gloomy room where daylight scarcely penetrates, his four-poster death-bed is still in place. Here he lay in agony, unable, it is said, even to bear the weight of a sheet on his ulcerated body, while priests said mass in the adjoining chapel.

From Yuste I set out to explore the other villages of La Vera, as this idyllic region is called. In Valverde de la Vera, a medieval warren of timber-framed houses, I took refuge in the doorway of a bar as a herd of fierce-looking long-horned cattle was driven through the narrow streets. Inside the bar, its floor ankle-deep in sawdust, shrimp heads and olive stones, wizened men of incalculable years drank beer and played cards with the easy ribaldry of a lifetime together.

But the best, to my mind, was Garganta la Olla. For me it was the archetypal hill village of northern Extremadura. A huddle of tiled rooftops, a granite church, and behind it and all around, the chestnut trees and cherry orchards glowing with soft autumn colours, like an antique tapestry, climbing to the high country where wild boar roam in the copper-glinting woods and eagles coast among the clouds.

I came to Garganta over the hills from Yuste, and when I stopped to look down, the sounds of the village came floating up on the sharp mountain air, cocks crowing, dogs barking, a stream hissing under the oaks. In the village itself, smoke was seeping through the tiled roofs where hams hung in soot-blackened attics, maturing in the pungent darkness. Cobbled streets ran like the uneven beds of mountain streams between balconied houses festooned with strings of peppers. Hand-written messages, scrawled on scraps of paper and stuck in shop windows, advertised local honey for sale. This was not a wealthy village, but it seemed that everything the land produced could be obtained here: fresh walnuts, trout, field mushrooms.

The villagers, too, appeared exceptionally friendly, and the old men sunning themselves in the square, learning that I was English, were eager to know more about *La Dama de Hierro*. Even here, it seemed, in this rural backwater in what is still one of the least populated regions of Europe, Mrs Thatcher's Iron Lady reputation had cast its formidable shadow.

Next morning I set off for another remote corner of the province, back-tracking through Montehermoso towards the sombre summits of the Sierra de la Canchera. Here, among desolate hills of pine and heather, I came to the villages of Las Hurdes, with the narrow mountain road following every twist and turn of the Río Hurdano in its wild gorge below. Up and up the road climbed, zigzagging into the clouds, leaving behind the sunlit terraces, the white towns of the warm south and the sacred groves where the black bulls roam. By the time I descended from the clouds and the familiar pattern of cork oaks began to reappear, I had crossed the border into Salamanca and was on the road back to the Atlantic coast, to Santander and home.

SPAIN – PICOS DE EUROPA

Alevia, high in the mountains of Asturias, is the kind of village where rush hour is a procession of cows with clanking bells, plodding home at milking time. From its narrow streets I climbed a path that led steeply into the Sierra de Cuera, a limestone range with its head in the clouds. On the way up, I passed cider orchards where red apples hung from bending boughs, mountain pastures strewn with mushrooms and, higher still, flocks of sheep pouring down the stony slopes. At last I came to the skyline and, far below through a gap in the clouds, I saw for the first time the Cantabrian sea, bluer than the gentians in the mountain grass, and the Asturian coast marching west to Galicia.

That first view of the sea was just one of the high spots of a week-long walk in northern Spain, from the Picos de Europa to the fishing port of Llanes. This is Green Spain – the Costa Verde – where Madrid's smart set comes to escape the heat of the Castilian summer, and it is as different from the rest of the country as Majorca is from the Isle of Skye.

At first glance it all looks strangely familiar: a lush coastal ribbon of pasture and bracken ending abruptly in stark slate cliffs and sandy coves. Like Cornwall, perhaps, or Pembrokeshire, or the wilder shores of Ireland. But only in Green Spain can you still see old-fashioned haystacks like shaggy anthills standing in meadows where 20 kinds of orchids bloom in spring. Only here will you pass Roman-tiled farmsteads with their free-range hens and traditional *hórreos* – the rat-proof corn-cribs of Asturias – raised four-square on staddle stones taller than a man.

The Asturians, too, are quite unlike the people of Mediterranean Spain. Not for them the wine and flamenco of the warm south. They still cling wholeheartedly to the culture of Europe's Celtic fringe. Like the Welsh, they dig for coal. Like the Bretons, they are great trawlermen, drink draught cider, play the bagpipes and have their own version of Breton pancakes called *frixuelos* – delicious with a topping of dark mountain honey. And, like the Galicians of north-western Spain, they fortify themselves against the rain with hearty stews of pork and beans and a few garlicky chunks of blood sausage thrown in for good measure.

Away from the coast, Asturias quickly becomes mountainous, a vertical Normandy, flowing with cream and cider and salmon rivers. On a clear day, it is said, you can pick out the snows gleam-ing on the Asturian mountaintops from 200km out to sea. For mariners returning from South America in the age of the conquista-dores, these lofty summits were their first sight of home. Hence their name: the Picos de Europe.

Behind the Picos hides the rest of Spain, brown and dusty, lean-ing towards Africa. But Asturias, on the seaward side, is painted in a thousand shades of green, a second Switzerland, with its alpine pastures and echoing cowbells. Yet to think of this massif of saw-toothed summits as an Iberian version of the Bernese Oberland is to do it less than justice, for the Picos are unique and there is nowhere left in the Alps that is half as wild or unspoilt.

It was here that Christianity made its last stand against the Moors in the eighth century, finally emerging victorious under King Pelayo after a battle near Covadonga that marked the beginning of the reconquest of Spain. Today these remote mountains form the core of Spain's biggest national park and, once again, they are a vital stronghold – this time for some of Europe's rarest wild creatures. Packs of wolves and even a handful of brown bears still roam the Picos, along with chamois, eagles and griffon vultures.

My week began with a 12km walk into the heart of the Picos from Poncebos, the park's northern gateway. Limestone is the keynote to understanding these high-rise landscapes, limestone that has been shaped and weathered into fantastic steeples and silver-grey pin-nacles that go rushing up into the sky. This whole area is riven by deep gorges, but by far the most spectacular is the one formed by the Río Cares. The Asturians call it La Garganta – The Throat – and this was the route we followed. In the European super-league of gorges, it is the champion; a limestone chasm 1,000m deep. From below comes the constant roar of the river cascading from pool to jade-green pool. High above, among the clouds and around the peaks and ridges, griffon vultures ride the updraughts on giant wings. And somewhere between the sky and the river runs the path.

To our left I passed the rock track to Bulnes, perhaps the most inaccessible village in Europe, with Naranjo de Bulnes – a 2,519m

Spanish Matterhorn – soaring above it. Soon, Bulnes and its 30 or so inhabitants will be connected to the outside world by a mountain railway, but until then, the only way in or out of the village is an arduous two-hour hike.

As I toiled on I could see our route unrolling ahead across steep aprons of scree, diving now and again into short tunnels through the living rock. In places this walk is a real cliffhanger, with dizzying drops along the way, but the path – built 80 years ago – is safe and sound and 2m wide.

So far the weather had been kind but, of course, it was too good to last. A sudden warning clap of thunder reminded me that this is where the rain in Spain mainly falls, and in seconds we were drenched. Luckily, warmth and hot coffee were available in the hamlet of Cain, only 10 minutes away, where the walk ended.

Throughout the week I stayed in *casonas* – comfortable small country houses providing B&B and an evening meal of traditional home cooking. *Casonas* are a uniquely Asturian invention. In style they range from converted farmhouses to *casas indianas* – handsome, 100-year-old mansions built with fortunes made in Latin America. None has more than 20 rooms and every one is family-run.

The *casona* where I stayed in Alevia had been a farmhouse for 500 years and was the home of Señor Gregorio Sanchez Benito. 'My wife was born here,' he said. 'When she was a girl, the ground floor was still occupied by cows and chickens. That is how we lived in those days.' But a few years ago, in an attempt to reverse the drift from the land, the authorities began to encourage rural tourism, and the old farm became a *casona*. Now, their breakfast – eggs and bacon, freshly squeezed orange juice, jugs of coffee, and bread straight from the village bakery served with home-made blackberry and apple jam – had been voted the seventh best in Spain by the national daily newspaper *El Pais*. But wherever I stayed the food was outstanding. Every evening I feasted on hearty suppers that usually began with mountain ham or shellfish soup, and ended with a choice of local cheeses – reflecting the fact that Asturias produces more varieties of cheese to the square kilometre than anywhere else in Europe.

After that first day's walk through the Cares Gorge, the rest of the week could have been an anticlimax. But my journey to the sea, through a gentler landscape of orchards and farm tracks, was the perfect counterpoint to the bare-boned grandeur of the Picos. I wandered along winding country roads strewn with sweet chestnuts and fresh-fallen walnuts still wet from their shells, with never a car to disturb the peaceful sounds of cowbells and trout streams. A footpath plunged into the September coolness of mushroom-smelling woods, to emerge on a heathery ridge where grayling butterflies lay aslant in the sun. Behind me, bracken spilled in deep folds into the valley out of which I had just climbed, and ahead I saw again the cliffs and coves of the Cantabrian coast and the immense blue arc of the Atlantic, but closer now.

I stopped to picnic on the ridge while a pair of eagles sailed overhead – a thrilling reminder of the wildness and diversity of Spain's timeless countryside. Then it was down through soft meadows and muddy lanes to my last night's lodgings. The walk was over but one last rite of passage remained. The sea was only a couple of kilometres away at Llanes, with its colourful harbour and tall houses graced by glassed-in balconies. So to Llanes I went, to bathe my feet in the cold Atlantic, and to celebrate the journey's end in a tapas bar, with a dish of *parrochas* – miniature sardines grilled in olive oil – and a glass of sharp Asturian cider.

SPAIN – ANDALUCIA

The path emerged from the woods beside a dried-up stream-bed choked with oleanders, and here we stopped for elevenses. We rested in the shade of a cork oak while Hugh unpacked one of the panniers slung over the the grey flanks of Pedro's mule, Paloma. Out came home-made lemonade, a rich Dundee fruit cake and a bottle of Domecq's La Ina, a chilled fino, poured into stainless-steel goblets. 'I don't think it's worth compromising, not to have the best sherry for the sake of a pound or two, do you?' Hugh said.

For several years now, Hugh Arbuthnott, former Black Watch officer and City gent, and Jane, his wife, have been leading walking safaris into the wilds of southern Spain from their home near the Andalucían mountain village of Gaucín. In July and August it is too hot for walking, but our trip took place in late September. Although the landscape was still painted in parched colours, the hillsides as bare and tawny as the skin of an old lion, the mountain air was sharp and clear, and the light, falling yellow across the valleys in the late afternoons, held the hint of autumn not far off. An ideal time, an ideal place to enjoy the last of the summer wine.

The first leg of the journey had taken us over stony hillsides, past whitewashed farmsteads, and then up through steep pinewoods to pick up the old tobacco smugglers' trail that runs from Algeciras to Ronda. At the top of the first high ridge we paused to drink, squirting water from leather *botas* carried by the uncomplaining Paloma. Far to the south, barely discernible in the afternoon haze, rose the pale blue sugarloaf of Gibraltar, where our flight had landed only the day before. Now the Rock and the crowded coasts were behind us as we headed north into the mountains.

Not until you leave the busy coastal highways and venture on foot into the interior do you begin to realize what a huge, hard, wild country Spain is. We tunnelled upwards through another pinewood, sweating in the resinous air and glad of the breeze that sighed like surf in the branches above our heads. And then, quite suddenly, we were out of the woods on a rocky ridge, a great void at our feet. Beyond, lit by the late afternoon sun, were the white houses and Moorish castle of Gaucín, with the mountain of El Hacho (the Axe) at their back.

Gaucín is one of the famous *pueblos blancos*, the dazzling, lime-washed hill towns of Andalucía that cling like swallows' nests among the barren crags. The Hotel Nacional, where we stayed, a modest building with just half a dozen clean and simple rooms, was previously called the Hotel Inglés, and its registers were filled with the signatures of British naval officers from Gibraltar who had stayed here on their way to Ronda.

'I spent a top-hole time here,' someone had written in 1920. On another, more recent page, Clementine, the elfin lady owner, proud-ly pointed out the signature of the Empress Pahlavi, the last queen of Persia. Beneath it, some wag called Robert had signed his own name, adding thoughtfully: 'One simply can't have too many queens on one page.'

After Gaucín the landscape changed, and we walked all morning through an Arcadian countryside of deep valleys filled with cork-oak forests. Deer live here, although we did not see any. In spring and summer there are cuckoos, nightingales and golden orioles, Hugh said, and eagle owls – fierce birds with orange eyes and a voice as deep as a hound's – which the Spanish call *el gran duque*. But now, apart from a distant carillon of goat bells, the woods were silent. Wandering among the endless aisles of gnarled cork oaks, I thought how easy it would be to become a tree-worshipper. Some of these forest giants, with their hollow trunks and misshapen limbs, looked as if they had stood here for centuries, relics from the days when Andalucía was ruled by the Moors.

Pedro, our muleteer, worked in these woods every year, harvest-ing the cork and packing it out by mule to Gaucín. We passed many oaks that had only just been stripped of their bark, their smooth, bent, terracotta trunks left looking uncomfortably naked, like old men caught with their trousers down.

Towards noon, having disposed of the Dundee cake and chilled fino, we continued across dry meadows of yellow grass where dead thistles stood like splintered spears, and came to a farmhouse, cool as a cave, with flagstone floors and melons ripening in nets hung from low beams. Cold beers from a gas fridge were set before us, with *tapas* of air-dried ham and cheese. Then it was on again, down an old drove road to the Río Guadiaro, lined with jungles of oleander and orchards of apples and ripe quinces, and home to slow-moving ghostly barbel.

Across the river the path rose once more into the hills, winding among scattered groves of evergreen oaks among which stood a Moorish watchtower, deserted now except for bats and owls. The tower and the name of the nearby village, Cortés de la Frontera, were markers in the landscape, identifying this as part of the last Moorish kingdom in Spain, which held out until 1492.

It took the Romans two centuries to conquer the Iberian Peninsula. The Moors did it in two years and stayed for 700 more. No wonder that, all over Andalucía, towns and place-names still resonate with their dark presence. Even Gibraltar, that staunchest of British citadels, owes its name to the Moors, who called it Gebel Tariq. Today, more than 500 years after the fall of Granada, these lonely mountains still have the watchful air of frontier country.

Ahead, on a rocky hill shaded by a canopy of oaks, stood Hugh's campsite. The cluster of green tents was a vision straight out of Africa, complete with the smell of woodsmoke and a cloudless sky in which a pair of griffon vultures were sailing on enormous, outstretched wings. There was roast lamb for supper, a velvet-smooth Rioja wine, a campfire to hold the September evening chill at bay, and a sky full of stars. As in Africa, much of the joy of these Andalucían safaris comes from the provision of luxurious comforts in the midst of wilderness. Boy Scout camping this was not; when I turned in that night it was to find a hot-water bottle in my bed and a duvet as deep as a snowdrift.

Next morning we set off early to eat a typical Spanish breakfast in a local bar in Cortés: toast rubbed with a raw clove of garlic, then soaked in olive oil to produce a kick like horse liniment, which only the strongest black coffee could exorcise. It was here that we exchanged our mules for a string of Andalucían donkeys and met Candido, the guide who would take us over the high pass in the Sierra de Libar. To the clatter of the donkeys' hooves on the cobbled streets of Cortés, we set off into the mountains, plodding steadily upwards towards the gaunt battlements of shattered limestone that seemed to bar our way.

The red tassels on the donkeys' harnesses swung gaily, as if we were on our way to a country fair, but the sun was hot now and the steep stone track lay ahead of us like a life sentence. The Romans had built it, Candido told us; a road to nowhere, toiling up into the sky where the air was so pure that it no longer carried even the the familiar incense of the pines. Eventually we reached the high pass at 1,000m and dropped down over the other side through a desolation of boulders to visit the Cima de Libar, a yawning sinkhole, which is one of the wonders of these wild Andalucían karst-lands. A young oak had taken root in the sinkhole's rim. I grasped it firmly, leaned out and stared down into the darkness while Candido tossed pebbles into its rock throat and their clatter echoed on and on.

Our route now lay across sun-dried pastures where ancient pollard oaks stood, each in its pool of shadow, with the mountains rising on either side and kestrels wheeling among their crags. 'This is the Llano de Libar,' Hugh said. 'It's what I call our secret valley.' It was a magical place, timeless and beautiful and so remote that you can only reach it on foot. In springtime, he said, the pastures are green and so filled with wildflowers that you can hardly move for fear of trampling on the wild orchids and hellebores that grow here.

Eventually, after walking for nearly five hours, we were greeted by Jane with a picnic lunch spread under the trees: ham and hard-boiled eggs, cold roast quails and a delicious white Rioja, followed by cheese and fresh walnuts eaten with golden chunks of quince jelly. And – since this was Andalucía – a siesta in the grass.

Then on by car we travelled in the late afternoon through a wonderful park-like country of scattered trees and rolling stubble lit by the deepening light. We drove westward straight into a September sunset, the sky the colour of a Spanish blood orange, the sierras sharp-etched in deepest indigo and the lights of Grazalema shining like fallen stars under the high peaks.

On our last day, having seen Ronda perched in the distance on its 120m-high cliffs, we entered the city like pilgrims at the end of a journey, to wash off the dust in the gracious old Reina Victoria hotel. Yet not even the romantic streets and courtyards, the famous bull-ring or the dramatic gorge that splits the town in two could dispel the sense of anticlimax. My head told me that I should be glad to be staying in one of Spain's finest tourist cities. But my heart was still in the high country with Pedro's mules, among the deep patrimonial forests and remote valleys where the old Spain lives on, proud, austere, unvanquished.

FRANCE – ISLANDS OF SILENCE

In Florac, on the upper reaches of the Tarn, I met an Englishman who has been coming to the Cévennes for 30 years. 'It's the orchids,' he said. 'They grow here like nowhere else I know. In England, if a military orchid is found, we fence it off and mount a 24-hour guard until it has finished flowering. In the Cévennes, military orchids are as common as buttercups.' So it came as no surprise that the first orchid I saw in the Cévennes turned out to be a military, a glorious spike of pinkish-purple, standing to attention in a lay-by.

I had flown to Montpellier to join a seven-day tour organized by Naturetrek, the Hampshire-based eco-travel company. It may have been billed as a Cévennes safari, but camping was definitely not on the programme. Instead we were based in Cocurès (population 160), in the extremely comfortable Hotel Restaurant La Lozette, one of the best two-star hideaways in France.

Cocurès is a pretty village of tumbledown houses with wooden shutters and kitchen gardens, and an ancient hound that howls whenever the angelus rings. Here, every morning began with a visit to the nearest supermarket, just down the road in Florac. Then, loaded down with picnic supplies (local cheeses and *charcuterie*, loaves, wine and luscious cherries), we would pile into our eight-seater safari vehicle and head for the hills in search of *la vie sauvage*.

The Cévennes, forming the south-eastern corner of the Massif Central, is a hard and beautiful land, but it is also filled with the dazzling light of the warm south and the sense of freedom that always accompanies vast open spaces. If there really is a heaven, then it probably looks like the flower-strewn rocks and meadows of these timeless limestone uplands. For anyone with even the remotest interest in wildlife this is a hugely rewarding region to explore, split by colossal gorges and criss-crossed by GRs (*sentiers de grandes randonnées*), well-marked routes for long-distance walkers that follow the old drove roads and shepherds' trails across wild and largely empty country.

This is the region made famous by Robert Louis Stevenson, who walked here as a young man in 1878 with his donkey, Modestine. The GR70, which traces the route he took through the Cévennes and over Mont Lozère on his way south to St Jean-du-Gard, has been named the Sentier Stevenson after him, and you can, if you wish, even hire a donkey and follow in the great man's footsteps up and over Mont Lozère.

We spent most of our time in the Parque National des Cévennes, which contains about 2,000 flowering plant species, including 47 different orchids, as well as spectacular birds such as eagle owls and griffon vultures, and 45 kinds of mammals. No wonder we needed two experts to accompany us: Michael Chandler, a Yorkshire botanist with 25 years of guiding experience; and Andy Tucker, a young ornithologist from Hampshire.

Now, with Andy at the wheel, we zigzag up a mountain road for our first glimpse of the Grands Causses, the great limestone table-lands that dominate so much of the Cévennes. Marooned in the skies of southern France, the Causses are another world. Islands of silence, the French call them. But their silence is an illusion. Listen again and what you hear are larks and sheep bells and the song of the wind running over the land.

On the Causse Méjean a pair of Montagu's harriers hunt over the hillsides, rocking and swaying on long wings, and quails call 'wet-my-lips' from meadows lit with purple pasque-flowers. This is sheep country, a lean, spare land with its ribs picked clean. Among its drystone walls and grey stone barns you may catch echoes of other limestone landscapes – Ireland's Burren and the Yorkshire Pennines – but on a much grander scale. It is also one of the last places in Europe where you can still witness transhumance, the age-old practice in which sheep flocks, having wintered in the valleys below, are brought up to graze on the high summer pastures. The thin turf barely covers the stony Causse, yet wildflowers thrive in unbelievable profusion: pink scatter-cushions of rock soapwort, mauve alpine asters, masses of tiny yellow rock roses and an endemic fly orchid that sends our botanists into raptures.

My fellow Naturetrekkers are a mixed bunch. Some have come to botanize, and some to look for rare birds such as stone curlews and rock thrushes. 'Some clients are incredibly keen,' says Michael. 'We had one chap who wouldn't eat lunch because he reckoned an hour each day for a week would give him the equivalent of an extra day to hunt for orchids.' But most, like me, are content to take pleasure in everything, from wildlife to wine and the joy of exploring open country in this stunning corner of *La France Profonde*.

At noon, having picnicked under a hawthorn hedge still snowed under with blossom in early June, we find a cluster of mauve and white lady orchids, each floret like a miniature flamenco dancer in a flouncy dress. Growing near by is the more subdued man orchid, known to the French as *l'homme pendu*, meaning 'the hanged man'.

Mid-afternoon brings us to St-Chély du Tarn, a viewpoint teetering on the edge of the Gorges du Tarn, where the river makes a U-turn in its stony bed 300m below. The Gorges du Tarn rank among nature's grandest follies; by comparison, Cheddar Gorge is a mere crack in the pavement. They are France's answer to the Grand Canyon – 50km of dizzying cliffs, buttresses, pillars and fingers of stained limestone with the Tarn River shining emerald-clear at the bottom.

Next day we set off to botanize on the slopes and ridges of Mont Lozère (1,699m), the sacred source of the Tarn. Our route lies up the valley of a smaller river, the Runes, half-hidden in sweet-chestnut woods. In former times chestnut flour was vital for the local economy in a region where cereal crops were hard to grow.

We cross the Sentier Stevenson and find ourselves in Le Pont de Montvert, a typical Cévenol village of sway-backed roofs with fish-scale tiles. It is market day, and we top up our picnic provisions with cheese and cherries from the roadside stalls. Above the village we climb through wet meadows filled with paintbox colours – pink tufts of bistort, deep-purple mountain pansies, yellow globe flowers and, most beautiful of all, drifts of narcissi like fallen snow.

Mont Lozère is made of sterner stuff than the Causses. A whale-backed hump of solid granite, it is the domain of the short-toed eagle, known in the Cévennes as the *péyriblanc* (white friar) because of its pale creamy underparts. We watch one in typical pose, hovering in the teeth of the wind as it searches for snakes on the boulder-strewn mountainsides. Higher still, at around 1,600m, we find daffodils still in flower, and wood anemones sheltering under stunted pines.

Later in the week we drive to the summit of Mont Aigoual (1,567m), where wild tulips grow. They are everywhere, scattered like golden stars in the grass. Our mountaintop picnic spot is graced with tremendous panoramic views. To the north, the ridges and valleys of the Massif Central roll away towards the Auvergne. To the south sprawls the Camargue, a far-away gleam of sea and salt marsh; and to the south-east, blue with distance, looms the mighty silhouette of Canigou, marking the beginning of the Pyrénées.

The weather, indifferent at the start of the trip, is now in full Mediterranean mode. On a day hot enough to melt the tar on the road we resist the temptations of Meyrueis, a little town full of restaurants and pavement cafés set out beside a tumbling stream, and toil up the Causse Noir. There we watch honey buzzards and find the scarce and beautiful yellow adonis – one of the region's most precious plants – growing in the company of Pyrenean bellflowers and spider orchids among dark stands of juniper and pine.

On our way back we re-enter the Gorges du Tarn and stop near the kayaking centre of Blajoux to admire a field of lizard orchids. Each flowering spike has a wriggly tail – and a scent like goat's cheese. But while the botanists have their noses in the grass, the birders are staring into the heavens. Above the rimrocks, on outstretched wings 3m wide, floats a vision of Africa, a spiralling flock of griffon vultures. Two decades or so ago these giant airborne scavengers were almost extinct in the Cévennes. Now, thanks to a successful reintroduction programme, some 75 pairs breed in the national park. Up on the Causses, where the griffon vultures search for carrion, life is as hard for the wild creatures as it is for the shepherds and their flocks who have together shaped these empty landscapes. In high summer the dried heads of carline thistles, which flowered the previous year, lie like spent suns among the stones and, except in the clay-lined dewponds known as *lavognes*, there is no water for man or beast. In its extremes of heat and cold this is a land without pity, as cruel as the butcher bird, or red-backed shrike, which impales its victims on thornbushes. Yet when the orchids are in flower and the grass shivers in the wind, there is nowhere lovelier in the whole of France.

On our last day, by popular request, we return to the Causse Méjean, with its standing stones and weathered crosses and huge, ever-changing skies. Of all places in the Cévennes this is the one I like the best. Its waving grasslands remind me of the Serengeti – an impression redoubled by what looks like a herd of zebras on the skyline. They turn out to be Przewalski's horses, a breed so ancient they appear to have stepped straight out of a cave painting. These limestone uplands are the closest thing in Europe to their native Mongolian steppe, where they are now extinct. But if all goes well and numbers increase, there is a plan to return the horses to their original home.

It is time to leave. In the golden light of late afternoon a flock of sheep comes spilling down the road towards us. Led by a shepherd and his dog, they pass in a patter of horny hooves, leaving behind a pungent smell that hangs in the air long after they have disappeared.

FRANCE – THE BASTIDES OF AVEYRON

All night the rain had beaten a furious tattoo on the slates of L'Oustal del Barry, our country hotel in Najac. Next morning, as we set out on the first leg of our four-day, 80km walk to the River Lot, the sky was still threatening, the oakwoods still dripping. Along the path, the overnight rain had brought out a host of edible snails. Twice the size of our humble English molluscs, they crawled in a leisurely way between the buttercups. But we planned to travel at rather more than a snail's pace. Our luggage had been sent on ahead. Now weighed down by nothing more than a picnic provided by our hotel, we wound our way down into the wooded gorges of the Aveyron.

Our objective was to plunge on foot into the green heart of midmost France, stopping on the way at one or two *bastides*. There are more than 170 of these medieval walled market towns scattered across south-west France. Built in three waves between 1222 and 1373, the *bastides* were the new towns of their day – founded to encourage an expanding population to settle the lands laid waste during the power struggle between the kings of France and the counts of Toulouse. Not all were built on green-field sites – many overlapped existing communities. But the classic *bastide* began as a series of allotments laid out in a grid system. Once the houses were built, the grid was preserved by a network of streets and alleys, pre-dating the American townplanners' model by several centuries.

During the Hundred Years War, the *bastides* suffered greatly. First came the Black Prince, then the Black Death. Yet, seven centuries later, these marvellous examples of medieval town planning are still with us. And, unlike the grim castles and Gothic cathedrals of the time, the *bastides* are living monuments depicting the architecture of the people. Najac, perched high on a rock ridge above the Aveyron, was itself a *bastide* – one of the prettiest villages in France, but not typical. Better examples lay ahead.

Splashes of red and white paint on rocks and tree trunks told us we were on the *Grande Randonnée 36*, one of France's long-distance footpaths. The clouds broke. The sun came out. The Aveyron was in spate, a brown flood roaring down its deep wooded gorge, swirling under the bridge over which we had crossed the previous day on the four-coach train from Toulouse. Looking back, we caught a last glimpse of Najac's castle on its hilltop, before the woods swallowed us up.

Later, we emerged on a back-country road that wound through a countryside of old-fashioned hay meadows. The grass had not yet been cut and was filled with buttercups, white drifts of ox-eye daisies and half a dozen kinds of orchid. At dinner the night before, we'd been puzzled by a mysterious dish of round, fleshy leaves the size of a five-franc coin. The menu described them as *ombilics de Venus*, meaning 'Venus's navels'. Now, as we trudged along the road towards Monteils, the mystery was solved: sprouting from a wayside wall was the very same plant – known in Britain more pro-saically as pennywort.

Further delicacies awaited us at our next stopover in Monteils, a sleepy village in the Aveyron valley, which we reached by mid-afternoon. Here, we were given local asparagus bathed in hol-landaise sauce, followed by roast breast of duck.

Next morning, we climbed out of the valley up steep, stony slopes where spider orchids grew under the trees. This was our first glimpse of the limestone landscape of the Causse, its rocky ribs cov-ered with juniper and scrawny truffle oaks. Nightingales sang from thickets of wild roses, enticing us ever deeper into *La France Pro-fonde*. Black-veined white butterflies – a species not seen in Britain for decades – flew in their hundreds about the roadsides and, as the day warmed up, grasshoppers gave the heat a voice, a mindless shrilling that rose in waves from the ripening meadows.

Picnic time became a high spot of each day. *Déjeuner sur l'herbe*, munching cold roast duck and crusty bread washed down with red wine. The sun was hot on bare arms and legs. I took a last swig from the bottle, lay back in the grass among the field orchids and watched a hoopoe, a cinnamon-coloured bird with black and white wings, flying over the trees.

It was easy to see why this idyllic landscape attracts so many Britons, its rural delights conjuring up vague memories of our own lost countryside. And it was no wonder the English fought the Hun-dred Years War. Who could blame us for trying to hang on to the indolent lands of Aquitaine? Great chunks have scarcely changed since the time of the Black Prince.

Most days we seldom saw a soul. Then, on the high road to Villefranche, I met a shepherd sitting under a walnut tree. He was 65, he said, fingering his beret with tobacco-stained fingers, though he looked much older. I remarked on the beauty of the Causse. 'But it is hard country,' he said. 'The soil is too thin. We have a little of everything: wine, cheese, fish, walnuts; but it is not a rich land.'

Soon afterwards, we came down into Villefranche-de-Rouergue on the banks of the Aveyron, now a sizeable town but still a *bastide* at heart. In the centre, the houses are still locked in their original gridiron pattern around the arcaded market square, which forms the hub of all true *bastides*. We pushed on to another, Villeneuve d'Aveyron, which is more intimate and peaceful than Villefranche. Villeneuve has grown up around the much older church of St Sepulchre, its interior decorated with faded wall paintings of pilgrims sporting broad hats and carrying long staves, bound for the shrine of St James in Galicia.

At high noon, as we trudged over the Causse in the quivering heat, the dusty road stretched ahead like a life sentence. But at last, the long day came to an end in a green valley, where a clear stream led past a romantic stone château to the cheering sight of an *auberge*. The owner, Monsieur Mouly, welcomed us with a pot of tea. The *auberge* was utterly peaceful. There were doves on the roof, a small dog and a horse with a spotted foal; but we were the only guests.

Next morning, we marched on through the high meadows, where sheep lay in the shade of ancient walnut trees. This was classic limestone country, criss-crossed with drystone walls and cut by deep valleys. It was reminiscent of the southern Pennines, but more generously wooded.

Much of our walk followed the GR36, but the local tourist board had also marked our route with additional signs where there was the chance of taking a wrong turning. Only on the final stretch did we hit a problem: coming down from Capdenac, in the valley of the Lot, the sign pointed along an impenetrable lane of chest-deep nettles.

But we made it. We had walked nearly 80km since our gastronomic welcome in Najac four days earlier. Next day, the train that took us back there covered the same distance in 40 minutes.

IRELAND – THE FINAL FRONTIER

By air it is only a 50-minute hop from Dublin to Donegal, but the difference could not be more dramatic if I were landing in Tibet. As we drop through the clouds to Carrickfinn airport, I see Donegal for the first time: green as the curl of a breaking wave, a sudden gleam of blanket bog, the iron ribs of rain-washed mountains; and everywhere, lit by fitful shafts of sunlight, vast tidal inlets, deserted beaches and tattered islands running out into the Atlantic.

Dublin may be the capaital of Ireland, but Donegal is the guardian of its soul. It is part of the Gaeltacht – where Irish, as spoken by the High Kings of Tara, is an everyday language – and revels in its remoteness. To come here is to stand on the outermost edge of Europe, where the Old World ends, the land falls apart, and the next Irish pub is in Boston. At its narrowest, down by Bundoran, Donegal is almost cut off from the rest of the country by the Ulster border. And north beyond Malin Head, a stormy name straight from the shipping forecasts, there is nothing but sea all the way to the Arctic.

Yet wherever you travel in Ireland's wild west, from Donegal to Co Kerry, there are oases of comfort in the Celtic tundra: a bed for the night, a bar that echoes to the beat of the bodhrán, where old, spine-tingling songs are sung and even the humblest pub may surprise you with a feast of crab claws cooked in garlic. This is one of the reasons I have come to Donegal: to track down a Frenchman who is said to run the greatest little B&B in Ireland. I drive up a couple of first-gear hills, then along a path between hayfields and fuchsia hedges to a garden where a wild-haired leprechaun, a Gauloise dangling from his lips, is mowing the grass.

Paul Chatenoud was born in Morocco, studied philosophy at the Sorbonne and owned a music bookshop on the Île-St-Louis in Paris. In 1984 he threw up his old life and came to Ireland to become a writer. Instead, on a whim, he bought the Green Gate, a derelict cottage outside Ardara, and ended up in the tourist trade.

The Green Gate is laid-back and eccentric in the best possible way. In my bedroom – formerly a cowshed – stands a posy of wildflowers in a jam jar. There are slate windowsills and rough-cast walls, and not a wardrobe in sight. A tall man could crack his head on the ceiling and the bath water is a rich peaty brown. But that's not the point. The Green Gate is not just a bed for the night. It is simply one of the things you must do in Ireland, like kissing the Blarney Stone or climbing Croagh Patrick. And, of course, what makes it so special is Paul Chatenoud himself, with his books and his classical music recordings, a one-man band who makes the beds and serves huge Irish fry-ups in his own cosy kitchen between witty and wonderful bouts of storytelling.

'There is no set time for breakfast,' he says. 'Just turn up when you like.' And what a breakfast it is: soda bread and fresh farm eggs, bacon and sausage, seven kinds of marmalade, and honey in the comb from Paul's own hive. A turf fire glows in the grate and a tame robin (named Christopher, naturally) hops through the open door to take crumbs from Paul's fingers.

Down the hill in Ardara there are soft tweeds to buy at John Molloy's factory shop, foot-tapping sessions of Irish music at Peter Oliver's Corner House bar, and a genius called Laurence Herron who carves otters and dolphins out of black bog oaks that were growing before the Pyramids were built. There are restaurants, too, but if you really want to eat well you must drive south to the Castle Murray House restaurant on St John's Point. Like the Green Gate, it is owned by a Frenchman, Thierry Delcros from the Dordogne, who is also the chef, and who buys his fish every day at Killybegs, where 40 per cent of Ireland's national catch is landed.

Time to move on, down midsummer lanes stitched with dog roses and honeysuckle. At Maghera, just west of Ardara, the tide is out. Cattle are wandering by the shore and curlews are calling over kilometres of wet sands. I pass the waterfall of Assarnacally spilling down from Slievetooey, and blanket bogs where the cotton grass blows like fresh falls of snow. And occasionally, among the des-res bungalows, like a ghost from the past, a low stone cottage peeks out, its thatched roof lashed down against the wind. But of all the sights in Donegal there is nothing to match the towering pinnacles and cliffs of Slieve League. They are the highest cliffs in Europe, plunging for nearly 600m into the Atlantic, and swarming in early summer with vast numbers of nesting seabirds. This is Yeats country, lorded over by Ben Bulben, a mighty, flat-topped limestone mountain looking down on Drumcliffe churchyard where the great man himself lies buried.

Later, on the road to Ballymote, in the depths of the lush, low-lying Sligo pasturelands, I cross a river covered in water-lilies, with cattle grazing on its banks. It is the Owenmore, the kind of river that Constable might have painted, but which no longer exists in England's tidied-up countryside.

Temple House Hotel, where I spend the night, is a genteel Victorian time warp. With its half-tester beds and family portraits, it looks much as it did when it was completed in 1863. I am given a huge room, known as the 'half-acre', looking out over the park to the ruined castle built by the Knights Templar in 1200, and the lake beyond, which is said to be full of monster pike.

'Welcome to the warm, wild, wonderful west', says a sign by the roadside. In Killala there is a round tower in which the monks hid when the Vikings came raiding, and out past Downpatrick Head lie the Stone Age fields of Céide, the world's most extensive neolithic monument, lost for 5,000 years under a blanket of bog.

The west coast bristles with stirring names. In Donegal I came across Bloody Foreland. In Mayo is Blacksod Bay, where cloud shadows race over the Nephin Beg Mountains in what is possibly the emptiest corner of all Ireland. At the south end of the bay lies Achill Island, anchored to the mainland by a little stone bridge. Sometimes on Achill it is hard to tell land from sky. What at first sight I took to be clouds suddenly resolve themselves as the rounded summits of Croaghaun and Slieve More. The islanders, who once caught basking sharks for a living, now do better from tourism. At Keel, wetsuited surfers are riding the rollers on a beach strewn with jellyfish, and the pubs do a roaring trade in seafood.

Back on the mainland again I follow the coast road past Croagh Patrick, the holy mountain where St Patrick prayed for 40 days and flung Ireland's snakes into Clew Bay. Some pilgrims still climb barefoot to its pyramidal 765m summit.

The narrow waters of Killary Harbour make a natural break between Mayo and Galway. To the south rise the blue summits of the Beanna Beola – the Twelve Bens of Connemara. Wherever you go in this most haunted corner of Ireland, on the bog road to Cashel or the coast road to Clifden, you can feel these peaks watching you. Barren it may be, with its granite bays and trackless bogs, but there is a beauty here that pierces the heart. In the stone-walled fields that slide down to the sea, a Connemara pony suckles its foal. Cuckoos call from the telephone wires, and on the road to Roundstone there is a lough with two swans sailing on it.

Galway City comes as something of a shock after the silence of Connemara. It has motorways and a rush hour and more traffic lights than the whole of Donegal. But beyond it loom the limestone uplands of the Burren, a lunar landscape of dolmens and ring forts on the roof of Co Clare. Except that all kinds of wildflowers – orchids, gentians, burnet roses – sprout from every crevice, transforming it into a giant natural rock garden.

The Burren marks my journey's end. Today I must fly home from Shannon, but before I go there is still time for one more treat. On the way to the airport I drive out through Lahinch to see the fortress Cliffs of Moher. This is the west coast's last hurrah before you hit the Shannon: 8km of vertigo-inducing limestone falling sheer into the sea.

Stand on the edge in the eye of the wind with the waves booming 200m below. Remember that the next landfall is America, 5,000km away. Then ask yourself: could there be a more dramatic frontier than this, between the Old World and the New?

EAST GERMANY – OVER THE WALL

The queue at Checkpoint Charlie moved quickly. Germany's most famous cold-war frontier post had been robbed of its former spy-thriller image, yet its seedy atmosphere still managed to provide an odd frisson as I crossed into the East.

Half an hour later I was watching the *Mauerspechte* (wall-peckers), souvenir-hunters dismantling the Berlin Wall with hammer and chisel. The sound of their tapping echoed beneath the Brandenburg Gate and across the empty space of what, until the previous November, had been a deadly no man's land. The sightseers were in a festive mood. There was a heady sense of living in momentous times. The wall, that monstrous schism between the two great power blocs, had been reduced to a linear billboard of graffiti. Already 'Gorbachev's Year' was beginning to fade, overlaid by increasingly urgent calls for reunification. Now, everywhere, the black, red and gold flag of West Germany was being flaunted from street windows. *Wir sind ein Volk* was the new rallying cry.

It was still only February but spring was in the air and the first flowers were blooming along the Unter den Linden. East Germany, too, was opening up, stirring in the unfamiliar warmth of a new political climate after its 40-year winter.

Soon we were heading south across the floodplain of the Elbe, speeding down the autobahns of the Third Reich into a lurid, photo-chemical sunset thrown up by the factory chimneys of Bitterfeld, an apt name for one of the most polluted towns in Europe. Atmospheric pollution in the German Democratic Republic was a fact of life. It emanated not only from the factories but also from the poisonous exhausts of old jalopies – Wartburgs and Trabants – the only cars most East Germans could buy. Above all, it came from burning brown lignite coal, one of the country's few abundant natural resources, which painted the air with sepia tones and gave every town and city an acrid bronchial reek reminiscent of the old London smogs.

It was dark when we reached Weimar, but morning revealed a graceful baroque town steeped in memories of Goethe and Schiller. Among Weimar's cobbled streets and squares the ghosts of German literature are eveywhere, much as Shakespeare's spirit presides over Stratford. The townhouse where Goethe lived for half a century until his death in 1832 is now a literary shrine, but I preferred the simpler charm of his summer retreat in the park beside the River Ilm. There, crocuses were in flower and nuthatches whistled in the woods. This was not the East Germany I had expected. I had come prepared for winter, only to run into the warmest February for years.

Later, we stumbled again on Goethe's all-pervading presence at Dornburg, high on limestone cliffs above the River Saale where three castles, Gothic, Renaissance and rococo, rake the sky with gilded spires. No wonder Goethe was a frequent visitor. Even in winter, its roses dormant and the terraced vines pruned to black stumps, it was an idyllic place.

But then came one of those unsettling mood-swings so typical of Germany. From Dornburg we had driven back through Weimar, past the sprawling Russian barracks at the edge of town and out into the wide Thüringen countryside. Away to the north a dark tower stood. It was the Buchenwald extermination camp memorial, a stark and solitary cenotaph laying bare the darkest corner of the German soul. The day was bright and the afternoon sun fell warmly across the open fields, but I could not bring myself to visit that terrible place.

By the time we reached Erfurt the western sky was apple-green, throwing into sharp relief the soaring pinnacles of the Gothic cathedral and St Severi's Church. Erfurt, hardly known in the West, will surely become one of the classic tourist showpieces of Eastern Europe. Its 14th-century cathedral windows – the finest in the German-speaking world – survived the Allied bombing raids of the 1940s, and the damage caused to the city's rich medieval core has been painstakingly restored. Today it is again a city of bells and towers and tall Renaissance gables, with a marvellous medieval bridge, the Kramerbrucke, piled high with half-timbered shops and houses like the old London Bridge of Tudor England.

In the evening I took a tram through the cobbled streets to eat at the 14th-century Gildehaus restaurant in the *Fischmarkt*. The place was packed, mostly with West Germans who had never been in the East before. Strangers in their own land, they were here on a free-spending voyage of discovery. 'It's so cheap for us,' said one, calling for a third bottle of wine between mouthfuls of black cherries and ice-cream. 'Eating out costs so little that we're finding it hard to get through all our money.'

With an exchange rate favouring the Deutschmark by three to one it was no wonder the roads were full of BMWs with West German number-plates. I heard of one visitor who sat down and ordered four dinners at a sitting. But it could not last. Already there was talk of East and West united under a Deutschmark economy. 'Soon the honeymoon will be over,' said a student from Göttingen. 'That's why we're here now.'

Most of the West Germans in Erfurt had crossed the border at Eisenach, birthplace of Johann Sebastian Bach, which stands at the western approaches to Thüringen. Above the town looms Wartburg Castle, the famous old fortress that has given its name to East Germany's most popular family car. I had hoped to stay at the castle hotel but it was not to be. The manager was very sorry. Every room had been booked by the West Germans, but he said if we came back the next day we could have breakfast and see the dining hall with its minstrels' gallery and sinister fairytale murals.

So next morning I left Eisenach while fog still lay thick in the valleys, making islands of every ridge and hilltop, and climbed up to the castle through the frost-crackling beechwoods. Founded in 1067 by Count Ludwig der Springer, Wartburg's keep is the best-preserved secular Romanesque building north of the Alps, revered throughout Germany for its romantic associations with the *Minnesanger*, the medieval troubadours whose exploits provided the inspiration for Wagner's *Tannhäuser*. It was at Wartburg in 1521 that the fugitive Martin Luther first translated the New Testament into German, letting loose the spirit of the Reformation. The room where he worked is still there, with his desk and Bible, but the ink-stains on the wall where he flung his inkpot at the Devil have long since gone, chipped away by souvenir-hunters in a manner reminiscent of Berlin's wall-peckers.

Meanwhile, the weather continued to confound us. This was to have been a winter's journey, a black and white portrait of East Germany under snow. Instead, the false spring that had begun in Berlin continued to pursue us deeper into Thüringen. In the early mornings the hills sulked in mist. Damp dripped from the trees and tired crusts of rotting snow still hung around on the highest north-facing slopes. But then the sun would break through, its slanting rays falling between the pines to banish the Teutonic gloom as the temperature rose to an unusual 19°C.

All day we followed the tortuous back roads from village to village. Giessubel, Masserberg, Heubach, Biberau – they were always the same. A narrow street, a rushing stream, a sombre church with a gilded belfry, its cool interior painted in chaste baroque colours, and every house covered in the ubiquitous fish-scale tiles of dark Thüringen slate. From the hillside above Heubach I watched the smoke rising from cottage chimneys as stoves were lit for the night. The sun disappeared behind the trees. The air grew cold. The wooded ridges turned blue and then black. A flock of fieldfares flew overhead, their wintry chucklings a comforting sound of home, and I realized how close in both name and spirit was this German *wald* to our own English wolds and wealds.

Thüringer Wald, the Thuringian Forest, is a range of rolling pine-clad ridges, the highest a shade under 1,000m, which dominates the south-western corner of the country. The forest hides many secrets. It is a refuge for the black woodpecker, a haunt of goshawks and salamanders. Red deer and wild boar roam its deepest recesses, and in spring and summer 20 different kinds of orchids bloom among its glades and meadows. In winter there is cross-country skiing. In summer, East Germany takes to the woods on foot. Everywhere, rustic signposts like wayside calvaries pinpoint the beginnings of hundreds of paths. Some run for miles beside tumbling streams. Others climb through Gothic aisles of beech to the high ground where the tall pines grow, closing ranks in dim perspectives that shut out the sky and fill the world with a resinous silence. The best is the Rennsteig ridgeway, a long-distance path that runs over the roof of the Thüringer Wald for nearly 170km.

To explore the eternal twilight of the Thüringer Wald is to peer deep into the German psyche. No other people in Europe love their dense forests with such pagan fervour. In those wolfish woods, thick with hobgoblin shadows and mushroomy smells, you might still catch an echo of the Brothers Grimm. But the lure of the pines does not last. After a couple of days I found their black magic oppressive, and was glad to be back in the more open country around Arnstadt.

There, pines still bristled along the hogbacked ridges, but in between lay a far-reaching countryside of huge, hedgeless fields, with sometimes a lonely watchtower where hunters waited for the deer to come down from the woods at dusk. Plum trees grew beside the roads, and between the woods you could see a long way, making it easy to imagine the glitter of distant armies wheeling on the sunlit plain. Church towers, each with a spire like a Kaiser's helmet, rose from every fold and hollow, where half-timbered farmhouses slept under steep red roofs in a nest of orchards, surrounded by duckponds, dunghills, free-range fowls and all the other rural stage-props long since banished from the British countryside.

On the road to Branchewinda we passed an old man and a boy in a horse-drawn cart. In the village itself, Siegfried Schulz was forking hay from a trailer hauled by a miniature tractor he had put together himself by cannibalizing an ancient motorbike. 'You can't buy anything in this country,' he said. 'For 40 years life has gone downhill. Now at last there is hope.' His farm has been in the family for generations. In the 1950s it had been collectivized, his land taken away by the state, all but his paddock with its hens and pear trees, and a handful of sheep. Now he worked as a lorry driver, but the farm was where he was happiest. 'I like to have my hands in my own earth,' he said.

Local people seemed genuinely pleased to see us. Frau Regina Voigt, who runs the village shop, told me I was the first Englishman she had ever met. Proudly she unlocked the village church to show me the treasured icon above the altar. The church clock still worked, its cracked bell sending a cloud of sparrows flying into the churchyard beech. Beneath the tree was a memorial to the German dead of two world wars: 28 men from a village of fewer than 150 souls. Greiner, Katzenmaier, Pohl, Stuberauch, I read their names and wondered where and how they had died, while skylarks sang in the open fields and the churchyard crocuses turned their faces to the sun.

Towards evening the light turned golden, bringing with it an inexpressible sense of serenity. This was the time I loved best in this forgotten countryside: a mistle thrush singing, the air smelling of pines, deer stealing out of the woods to feed and the lights of distant villages beginning to shine in the gathering dusk.

Much of East Germany, even in its most historic cities, seems frozen in a 1950s time warp. But in these uncharted Thüringen villages one stumbles constantly upon an older, Arcadian past contemporary with Constable's England, which has somehow survived two world wars and 40 years of Communism.

'You know, in olden times Thüringen was known as the green heart of Germany,' said Artur Volker, former burgomaster of

Neuroda. Aged 76, he was still living with his wife in the half-timbered farmhouse they first moved into when they married in 1936. They still worked with heavy horses until the farms were collectivized in 1958, but today their balconied farmyard is silent. A wind blew through the village, shaking the slate wall-tiles with a skeletal rattle. 'You can't imagine how terrible it was to lose your land,' said Volker. 'We were supposed to give it up willingly but it was more like a prison sentence.'

After the pastoral landscapes of the past few days it was a shock to be heading back by way of Jena and Gera through a dour landscape of coal tips and pit-head winding gears. Somewhere between Karl-Marx-Stadt and Leipzig we turned off down a cobbled road in the direction of Colditz.

The weather, which had been so kind to us in Thüringen, now changed with a vengeance. It was Rose Monday, two days before the end of the German pre-Lenten *Fasching* festivities. Although we did not know it, Britain was being battered by one of the worst storms of the 20th century, and those same winds now fell on us in a fury. The sky turned black, and we drove on through a lashing hailstorm that shook the roadside birches as if it was trying to pluck them out by the roots. By the time we reached Colditz it was late afternoon and the grim old castle was already a brooding silhouette against the sky.

If there is one place in East Germany whose name is universally known in Britain, it must be Colditz, the prison in which Allied officers were incarcerated for trying to escape from Germany during World War II. The Nazis believed Colditz to be escape-proof, but many brave men proved them wrong by making successful 'home runs' to freedom.

No wonder the inmates were so keen to escape. Although it had now become a hospital I found it the most incredibly sinister place I had ever seen. Its dank walls, pierced by small, barred windows, exuded a feeling of evil and despair. Walking through the stone gateway beneath its snarling heraldic lions, I thought of the prisoners who had passed this way half a century ago, and found it hard to suppress a shiver.

Outside, back in the bleak little town square, dusk was coming down fast. Under lamps so dim they might have been gas-lit, the cobblestones gleamed black in the rain. The tall buildings can hardly have changed since the war, and it was all too easy to conjure up the grey ghosts of Nazi soldiers, the stamp of boots and the long red banners emblazoned with swastikas hanging from the upper windows.

Next morning the high winds were still blowing, but Colditz was back in the past where it belonged and we were having breakfast at the railway station in Lübbenau (soup, black bread, fried eggs and coffee) among blue-overalled workers drinking beer and schnapps after their early morning shifts. Lübbenau is the gateway to the Spreewald, the dreamy waterlands of the River Spree, which flows on to Berlin only 80km away. Not that you would ever guess Berlin was so close once you enter this timeless fen. The Spreewald is one of the most magical places in Eastern Europe, a roadless maze of canals, ditches and willow-bordered water-meadows, where punts are the only form of transport and even the children go to school by boat.

Most of the inhabitants of the Spreewald are Wends, a forgotten minority of swamp-dwelling Slavs who spoke their own language until the last war and are still proud of their separateness. Their wooden houses are unlike any others in Germany. Where the gable-end timbers meet they are carved in a crosspiece with two snakes' heads as a charm against lightning, fire and flood, and their log-cabin walls, although no more than 300 years old, are built with massive split trunks, just as our own Saxon ancestors built the wooden church at Greenstead in Essex.

At Lehde, a village Venice of thatched houses and waterside farm-steads, storks had built their nests on the fire-station roof. Three swans were feeding in a flooded water-meadow already gilded with the year's first kingcups. Occasionally a farmer would drift past, taking dung to the fields in a long black punt. In Max Lehman's garden, hens were scratching among the snowdrops. The alluvial soil was fine and dark. 'We're good at growing cucumbers here,' said Lehman, tapping tobacco into his pipe with a horny finger. 'And horseradish. All the horseradish grown in Germany comes from the Spreewald.'

In 1960 the State tried, but failed, to collectivize the local farms. The moated patchwork of pocket-sized fields was impossible to mechanize. In the end the government gave up, and Lehde and the neighbouring village of Leipe became the only ones in the whole of East Germany where farming was returned to private ownership. Even now, modern farming methods are shunned. No agricultural poisons pollute the Spreewald, no pesticides, no artificial fertilizers. Instead, a canny system of dykes and sluices channels winter floods across the fields, leaving a rich silt from which the summer grass springs tall, to be cut by hand and brought home by boat to feed the cattle in their stalls. Today, said Lehman, the biggest threat comes from the giant power station, upstream beyond Lübbenau, which regularly disgorges torrents of filth into the river. But somehow the fen has survived.

In the afternoon Herr Lehman took us by boat on a tour of the village. With blankets over our knees, we slid through the silent water as he poled us with effortless, rhythmic grace down reedy dykes where mallard sprang up at our approach, past black oak cottages and gabled farmhouses and out into the shining meadows. The day had turned bitterly cold, and the snow which had been so perversely absent in the Thüringen hills now came whirling out of a rapidly darkening sky in soft, fat flakes that soon covered the bottom of the punt. The chill bit to the bone; and yet I was mesmerized by the beauty of the place and the moment. Soundlessly we drifted on as if in a dream, past rows of domed haystacks and solemn poplars, the snow falling and the flat fields fading into a midwinter world of muted shadows.

Afterwards, thawing out in front of a brown-tiled stove while Frau Lehman prepared coffee and sandwiches, Max Lehman told me how life had changed since the fall of Erich Honecker's regime. Next month they were going on a two-day trip to Vienna. It would be the first time either of them had set foot in the West. 'It's Gorbachev we must thank for our freedom,' he said. 'Six months ago we could not have had this conversation. I could not even have asked you in for fear of being reported to the Stasi. Even now I find it hard to believe what has happened. It was like living under Hitler. We were always afraid. Now it's over.'

HUNGARY – THE CRANES OF HORTOBÁGY

Out of the golden October twilight falls a wild music, at first so faint I can hardly hear it, a few random chords of high horns blowing beyond the horizon. Then louder, more insistent, drawing closer with every second until there is no mistaking that growing clamour. It is the hounds of heaven in full cry – flock after flock of common cranes, flying in to roost in Hungary's Hortobágy National Park.

Every year the cranes migrate south from their breeding grounds in northern Finland, Belarus and western Russia, heading for warmer climes. But on the way they stop over in Hungary, where as many as 50,000 birds may gather before moving on to complete their immense journey from the tundra to the sun. Of all Europe's wildlife spectacles this nightly autumn fly-past is surely the greatest, a Hungarian rhapsody without equal. Yet nobody, apart from the locals and a few dedicated birdwatchers, seems to be aware of it.

Among those in the know is Gerard Gorman, the birdman of Budapest, a Merseysider with a wry sense of humour whose years in Hungary have not erased his Scouse accent. Gorman's bird-watching expertise is uncanny. He can literally charm birds off the trees, whistling up a black woodpecker on the banks of the Danube, or pointing out a goshawk as it dashes through the beechwoods of the Buda Hills. He came to Hungary to translate poetry, married a Hungarian, and now lives in Budapest, writing bird books and leading ornithological tours all over Eastern Europe. But his spiritual home is the Hortobágy, with its huge skies and immense horizons.

The Hortobágy is a three-hour drive from Budapest, out into the flatlands of eastern Hungary on the road to Debrecen. On the way we stop by the roadside to watch a pair of saker falcons perched on an electricity pylon. Sakers are fierce birds, says Gorman. Once he watched one beat up a buzzard. 'The buzzard flew down and drove the saker off its kill, but that was not the end of it. The saker turned and hurtled full-tilt at the buzzard, which was so startled that it fell on its back with its legs in the air as it tried in vain to defend itself.'

By now we are deep in the Magyar countryside. There are no hedgerows, just open fields of maize and sunflowers, and poplars lit with melancholy autumn colours. We cross a big, slow river, the Tisza, and beyond it, spreading towards Romania and the Ukraine, lies the Hortobágy – the Great Hungarian Plain.

The landscape of the Hortobágy is a mosaic of marshes, acacia copses, reed-fringed carp ponds and vast sweeps of semi-natural grassy steppe – the *puszta* – grazed by free-ranging herds of horses, grey Hungarian cattle and racka sheep with spiral horns. 'The national park protects about 70,000ha of it,' says Gorman. 'That's about one-quarter of the entire Hortobágy region.'

In places the skyline is broken by fleets of willows, like galleons becalmed in a sea of grass. Elsewhere are scattered farmsteads with long, low, thatched barns surrounded by noisy flocks of domestic geese, and gleaming dykes echoing to the rasp of frogs. Occasionally you pass low mounds known as *kun halom*, raised long ago by the Cumanians, who occupied the Hortobágy before the coming of the Magyars, the Seven Tribes who rode in from the east to found Hungary 1,100 years ago. But out on the *puszta* there is not a hill in sight, and nothing taller than the long poles of the sweep wells, markers in a low-profile landscape that seems to run on forever.

People are few: a man on horseback or a solitary shepherd, his face shaded by a hat with an upturned brim, a couple of black puli dogs yapping at his heels as he strides in the wake of his flock. But a whole way of life has grown up around the Hortobágy, whose daredevil horsemen and thatched *csárdas*, or country inns, with their gypsy music and goulash suppers, are etched deep into the Hungarian national psyche.

Next morning we are off early into the cold autumn dawn. In the village of Nagyiván, nearly every telegraph pole in the main street is crowned by a stork's nest. The storks have long since flown south to escape the harsh Hungarian winter, but other, rarer birds remain in the Hortobágy all year round, and Gorman knows where to find them.

A brown hare jinks away through the maize stubble as we cross the treeless fields. From the top of a haystack we scan the surrounding plains for movement. Suddenly Gorman jabs his thumb in the air with a gesture of triumph. 'Got 'em,' he says. Through my binoculars I can pick out what look like a dozen white-and-chestnut-coloured turkeys about 500m away. They are great bustards, Europe's heaviest birds. It's a special moment, watching them strut across the plain, though the autumn mist makes them hard to see.

Long ago, great bustards lived on Salisbury Plain. Now Hungary is one of their last strongholds – with 200 in the Hortobágy.

Later we watch a goshawk racing low over the plains to settle on a haystack, where it squats like a malevolent gargoyle, glaring at the world through mad yellow eyes. Further off, two hen harriers are hunting along the edges of a dyke, and we are so absorbed that we barely notice how quickly the sun is burning off the mist. Before we know it, midday is upon us. Time to eat, and shade is in short supply. Eventually we find a poplar grove and stretch out under the trees. Picnic-time on the *puszta* is a hearty affair: crusty loaves, salami strongly impregnated with paprika, smoked cheese and tomatoes, washed down with mugs of rough red wine.

It would be pleasant to linger but there is more to see. We drive on through the village of Hortobágy, crossing its beautiful nine-arched bridge and passing a Russian tank by the roadside. The tank is a relic from World War II, a memorial to the Red Army, which lost 15,000 men as its armoured squadrons poured across the *puszta* to push the Nazis all the way back to the Danube.

Not far from here are the fishponds of Hortobágy-Halasto, dug, it is rumoured, by political dissidents in Hungary's dark days after the 1956 revolution. Now, nearly half a century on, it is hard to imagine a more peaceful spot than these dreamy lakes, with their flocks of wildfowl and whispering reedbeds.

'There's a certain irony here,' says Gorman. 'Communism might have been a bad deal for the Hungarians but it was good for wildlife. When the state owned the fishponds nothing much happened, and the birds were more or less left alone. But when the Russians left in 1989 and privatization returned, there were worries that the new owners would be more concerned with profits, and less tolerant of wildlife.'

We stroll past a pond where unshaven men in blue overalls are scooping up carp with a mechanical digger and dropping them into plastic tubs on the back of a lorry, ready for transportation to market. Yet here, at least, the wildlife remains unaffected. From a thatched hide overlooking a vast reach of shining mudflats the view is of wall-to-wall ducks and waders. Near by sits a peregrine falcon, preening its slate-grey wings. Suddenly it takes off, skimming over the mud in a low glide, putting up every bird in sight. Effortlessly the peregrine soars among the frantic flocks, turns and scythes through a cloud of lapwings, flies on and then falls like a stone on a flight of redshanks, misses and races on behind the reeds.

The Hortobágy is a rich hunting ground for many kinds of birds of prey. By the end of the day we have added two imperial eagles to our list, plus a white-tailed eagle, a long-legged buzzard and a saker chasing a flock of starlings, which fly apart like exploding shrapnel as the falcon tears into them. By now we have also seen our first cranes – grey ghosts with crimson skullcaps – gleaning maize in the stubble fields. But these are only a foretaste of what lies ahead. Every evening the cranes gather in strength as they fly in to roost among the fishponds, and Gorman knows exactly where to place us under their flightpath.

An hour to sunset and we are in position at the edge of the *puszta*. The first birds to come over are white-fronted geese, 200 of them yelping and squealing as they spill the wind from their wings and drop in free-fall across the grazing marsh. Hot on their heels come the first parties of cranes, rippling in dark lines over the yellowing poplars. They fly close together in family groups of twos and threes, in parties of 20, in wavering chevrons, hundreds strong, etched against the sky.

Some land close by among the sheep flocks, falling across the *puszta* like a soft grey shawl. But most pass on overhead, making for the fishponds as even greater numbers appear over the horizon, approaching on a kilometre-wide front. They call as they fly, bugling their excitement as if caught up in some mighty drama. Aldo Leopold, the American conservationist, described the voice of the crane as 'the trumpet in the orchestra of evolution', and as they pour overhead the sound is deafening.

The sun sets. The air turns cold. Farmhouse lights begin to blink across the plain, like fishing boats in the gathering dusk, and still there is no end to the cranes. When at last we drive home in the dark, Gorman reckons we have seen 12,000 fly past.

Cranes are evocative birds. There's a magic about them, a hint of the unearthly, as if they have stepped straight out of the pages of an East European fairy tale. But why should the sight of them strung out across an autumn sky tug so strongly at the heartstrings? Maybe we recognize them as symbols of something we have lost. Free spirits of the boundless steppe, they owe no allegiance except to the seasonal imperative that has brought them south every year since the Ice Age.

In Hungary the coming of the cranes is a sign of winter not far off, but they will continue to feed and roost in the Hortobágy until the first hard frosts begin to bite, usually in late November. Then, one cold night when the moon is full and hoar frost turns the steppe to iron, they will take off with a rush of wings, calling as they gain height, and pour away under the stars, heading for Tunisia and the warm south.

THE SWISS ALPS – A BRUSH WITH EUPHORIA

It happened several winters ago, but I can recall the moment as if it were only yesterday. It was the morning – all too fleeting – when I finally reached the Elysian Fields of my skiing dreams. The fact that this event took place at Wengen was purely coincidental. But this was not true of the presence of Ali Ross, Britain's best-known ski teacher. Without Ali, a wiry Scot with gunslinger's shanks, who became the first Briton ever to be employed by the Wengen Ski School, it would never have happened at all.

Suddenly, after years of frustration as a stalled intermediate, everything clicked – confidence, knee-steering, good forward lean from the ankles – and I found myself carving turn after effortless turn through an overnight dusting of diamond-bright powder. It was as if I was skiing on automatic pilot, one turn leading instinctively into the next, to a rhythm as precise as a pendulum, and no thought beyond the high-octane euphoria of that headlong rush down the fall line in the shadow of the Eiger.

Fellow fanatics will know the feeling. It happens when the snow is flattering and forgiving, when edges bite, when confidence is absolute and every swooping turn induces that stomach-lifting sensation – not of skiing down the mountain but flying, held fast to the snow by nothing but the whisper of gravity under your skis. But recreational skiers such as myself will also know that such moments are brief and dearly bought, hedged around by days and even weeks when nothing goes right, when confidence crumbles and technique degenerates into an undignified scramble for self-preservation. The day after I learned how it felt to ski well I flew home to England. When I returned the following winter, filled with high hopes, I knew from the very first run that I had sunk back into my bad old ways.

All holiday skiers are prone to this malaise, but it is the middleweights, the great lumpen mass of intermediate skiers – to which I belong – who suffer most. We strive for the long-awaited moment when the truth is revealed and we will know at last what it is to inscribe elegant turns all over the mountain. Yet even when we know the theory – carving turns, knee-steering, angulation and the rest – the breakthrough into the superior world of the expert remains as elusive as ever.

Why should this be so? It helps to be super-fit and blessed, like Ali Ross, with the reflexes of the natural athlete, but this is not essential. Skiing is a knack, an indefinable fusion of balance and timing, which has its equivalent in the footballer's sweetly struck volley or the angler's perfect cast. You know when it happens because you *feel* it. But repeating it, run after run, year after year, on all kinds of snow and on all kinds of pistes – there's the problem.

Many factors contribute to the depressingly familiar style of the British on skis – able to muddle through almost anything, but with gritted teeth and ramrod legs, shoulders askew, bums in the air or, at regular intervals, in the snow. Of late a new and even more alarming variation has appeared: the *Ski Sunday* aficionados, who try to emulate the World Cup racers but succeed only in skiing out of control.

Lack of time is one reason for our lamentable performance. Most of us, I am sure, given a whole winter on skis, would make the quantum-leap forward into the dizzier realms of the black mogul runs and powder gullies. As it is, with only a week or a fortnight to spare, the holiday is invariably almost over by the time we have rediscovered our ski legs.

It has to be said that lousy tuition is another factor that holds us back. Too much confusing advice, too much national pride, too many changing fashions in ski teaching. Remember up and down unweighting? The French sit-back turn? The Austrians with their knees glued together? No wonder we are so obsessed with style, trying to imitate what we think we are seeing without understanding what the skier is actually doing, which is responding to the interlocking forces of speed, gravity and direction. No wonder so many of us are locked in the lavatorial position – the result of bending ze knees but not ze ankles!

Above all, I remain convinced that the eternal intermediate is a hostage to that old familiar enemy: the funk factor. Fear sometimes strikes for the daftest reasons, yet it is a perfectly natural reaction. It is right and proper to be afraid if we perceive a real danger – in this case fear of falling.

But surrendering to fear – even unconsciously – inhibits the very skills that would see us safely through. We tense up when we should relax. We sit back, ski defensively, hurry our turns through the fall line in that unnerving split second when we and our skis are facing directly downhill. Technique that enables us confidently to perform neat parallel turns on a gentle blue run of fresh-pisted snow falls to pieces when the run becomes a staircase of giant moguls or a fiendishly narrow woodpath of blind bends and icy tramlines.

At such bleak moments a little gentle psychology is not amiss. If you cannot yet call yourself an expert, at least you are no longer a floundering beginner. You can execute a passable parallel turn, sometimes you may even feel rather pleased with yourself, and you could – at a pinch – find your way down almost any slope. And isn't that what skiing is all about? It is being able to enjoy the dazzling world of the high mountains, lunch at your favourite mountain restaurant, bask on a sunny terrace and then ski back home through the trees.

As for those powder turns, I tell myself, there is always tomorrow. In middle age I have settled for the role of a red-run cruiser. My kind of resort is somewhere like La Plagne, with its miles of undemanding boulevards. But I know I have the potential to become a more effective skier. That is what Ali Ross taught me on that magic day in Wengen. Now all I need is the time – and maybe a little more of that forgiving snow.

ON
SAFARI

BOTSWANA – JACK'S CAMP

In the Kalahari a road may be no more than twin ruts in the grass; a set of tyre tracks worn deep in the sand. But these roads can tell you much about who has been there before you. On the way to Jack's Camp we crossed the huge prints of a Kalahari lion. We did not see him – his prints disappeared into a thorny tangle of acacia scrub where we could not follow – and perhaps it was just as well, for these desert lions have a long history of unpredictability. It was a Kalahari lion that nearly put an end to Livingstone in 1843.

Botswana has lots of safari camps and most of them can show you lions. But there is only one Jack's Camp and, apart from the rainy season, when the big cats follow the migrating zebras from the Boteti River, you don't come here for game. Instead, what Jack's Camp offers is total solitude and the biggest skies in Africa. What it also has is the charisma that Jack Bousfield, its founder, brought to this remote hideaway on the edge of the great Makgadikgadi thirstlands, ancient lakes sucked dry in the hot Kalahari sun. A photo of him adorns the bar – a bearded adventurer, larger than life, holding up the giant prehistoric hand-axe he discovered on Ntwetwe Pan, one of the nearby dried-up lakes.

The site Jack chose is idyllic: an island of palms in a yellow sea of grass. Under the palms stand eight roomy twin-bedded tents, each one furnished with Persian rugs and old-fashioned beds with chambray sheets. Every morning, copper jugs are filled with hot water for washing and shaving, but there is also the luxury of a private shower – albeit dispensed from a canvas bucket – and a modern flush loo tucked behind a screen of mopane poles.

In as little as three days here you can feel the desert taking hold of you, a kind of madness, like the beginnings of a love affair in which you cannot tear your eyes away from the beauty of the vast horizons. True, without water you could die here in a couple of days. But the Makgadikgadi is no ordinary desert. Rimmed by golden grasslands and by leggy clumps of hyphaene palms, it is the ghost of a prehistoric lake, an immense sea twice the size of Lake Victoria. Into it once poured all the waters of the Chobe and the Okavango rivers. Then, some 15,000 years ago, came a cataclysmic shift of the earth's crust. The rivers changed course. The lake died, its vanished deeps replaced by a desolation of glittering soda pans. The two main pans, Ntwetwe and Sua, stretch for more than 15,000sq km and are the biggest in the world. Together with their satellite pans they cover an area the size of Switzerland.

For most of the year the pans are as dead as Mars. But come November, if the gods are kind, the gift of rain brings them back to life. Overnight, Makgadikgadi becomes a lake again. Flocks of flamingos arrive to gorge on the brine shrimps as they hatch in their billions in the brimming shallows, and the surrounding grasslands echo to the thunder of migrating zebras.

My visit came in late July – well into Botswana's dry season. In camp, resting in my tent during the midday heat, I could hear the wind sighing in the palms like passing rain. But apart from a freak shower in May, not a drop had fallen since April. The flamingos had gone and the zebras had long since trekked back towards the Boteti. In the evening, during the golden hour that always precedes the African sundown, I drove across the plain with Ralph Bousfield, Jack's son, to visit an ancient baobab tree known as the Seven Sisters, which stands not far from camp.

The Seven Sisters is a colossus, a living cathedral as old as Stonehenge. By day the desert winds rush among its seven crooked spires with a sound like distant surf, and lanner falcons nest among its spreading branches. By night its gnarled fingers clutch at the stars. In the flatness of the Makgadikgadi it is the only significant landmark for miles and its massive outline was well-known to early explorers. Livingstone, who described the baobab as 'that giant upturned carrot', rested beneath its ample shade in 1858, and others carved their initials on its swollen trunk. 'Nowadays,' said Ralph, 'microlight pilots use it as a marker.' By the time we arrived the sun was down, but the tree still glowed like a kitchen stove, and we sat for a long time in its comforting shadow, warming our backs against its trunk, the colour of pink granite, while Ralph reminisced about his father.

Jack Bousfield was never cut out for a quiet life. During World War II he fought in North Africa with the Long Range Desert Group. When the war ended he couldn't settle down, so he became a hunter, first in Tanzania and finally in Botswana. But Africa was changing. Clients no longer wanted to pursue their trophies on foot, so Jack left the hunting business and turned instead to photo-safaris.

Yet even in Botswana, true wilderness as measured in Jack Bous-field's terms was becoming harder to find. Then one day somebody mentioned the Makgadikgadi. Jack asked what was out there. 'Nothing – only idiots go there,' they replied. 'Fine,' thought Jack, 'that's the place for me.'

Jack found it harsh, wild and empty and he loved it from the moment he first saw it. With Ralph's help he set up camp and was soon attracting a stream of visitors. But in 1992, tragedy struck when their plane crashed in the desert. Ralph survived but Jack was killed.

Today it is Ralph who runs Jack's Camp. Now aged 40, with shoulder-length hair and striking good looks, he shares his father's passion for the desert. 'In the coming century,' he said, staring out into the gathering dusk, 'the world's greatest luxury will be space. Out here there is still room to breathe, to count the stars and be yourself.'

By now the moon was up, its silver glow spilling through the branches, and still the old tree was warm to the touch. When at last we stood up to go, it seemed to stretch out its long roots, as if reluctant for us to leave.

In camp next morning, Ralph spoke to me at breakfast. 'I've arranged for you to go walking,' he said. 'Come and meet your guides.' Under the palm trees stood a wizened little man dressed in brown overalls and broken-down shoes at least two sizes too large. 'This is Mister Toh,' said Ralph. 'He is in his late seventies and I'm afraid he doesn't speak English, but Cobra will translate for you.' Cobra was younger than Mister Toh, but had the same apricot skin, distinctive high-boned cheeks and almond eyes. They were the first true Bushmen I had ever met.

Together we set off into the shimmering distance. By day, apart from a few distant ostriches, these Kalahari grasslands seem devoid of life. But after dark a host of animals emerge from their burrows to forage across the plains. Wading through the knee-deep grasses, we crossed endless webs of footprints they had spun in the night. Jackal, aardvark, brown hyena – my Bushman guides could read their tracks as easily as you or I can flip through a newspaper.

It seemed that the old man was something of a legend among his people. 'He was a famous hunter,' said Cobra. 'He could even out-run an eland.' Looking at him now, in his European clothes and out-size shoes, it was hard to imagine Mister Toh as a young man, racing barefoot over the plains. Yet his eyes were still sharp and he trod lightly on the earth, at ease in his desert world.

The following day an expedition had been planned, travelling on four-wheel-drive quad bikes into the hot, white heart of Ntwetwe Pan. The quad bikes would enable us to go where ordinary vehicles might break through the pan's crusty surface and become bogged down. To keep the dust out of our hair we wrapped *kikois* around our heads, Arab-style. The transformation was extraordinary. Tourists no longer, we were the Quad Squad, intrepid desert explorers. The bikes were comfortable and surprisingly easy to handle. One by one they roared into life. Then, with a 'Wagons Ho!' wave from our leader, we were off.

An hour later, far out in the yawning emptiness of Ntwetwe, we stopped to watch the sun go down and saw the earth's shadow flung out against the eastern sky. Then the moon rose, a huge, distended orange bubble that floated into view like a second sun, flooding the pan with an unearthly glow.

Ntwetwe must be the quietest place in Africa. Back in camp there were always natural sounds: the cluck of hornbills, keening jackals. Here there was nothing. Nobody spoke. Even the wind had died, and the sharp night air was cold and clean, like breathing pure oxygen.

I lay on my back and gazed up at the sky, where the torrents of the Milky Way now fumed and glittered with unbelievable brilliance. Listen, say the Kalahari Bushmen, and you can hear the stars hunting. I cupped my hands behind my ears, but all I could hear were gasps of wonder from my companions, and the beating of my heart.

Later, after a barbecue supper, we discovered to our surprise that our beds had been smuggled out of camp and placed in the middle of the pan. So, that night, instead of turning in under canvas, I slept beneath a canopy of stars, bathed in a dazzling moon-glow that lit up the soda crystals like snow.

Next morning we set off across the pan on foot, crunching across a wide bay towards a distant line of grassy dunes. In prehistoric times, said Ralph, when Ntwetwe was still a permanent lake, wandering bands of Stone Age people hunted and foraged along its shores. Their weapons – stone blades, hand-axes, awls and scrapers – lay everywhere, embedded in the soda crust, as if they had passed this way only a few weeks ago.

I stooped to pick up a spear point, teardrop-shaped and fashioned from a polished black stone like obsidian. Its scalloped edges were still razor sharp, and as it lay in the palm of my hand I thought about the last man who had held it, maybe 5,000 years ago.

BOTSWANA – THE LIONS OF SAVUTI

From the air, Savuti seemed as dead as Mars. As we flew in over the great Chobe National Park, the land below resembled a threadbare lion pelt, furred with grasses, veined with game trails. Yet from the moment I arrived and stepped out into the oven-dry air of late July, there was life. Flocks of quealeas – small finches with coral-red bills – took wing like puffs of smoke. Impala bounded across the roads and elephants stood under the camel's thorn trees, swinging their huge ears to keep cool.

Beyond the trees a level plain reached to the horizon. In the wet season, it is a marsh where thousands of migratory zebras feed and fatten, where the grass is as green as Ireland and tall enough to hide a stalking lion. But that was three months ago. Now it was an emptiness of yellow stubble, dotted with anthills and blackened tree stumps.

Without animals, Savuti is like an arena when the players have departed. An indefinable air of sadness hangs over it, as if this is how Africa will be one day when the game is gone. Here and there, small groups of animals moved in the distance: warthog, impala, a few tsessebe – Africa's swiftest antelopes. But most of the game had trekked north into the Linyanti Swamps.

It was not always so. Until the 1980s, winter floods from the Linyanti dribbled down the Savuti Channel, providing enough water to see the game through the dry season. Then tremors deep under the Kalahari caused a seismic shift on the surface, cutting Savuti's lifeline. When the channel finally dried up in 1982, the Savuti hippos walked for nearly 60km to seek refuge in the Linyanti Swamps. Two crocodiles wandered off and hid in a cave, where one is said to have survived for two-and-a-half years – until it was killed by a leopard. Now, when drought grips the land, the animals that remain in Savuti gather around Pump Pan, whose waters are piped from a nearby borehole.

We drove there one evening to see the show. Already, more than 50 elephants stood quietly around the pan and others were still trekking in. Big bulls, mostly, they crowded around the water's edge, while flights of sandgrouse whirred in to drink between a forest of legs. One bull, bigger than the rest, passed within metres of us. Six tonnes of silence, leaving a set of prints the size of dustbin lids.

Back in camp beside the bone-dry Savuti Channel, I discovered why Gametrackers, the owner, had named it Elephant Camp. After dinner, with everyone seated comfortably around the campfire, there came a sudden crash, followed by the giant silhouette of a fully grown bull elephant advancing through the hole he had made in the camp fence. With scarcely a glance in our direction, he strode past in the flickering firelight and began to shake down showers of seedpods from the overhanging camel's thorn trees.

'We get elephants turning up every night in the dry season,' said Rowan Vickery, the camp manager. 'We employ seven men here who do nothing but repair our fencing. Every night they put it back up. Every night the elephants come and knock it down again.'

As he spoke, three more elephants wandered in. Among them was a ragged-eared bull with broken tusks. 'That one can be a bit cheeky,' said Rowan, whose laid-back attitude concealed a profound respect for his nocturnal visitors. 'If you shout at him he may "mock-charge"; but if you just talk to him nicely he'll move off.'

Later, after everyone had turned in, I lay in bed and listened to the symphony of shaking branches and contented belly-rumbles as the elephants continued their midnight feast only metres from my tent. The last sound I heard before falling asleep was the dull roar of a lion, signing off with a deep, grunting coda.

Savuti is renowned for its lions, and many scientists have come here to study them, intrigued by their extraordinary ability to survive for long periods without water. For the past 20 years, the lives of the Savuti prides have been lovingly chronicled by Dereck and Beverley Joubert, two of South Africa's finest film-makers. Closest to the Jouberts' heart was Maome's pride, a savage sisterhood led by Maome herself and watched over by two magnificent pride males, Mandevu and his brother Ntchwaidumela (He Who Greets with Fire). But lions lead brief lives. In 1991, Mandevu and his brother were shot when they strayed outside the park. Maome, too, is long gone. New prides ruled Savuti and I was eager to see them.

Maome's successors included a pride of 26 lions with exceptional hunting prowess. A few months earlier, they had even managed to kill an elephant, grabbing it by the trunk and suffocating it. This pride, I was told, had since split. Most had gone north with the migrating plains game, preferring to skirmish with the Linyanti prides rather than starve in Savuti. But a few had stayed behind. So, rugged up against the cold winter dawn, we set out to look for these elusive survivors.

There was no wind to stir the dry leaves of the Kalahari apple-thorn bushes, no sound except the chanting of doves in the rain trees. Long reefs of light lay along the eastern horizon. Then the sun rose, throwing into sharp relief the maze of prints on the trail. Almost at once we found fresh lion tracks in the soft Kalahari sand and followed them for over an hour, crossing and recrossing the Savuti Channel – until a sudden movement caught my eye.

Out of the backlit bushman grass, two lionesses came padding. In the morning light the plain was grey, and grey was the dust that hung in their wake as they moved gravely between the leadwoods. At first, although they must have been long used to the presence of tourist vehicles, they seemed ill at ease and slunk away to hide in a thicket. But after a while they began to relax, rubbing heads and grooming each other with pale pink tongues, before flopping down to rest. They were litter mates, 10 years old, and turned out to be Maome's sole surviving daughters.

For the Savuti lions, the African winter brings hunger and hardship, but in the Moremi Game Reserve, only 40km away, the rules are reversed. At the height of the drought, while Savuti is gasping for water, the miraculous arrival of the Okavango floods heralds a dramatic change of fortune for the big cats that hunt along the River Khwai.

The Khwai is the outermost finger of the Okavango Delta, an immense oasis of lagoons, papyrus channels and palm-fringed islands in the heart of the northern Kalahari. It is fed by the summer rains that fall on Angola, but Botswana is so flat that the floods do not reach the River Khwai until four months later in the middle of the dry season. For a few weeks more, the river flows before the floods recede. In vain it tries to push up into the Mababe Depression, only to exhaust itself and die under the hot African sun. But on its journey it creates a thin green line of reedbeds and hippo pools, attracting animals from miles around.

Gametrackers has a lodge here, too, shaded by groves of lead-woods at the edge of the floodplains, across which, every day, a procession of thirsty animals marches out of the woods to drink. Giraffe and buffalo, proud kudu bulls with spiral horns, herds of foxy red lechwe antelopes and troops of zebra all risk death in the tall reeds where the River Khwai lions lie in ambush.

When the river runs and the game is plentiful, the pride grows fat on a glut of kills. In all, said Mothupi, my guide at Khwai, there were nine lionesses and four awesome pride males known as Bafana-Bafana (Our Boys) after the South Africans' name for their national football team. 'The lodge is the core of their territory,' said Mothupi. 'They often walk in at night.' And sure enough, after supper, a lioness wandered towards us as we sat around the campfire. She roared as she came, padding steadily through the firelight on her big soft paws, and strode on past us into the darkness.

Mothupi was an ideal companion. His family were BaYei, or water Bushmen, and he had spent all his life in the delta. 'When I was a boy, I lived by hunting and fishing,' he said. 'Life was simple. I had no clothes. We dressed in skins. The floor was our table and we ate with our hands. We ate lots of fish and every kind of animal. We ate bullfrogs, pythons, even leopards.' He turned and gave me a huge African grin. 'That's why it is so hard to see leopards today,' he said. 'Because I ate them all!'

But times change. When the Moremi reserve was created in 1962, Mothupi got a job at a safari lodge, taking visitors for boat rides in his *mokoro*, the traditional delta dugout canoe, and eventually became one of the Moremi's most respected guides. 'So you could say I have had two lives, one old and one new,' he said. 'Yet even now I cannot say which life I have enjoyed the most.'

Next morning, we drove into the Moremi, crossing the River Khwai on a rickety bridge of mopane poles, and found three more lions resting beside the remains of a zebra. 'They must have killed early this morning,' said Mothupi. 'See how full their bellies are.'

How different they looked, these fat cats of the Moremi, compared with the lions of the Savuti thirstlands. But their day would come. Three months from now, when the drought broke, when Savuti Marsh was green again and the plains game returned from their dry-season exile, Maome's daughters would have 5,000 zebras to choose from.

BOTSWANA – ABU'S CAMP

First light in the delta. Across the lagoon the palms stand tall, etched in black against the sky as the dawn chorus of doves, swamp boubous and Heuglin's robins echoes under the mangosteen trees. Botswana's Okavango Delta is one of the loveliest big-game sanctuaries on earth, a miraculous oasis of reeds and lily-ponds and marshy plains, scattered with a million wooded islands and threaded with spillways and shining channels whose waters fan out for more than 26,000sq km across the northern Kalahari. And in the midst of it all lies Abu's Camp, a luxurious springboard for the ultimate African adventure.

Abu is an African bull elephant, a majestic tusker in his prime. With him are nine other elephants, in age ranging from 41-year-old Benny to baby Kitimetse. For five never-to-be-forgotten days in April 2000 I rode, walked and swam with Abu and his herd, rocking and swaying through the reeds, listening to his contented belly-rumbles, feeling his huge spine flexing beneath me as we splashed across the delta's floodplains on a slow march though paradise.

You may hear it said that African elephants are untamable. Unlike their smaller Asian cousins they are treacherous, unpredictable, not to be trusted. But Randall Jay Moore, an American biologist, former animal trainer and erstwhile Vietnam War protester, has confounded convention by offering elephant-back safaris in Botswana. At US$6,500 per head for a five-night stay it's the most expensive camp in Africa, but guests love it. One German couple who met on safari returned for an elephant-back wedding, with the bride seated on Cathy, the herd matriarch, the groom on Abu and the priest officiating from Benny.

Every morning at sunrise my fellow guests and I would be poled by *mokoro*, the traditional Okavango canoe, across the short distance that separated our camp from the elephants' living quarters. There, at the command 'Stretch down', Abu and his companions would lower their bodies onto the sand and allow us to clamber aboard. Then Big Joe, the leading mahout, would kick-start Abu with a nudge of his toes behind each giant ear, urging him forward with a cry of 'Move out', and off we would march in a trunk-to-tail convoy, with little Kitimetse hurrying along at the rear.

Travelling by elephant is the ideal way to explore these languid African everglades. Padding softly over the sandveld, wading belly-deep through oxbow lagoons, Abu is in his element, a perfect, 6-tonne, all-terrain safari vehicle of awesome power, thoroughly eco-friendly and, apart from ocasional bouts of flatulence, entirely pollution-free. For me, after 30 years of safaris, this was the greatest of them all. Released from the tyranny of roads, you can go where you please, passing soundlessly into the shade of riverine forests, crossing watercourses, eating up the distance at a tireless 5kph. Furthermore, lounging 3m above the ground in a padded howdah as comfortable as a club armchair gives you a new perspective on the bush. Looking down into the amber floodwaters I could see quick, darting bream, and tiny frogs like Fabergé jewels clinging to the reed-stems.

Game was scarce, having dispersed after the rains. On previous trips clients had seen lion, leopard – even wild dogs. Now only red lechwe antelope remained, plunging like porpoises across the floodplains, and the periscope necks of giraffes rising from thickets of silverleaf terminalia. But I didn't care. For once the presence of wild animals seemed almost superfluous. The main attraction was, overwhelmingly, being with Abu and his companions.

Abu is probably the world's most famous elephant, having starred in a number of feature films, most notably *White Hunter, Black Heart* with Clint Eastwood. He was born in the wild in 1960, but then captured and transported to the USA, where he grew up in a Texas safari park. That is where Randall found him, chained in a barn, smothered in his own dung, sleeping on a bare concrete floor. Abu's handler told Randall he was uncontrollable. 'But all I saw,' he says, 'was a sad, mistreated animal.'

On an impulse Randall offered to buy Abu for US$10,000 and his owners accepted. 'It was the best deal I ever made,' says Randall. It was also the beginning of an extraordinary partnership that would ultimately lead both of them to a new life in the Okavango, where Randall established the first Abu's Camp in 1990.

With him from the States Randall brought two other captive African elephants. Benny, born in 1959 and captured as a baby in South Africa's Kruger National Park, also came from Texas. When

Randall found him he was 3m tall and weighed 5 tonnes, but was hardly the stuff of movie stardom, with one floppy ear and no tusks – the result of years of frustration and boredom in a cramped exhibition cage. The third elephant was Cathy, the same age as Abu, captured in Uganda and obtained from a safari park in Toronto. These three riding elephants formed the nucleus of Abu's herd, which expanded in Botswana with the arrival in 1990 of what Randall called his 'brat pack' – seven adorable orphaned babies from the Kruger National Park.

Later, from South Africa's Pilanesberg National Park, came two feisty teenage bulls, the colourfully named Nyaka Nyaka (Full of Shit) and Mthondo Mbomvo (Painted Penis), so called because a lack of pigmentation has left him with large pink splotches on his private parts. And finally, in 2000, Kitimetse (I'm Lost) arrived, the only true Botswana elephant, a four-year-old orphan found abandoned near the camp.

Now, 10 years on, Randall is a legend in Botswana. In his own way he has become the George Adamson of the new millennium, doing for elephants what Adamson did to raise the profile of lions in the 1980s. Twice married, twice divorced, he has mellowed since we first met in 1994. At the age of 49 he has shaved of his Zapata moustache and chopped off his ponytail, although he still smokes his favourite Cuban Monte Cristo cigars and is currently engaged to a beautiful 19-year-old Mauritian girl.

The turning-point in Randall's life came in 1971. The Vietnam War was raging, causing Randall's kid brother to volunteer for the marines and turning Randall into an anti-war protester, tripping out on drugs and generally raising hell. He was a student in Baltimore – a far cry from his home in the backwoods of Oregon, where he had grown up hiking, hunting and fishing with his father. One day a fellow student told him about a wildlife park in Washington state where tigers and elephants lived on a snow-covered mountain. On a whim, he drove there. It sounded like a fantasy, but when he arrived it was exactly as his friend had described. There in a barn were nine young elephants, including three from Africa, named Durga, Tshombe and Owalla. 'I knew there and then what I wanted,' said Randall. 'To work with elephants and go to Africa.'

So began Randall's education in the ways of elephants, training them for circus acts. Shortly afterwards he stumbled upon Karen Blixen's classic tale *Out of Africa*, which made him even more determined to go there. Meanwhile, both of Randall's mentors were killed by elephants, but Randall was undeterred. He clinched a film contract with ABC Television, raised enough money to buy Durga, Tshombe and Owalla, and in 1980 they sailed together from New York to Mombasa. Then followed a whole series of adventures and film episodes in Kenya and South Africa, at the end of which Durga, Tshombe and Owalla were released into the Pilanesberg National Park and Randall finally moved on to Botswana.

At that time the only other elephant-back safaris in the world were in Nepal's Royal Chitwan National Park, and nobody believed the same thing could be done using African elephants. That is, except for Randall. It was a chance remark by Peter Beard, the distinguished American wildlife photographer, that had sowed the seed. Sitting around a campfire one evening in Kenya, Beard was asked for his idea of the ultimate safari. 'To ride across Africa on an elephant,' he said. 'And I thought, OK that's what I would do,' recalls Moore.

His elephant-back safaris have now been running since 1990, although not in the same spot. The present site, where he moved in 1997, is in a wilderness concession of 2,000sq km overlooking a permanent lagoon whose Tswana name translates as 'The Place Where the Women Come to Gather Reeds'.

The camp itself epitomizes Botswana's enlightened, low-density, high-price approach to eco-tourism, with a central dining area and room for just 12 guests in half a dozen en-suite tents, designed in a revolutionary style Randall likes to describe as 'Afro-Bedouin'. Lots of celebrities have stayed here. Jack Lemmon loved it, and in 2000 Prince Harry and Prince William came out and rode on Abu and swam in Randall's private pool on the other side of the lagoon, where he has a house adorned with African artefacts and coffee-table books on big game.

It was here, lounging in the shade of the mangosteens, that Randall spoke of his feelings for elephants. Of their resilience – both mental and physical – and of their ability to understand more than 60 commands. 'They're a lot smarter than a lot of people I've met,' he says. 'I can say I generally prefer elephants to people. Elephants never lie or let you down.'

'Their social structure is so like ours in so many ways,' he continued. 'They love their young, become teenagers just as we do, grow old at the same age as us and grieve for their dead. All the best qualities we have as humans I see every day in my elephants. But at the same time I don't see the bad qualities. I sometimes say to myself that I built this whole business on the backs of Abu, Cathy and Benny. They are my children.'

I asked him what was the most amazing thing about elephants. 'Look,' he said, 'there's a mystery here. I'm not a big guy. Elephants are very large animals. And yet there's this relationship where they allow us to dominate them. It seems absurd, especially as we are so puny and they are so intelligent. So why do they do it?'

Moore's elephant enterprise is worth around US$8 million. In addition to his Okavango bush home he has a town house in Maun, owns a fishing lodge in Patagonia and has just bought a colonial mansion in Cartagena, Colombia. 'Not bad when you consider I started with nothing,' he says. In the beginning it was the movie business that generated the money. Since 1989 Randall's elephants have starred in nine feature films. The latest is the Walt Disney production, *Whispers*. But now it is the elephant-back safaris that are bringing in the dollars.

Moore's newest venture is the Botswana Elephant Training Camp (BETS for short), where young elephants are groomed for riding and film work. 'Elephant games can get boisterous so these little guys have to go to school to learn some discipline,' says Dirk Erdmann, their German trainer. 'Only when they reach their mid-teens are they ready for riding.' Dirk, whose wife Ricarda is the only female mahout in camp, describes the training regime as 'mellow', handing out treats every time the youngsters respond to his softly spoken commands.

Abu usually gets the starring role when filming is taking place, but in *Whispers* it went to a precocious little bull called Seba, who is currently being looked after at the training camp along with two of Randall's original brat pack, Mufunyane and Sirheni. In 1998 Sirheni produced the first baby elephant ever born at Abu's Camp. Sadly, it died 12 days later, but then Sirheni mated with a wild bull and to everyone's delight produced another, Pula (Rain).

Life at Abu's Camp has an easy rhythm. Up at dawn for a three-hour ride, followed by lunch and a siesta before heading out again in mid-afternoon. Back in camp there are hot baths at sundown as the bell frogs awake with a sound like ice cubes clinking in a million glasses. Then dinner under the stars – barbecued steaks, imaginative salads – followed by coffee around the campfire and sometimes, when the choir of frogs falls silent, the distant rumble of lions.

Every ride follows a different route, exploring islands marooned in the floodplains, padding soundlessly over the Kalahari sandveld.

Out in the drowning seas of grass Abu's family becomes a flotilla, ears flapping like the sails of old-time barges as we roll on towards the wide horizon. From time to time the elephants pause to snatch up a trunkful of bayonet-sharp palm fronds – a takeaway snack to be munched *en route*. 'Get it and go,' cry the mahouts, and on we ride, with Jika rumbling a message to Abu and Kitimetse's fat little body outlined in a halo of ginger hairs.

One morning we rode out for a barbecue lunch on an island of ebony trees deep in the delta, where a table awaited us, decorated with jugs of water-lilies, and blankets and cushions were spread out in the shade. Afterwards we swam in the warm Okavango waters while shoals of tiny fish nibbled gently at our bodies, and Randall, submerged to his armpits, sat in the shallows and smoked a cigar.

Sometimes, instead of riding, I would walk with Sandor Carter, Randall's camp manager. Sandor, a former British army officer, always carried a rifle in case of emergencies, but never had cause to use it. It was then, as we followed in Abu's giant footsteps through a backlit haze of golden grass-heads and surrounded by a forest of pillared legs and flapping ears, that I sensed what it might feel like to be an elephant, a member of a close-knit family bound by kinship ties as complex as our own. Looking up into Abu's benign brown eyes with their long dark lashes, I felt humbled by their tolerance. There is something almost spiritual about being accepted into the company of elephants, and to walk with them is to come tantalizingly close to bridging the gulf that separates us from the rest of the animal world.

But the high point of the whole safari was the day I swam with Abu in a deep lagoon shared by two bemused hippos and a 3m-long crocodile. They all kept a respectful distance as Sandor, Big Joe and I rode bareback into the water and then submerged on Abu's back as he sank like a submarine beneath us.

On our final morning in camp the mahouts demonstrated some of the skills (never tricks, insists Randall) learnt by the elephants for their roles as film stars. Lined up like a firing squad, we stood and watched Abu bearing down on us in a full-blooded charge, until suddenly he was towering over us, a monstrous shadow with ears outstretched, skidding to a halt at Randall's command only a few feet from our camera lenses.

Today Abu's age is beginning to show. The broken tip of one of his tusks now adorns the camp dining-table and the other is held together with a metal brace to prevent further cracking. But high-tech prosthetics and Hollywood ingenuity have created a perfect pair of imitation fibreglass tusks that he wears for his moviestar roles. Eventually Randall hopes to return him to the wild. 'I feel I owe it to him for all he has done for me,' he said. 'And not just Abu. Letaba could be the first to be freed. Then maybe Thando and, if all goes well, Abu and Benny, too. At least, that's the dream.'

He appears surprisingly sanguine about the prospect of letting Abu go. 'At the end of the day we can walk away in different directions,' he says, 'Abu to his freedom and me to a different future. Just so long as I know he'll always be out there and I can take a *mokoro* and pole out into the delta and maybe look at him through binoculars. To know Abu has finally gained his freedom will be satisfaction enough. God knows he's earned it. He's earned it every day of his life.'

But I found it hard to say goodbye. I was close to tears when I shook hands with the mahouts, Big Joe and David and Sumanadhasa, closer still when I made my farewells with the elephants. I thought of Jika splashing through the floods, kicking up water like a kid in a paddling pool; little Kitimetse plucking a water-lily and carrying it in the curled tip of her trunk; ugly, lovable Benny with his sad eyes and floppy ear; and, of course, Abu, the wise and gentle giant, eating up the ground with his massive swinging stride. Even now I miss them more than I can say.

KENYA – THE MASAI MARA

Even before the six-seater bush plane had landed on the Governor's Camp airstrip I had spotted a lioness at rest on an anthill. As the plane came to rest, fat African raindrops the size of Kenyan shillings began to drum on the dust, but I did not care. I stepped down onto the wet earth, thrilled to be back in the territory of the Musiara lion pride, whose lives I had once chronicled with the photographer Jonathan Scott.

We called them the Marsh lions, one of several large prides that roam across the 1,500-odd sq km of the Masai Mara National Reserve. But the pride males who had once been as familiar as old friends – Mkubwa, with his battle-torn muzzle, Brando, the majestic Scar – were all dead. New males now ruled the Marsh, and even as I waited for the baggage to be unloaded, two huge lions I did not recognize, each with a splendid shaggy mane, trotted across the end of the airstrip less than a hundred metres away.

The high country of the Mara usually enjoys good rains, but until my arrival Kenya had been enduring a drought of such severity that the buffalo – normally such powerful animals – had been reduced to walking sacks of bones. Now the drought was over and the grass rains had begun, bringing relief to the parched plains and encouraging the handsome topi antelope to give birth to their gangling ginger calves. It did not rain continuously. The days were hot and sunny, but every afternoon storm clouds piled up over the Siria escarpment as zebra galloped in full sunlight over the greening plains, their striped coats standing out in brilliant contrast against the deepening indigo skies.

These high-country skies are never empty. As the lions are to the grasslands and brush-choked *luggas* (seasonal watercourses), so the eagles are to the currents and thermals that swirl in the upper airs above them. Here live the tawny eagle and the black-chested harrier eagle, the handsome bateleur, rocking and tilting on outstretched wings, and the great martial eagle, the lord of the steppe, with his ermine chest and executioner's hood. Augur buzzards flaunt their bright chestnut tails. Exquisite little black-shouldered kites hover with the ease of kestrels. And always there are the vultures, Africa's dark angels of death, spiralling over the plains in search of carrion.

For many years, setting out at first light to look for the Marsh lions, I had watched with envy as the two multi-coloured hot-air balloons rose like twin suns from the riverine woodlands behind Little Governor's Camp, taking their passengers high into the eagles' kingdom on a 90-minute joyride over the plains and ending with a champagne breakfast. It had always seemed so sybaritic and unnecessary, a touch of the fairground, an exercise in gimmickry far removed from the simple, uncluttered existence that life in the bush ought to be. It was also very expensive. Yet I longed to see the mosaic of grasslands and game trails as they must appear to the high-wheeling vultures. And in the end I gave in, and was not disappointed.

Ballooning over Africa, I decided, is like going to heaven in a picnic hamper. Leaning comfortably on the basket's chest-high wicker rim, I could see the coils of the Mara River glittering among its luxuriant woodlands, the blue walls of the Siria escarpment and the great plains reaching down into the Serengeti. Even without binoculars it was possible to pick out the distinctive shapes of animals: a lone topi standing motionless on an anthill; a group of giraffes throwing long shadows across the grass in front of Kichwa Tembo Lodge; and, best of all, a sudden stampede of zebras immediately beneath us, where our shadow flew across the grass towards a pair of hunting lionesses.

Eavesdropping on the big cats from such an unusual viewpoint reminded me that it was lions that had first lured me to the Mara in the early 1970s, and it was here one cold, bright morning that I heard my first wild lion. The dew still clung to the tall stems of red oat grass, and the lion was standing on a termite mound perhaps half a kilometre away. Being new to Africa, I was surprised at the manner in which he roared, not gaping open-mouthed like the old MGM movie lion, but expelling the sounds from deep down in his chest through half-closed jaws; and with every grunt I could see his breath condensing in distinct puffs of warm air. Now, 30 years on, I am still drawn back to the Mara by the song of the lion, and its magic never palls.

It was here, too, that I had first met Jonathan Scott, and it was sitting around a campfire one evening that the idea of a book about the

lions of the Masai Mara first took root. Jonathan showed me his photographs and also the diary in which he had entered brief details of
everything he had seen during his time in the reserve. Time and
time again the words 'Marsh lions' leaped from the pages. The name
intrigued me. It had a resonance and an element of the unusual.
People did not usually associate lions with marshes, and I began to
see Jonathan's favourite pride as he saw them, not as an anonymous
group of animals but as individuals, each one recognizable, with its
own dramatic story of hunting, mating and fighting to be told.

By then I was completely hooked on Africa and desperately wanted to write a book about it. Jonathan, too, was eager to win recog-
nition and a wider audience for his superb photographs. So the idea
of *The Marsh Lions* was born, a collaboration that continued over the
next four years as we followed the fortunes of the Musiara pride and
told their story as truly as we could.

Of course, the Musiara lions were not the only pride in the
reserve, which at that time had a population of around 500 if you
included nomads from the Serengeti. Across the river from Governor's Camp lies the territory of the Kichwa Tembo pride. Downstream, on opposite sides of the river, live the Seronera lions and the
Paradise Plain pride. To the north, just outside the reserve, roam the
Gorge pride and the Mara Buffalo pride. Away to the south-east,
other large prides hunt along the Talek River and in the hills around
Keekorok Lodge.

Those days spent in the company of the Marsh lions were
among the happiest of my life. Tourism in the Mara was still in its
infancy. The grasslands were not yet criss-crossed with tyre tracks
or overrun with visitors, and we could be alone with the pride
from dawn to dusk. It was an extraordinary privilege to enter their
world and observe their complex social behaviour at such close
quarters. Sometimes, as we followed the pride males out onto Miti
Mbili (Two Trees) Plain they would turn and walk towards us,
tongues lolling in the heat, to slump in the shade of our vehicle.
There they would sprawl, resting their huge heads on their paws,
treating us with stunning indifference. The latent power concealed
under their smooth tawny coats was unimaginable. From time to
time, the lion we knew as Scar would look up and open his jaws
in a cavernous yawn, revealing yellow canines the size of my
thumbs, and I would remember the words of Myles Turner, the
legendary warden of the Serengeti: 'There is nothing in the world
as pitiless as the baleful stare of a lion.'

Scar was the epitome of a male lion in his prime. From his thread-bare muzzle to his black tail-tuft he was nearly 3m long. His mane was so thick it almost hid his ears, a glossy rug of tobacco-coloured hair, shot through with auburn glints. He was everything a pride male should be: deep-chested, powerful, with an aura about him, and a way of walking with a magisterial, almost insolent swagger that reflected his fearless self-confidence. Looking at him and Mkubwa, his pride companion, I would try to imagine what it must feel like to be a lion. Like me, Scar would have heard the wind in the grass and the mournful descant of doves in the *luggas*. Were we not warmed by the same sun? There were many sensations we must have shared, but it was impossible to know what went on behind those implacable yellow eyes.

Out on the plains the air quivered and scintillated along the stony ridges. Nothing moved. Everywhere, animals rested, seeking the shade of croton thickets or solitary acacias. Warthogs withdrew into their burrows. Buffalo lay in their wallows. Elephants moved deeper into the riverine forest, cooling themselves with flapping ears. And still the lions slept on, conserving their energy, waiting for darkness. They would move again only when compelled to do so by the imperatives of hunger or sex, or the need to assert their territorial authority.

Towards sunset the cooling air would rouse them. They would yawn and stretch and sit up to see the game on the move again, the grassy horizons spiked by the horns of topi and gazelles. Then, unhurriedly, they would haul themselves to their feet and sniff the breeze and listen with eyes half-closed as if in concentration, catching the distant sounds of zebras and wildebeest down in the marsh, and roar until the air shuddered. Soon their lionesses would be hunting and they would set off at a leisurely pace towards Musiara, two dark, shaggy shapes in a lion-coloured landscape of swaying grass-heads and lengthening shadows.

Sometimes, too, during the wildebeest migration, we would follow the Marsh lionesses as they prepared an ambush. There were five of them altogether – the Talek Twins and the Three Sisters – five tawny cats fanning out through the long grass, bellies down, heads low, ears laid back. Then would come the sudden rush, the wild stampede of panicking wildebeest running for their lives. All except one, clasped by a lioness in a terminal embrace as she applied the classic, choking bite to the throat, the dust drifting away to reveal the rest of the pride closing in for the feast.

The great migration transforms the Mara. It is the high point of the year, marking an end to the cool, overcast weather of July and bringing a return of hot, bright days until the onset of the grass rains in October. No two migrations are ever the same, but the zebras are invariably the first to arrive, a restless vanguard, 250,000 strong, cantering north from the Serengeti to chomp down the coarse stems of the red oat grass. In their wake come the wildebeest, massing on the banks of the Mara River like an army laying siege.

The river crossings are spectacular beyond belief, but tinged with tragedy. Over come the wildebeest in a grunting mass of struggling bodies, an avalanche of desperation, heads tossing and eyes rolling as they swim shoulder to shoulder for the opposite bank. Many never make it. Every year, thousands are crushed or drowned, or pulled under by the huge Mara crocodiles. In the aftermath of a major crossing the air is heavy with the stench of death.

For the predators, the arrival of the migration heralds a season of plenty. Wherever you look the plains are black with grazing herds, and the lions grow fat. Every morning, a vortex of descending vultures pinpoints a fresh kill on the plains. Every day the Marsh lions lie in wait among the reeds of Musiara, or along the Bila Shaka *lugga*, whose name means 'Without Fail' because you can always find lions there.

But towards late September the wildebeest grow restless. What was grass is now stubble, and soon the plodding columns are heading south again, disappearing into the northern woodlands of the Serengeti. From there they head on across the Seronera valley to gather on the open plains around Naabi Hill and the Gol Kopjes, where they give birth in February. So it continues, as it has done since the Pleistocene, an ancient story with no beginning and no end – only the golden sunsets and the blood-red dawns, the wind in the grass and the endless wanderings of the wild herds as they chase the rains across this enormous land.

The sense of space is intoxicating, the light dazzling. Above all this is grassland country, in which you can drive for hours with the seedheads hissing and waving around you like the billows of the sea, rolling away in long crests and ridges to a horizon so faintly blue and far away that it seems like the edge of the world. Once, all this land belonged to the Masai, nomadic pastoralists with red cloaks and shining spears, who still call vultures 'the birds of the warriors', recalling the days when blood feuds and cattle raids left their toll on the plains and the winged scavengers would come to peck out the soft eyes of the dead.

Today the Masai still graze their cattle on the surrounding range-lands, sharing the grass with the wandering game. But progress has blunted the old, sharp sense of pristine wilderness. To the east, much of the Loita Plains country has gone under the plough and been turned into wheatfields. In the Mara reserve itself, the grass-lands are scarred by a maze of tyre tracks, and at night, what was once a comforting void of darkness now glitters with the lights of lodges. With each passing year the problems become more acute. Kenya depends on the tourist dollar and so does the Mara. Without it the land would surely be claimed for agriculture to feed the country's fast-growing population – so making wildlife pay its way is the best chance of ensuring its survival.

Yet there comes a point – and many conservationists who care about the Mara believe it has been reached – when the reserve can absorb no more visitors without becoming degraded, and when the wilderness experience itself is at risk of being devalued by sheer weight of numbers. In Africa, such decisions are tough indeed, but Kenya has an honourable reputation in the field of conservation and the Mara is still its finest big-game stronghold.

Kenya is not my country. My roots are in England, where I was born and where I still choose to live. But there is hardly a day when I do not think of the Mara with an unbearable longing. At such times I miss the clear morning air, the way the light falls through the lacy canopy of the acacias, and the warm smell of the sun on the grass. I miss the cheerful sound of Swahili voices around the camp, the distant squealing of zebra stallions and the calls of boubou shrikes, doves and fish eagles. And I wish I was there, knowing that even now everything is in its place – the leopards resting on their rocky ridges, the cheetahs on the plains and the lions roaring across Musiara Marsh.

The Kenyans know what the lions are saying: '*Hii nchi ya nani? Hii nchi ya nani? Yangu… yangu… yangu.*' 'Whose land is this? Whose land is this? It is mine… mine… mine.'

KENYA – LAIKIPIA

High above the Great Rift Valley, on a ranch the size of a small English county, sits Kuki Gallmann, the blonde enchantress of Laikipia, weaving her stories of Africa. She is the new millennium's Karen
Blixen, a blue-eyed Italian whose autobiography, *I Dreamed of
Africa*, was recently made into a film starring Kim Basinger.

'To a wild land we came,' says Gallmann. 'Wild men we married.
Wild sons we bore.' She is talking of the pioneer spirit that arrived
in 1896 when Lord Hugh Delamere became the first person to settle in what later became known as the White Highlands. Today,
more than a century later, Kenya has altered beyond recognition,
yet the wildness lingers on in this last frontier of the old East Africa,
where the descendants of those up-country settlers still live.

The Laikipia Plateau is enormous. It stretches from the Great Rift
Valley to the slopes of Mount Kenya and is larger than all of Kenya's
protected areas except Tsavo National Park. Although divided into
a patchwork of farms and cattle ranches, Laikipia is unique
because, unlike elsewhere in Kenya, wildlife numbers have actually increased over the past two decades. It is one of the last refuges
of the critically endangered black rhino and has the largest elephant
population outside the parks – 2,000-plus at the last count. Yet in
tourist terms Laikipia has remained almost unknown.

Now change is in the air. Since the founding of the Laikipia
Wildlife Forum in 1991, the indigenous Samburu and Laikipiak
Masai tribespeople have been making common ground with their
European neighbours to build a wildlife stronghold the size of
Wales. These days, when chasing the tourist dollar is more
profitable than farming, it makes good sense to transform your
ranch into a private game reserve. Ol Ari Nyiro, the Gallmann
ranch, is such a place, set in one of the wildest, emptiest landscapes
you could imagine, bounded by the wooded depths of the Mukutan Gorge. Sometimes, says Kuki, when the evening light catches
the ribs and folds of the hills, you can see rhinos browsing on the

far side. 'It's such a privilege to live here,' she says. 'I feel a ferocious sense of guardianship about it. Yet nobody owns it. It owns you.'

Kuki's guests stay at the Mukutan Retreat, a luxury lodge with a swimming pool and three spacious cottages clinging to the lip of the gorge. Here, solitude is absolute. The air is heavy with the sweet scent of flowering carissa bushes, turacos fly across the void and at night the gorge echoes to the blare of elephants.

East of Mukutan, on a cliff overlooking the Ewaso Nyiro River, is a lodge called Sabuk, run by Simon Evans and his partner, Kerry Glen. If you want to go on a camel safari, Sabuk is the place to choose. Simon had gone hunting in Tanzania when I arrived, leaving Kerry in charge, and together we set off with a string of camels and a posse of Laikipiak Masai warriors led by Shillingi, a thin man wrapped in a cotton *shuka*, who once poached elephants for a living.

Camel-trekking has one big advantage over horseback riding: no previous experience is needed. All you do is hoist yourself aboard and cling on tight as the animal lurches to its feet. The camels are led by a man with a rope and simply amble along in a tireless soft-shoe shuffle. Even so, after an hour of this I found it more comfortable to walk.

There were no roads, only well-trodden elephant paths, weaving through the tangled commiphora thickets. The elephants themselves had moved on because of the drought, but the presence of buffaloes caused us to walk warily, even though Kerry carried a rifle. By mid-morning we had reached camp by the river, in whose croc-free pools we swam until lunch was served under a thorn tree.

Later, we walked into the hills for a sundowner. We sat on a rock and drank cold beers straight from the can. The moon rose. Stone partridges began to call and a tawny eagle sailed past in the updraughts. To the north rose Ol Doinyo Nyiro, the Dark Mountain, and closer to hand loomed a distinctive granite sugarloaf. 'The Masai call it Ngai Susa,' said Kerry. 'The Place Where God Blows the Wind.'

At Loisaba, a private lodge not far from Sabuk, I swapped my camel for a joyride over the Great Rift Valley in a five-seater, air-conditioned helicopter. My pilot was Humphrey Carter, ex-Irish Guards, very dapper in his snazzy flying suit. 'Let's have some music,' he said as the blades started to rotate. Next moment, with Bruce Springsteen in stereo on the headphones, we are swooping out over Losiolo, where the Rift Valley walls drop for 1,800m – deeper than the Grand Canyon.

Enclosed in our glass bubble of comfort, we float across inaccessible ravines, above fathomless forests of cedars and euphorbias, over a John Wayne landscape of buttes and badlands, towards range upon range of shark's-fin mountains. This part of Kenya is so impossibly remote that a helicopter is the only practical way of seeing it. On we skim over the Suguta valley, where Turkana tribesmen and their camels eke out a precarious existence on the desert floor. 'This is one of the hottest places on earth,' cries Captain Carter as we land on a black volcanic cone amid the rolling dunes. Stepping outside is like landing on Mars as we sip champagne in the 45°C heat. We watch Cathedral Rock turn deep orange in the setting sun, and when we take off again, turning for home over the swirling flamingos of Lake Suguta, it is like a scene from *Out of Africa*. If you are planning a list of 'Ten Best Things to Do Before You Die', put this near the top.

Loisaba, where the helicopter is based, was the home of an Italian nobleman, Count Ancilotto, who came here to hunt but fell in love with Laikipia and stayed on to become a rancher. When the count died, Peter Silvester, a former professional safari guide, moved in to run Loisaba as a wildlife estate. As Silvester told me, 'Nowadays a dozen tourists are worth more than 2,500 head of cattle.'

On the neighbouring ranch at Ol Malo, Colin and Rocky Francombe run what is probably the most luxurious lodge in Laikipia. Its cottage suites are the most spacious, its views the most sweeping, and it is set on the rim of a rocky escarpment that overlooks a waterhole where elephant, buffalo and leopard come to drink. From Ol Malo it is only a short hop by light aircraft to Mugie, the 19,000ha wildlife ranch where Stephano Cheli, one of Kenya's most respected safari operators, has set up camp in a glade of yellow-barked acacias. Mugie is an upmarket version of the old-fashioned hunting safari camp, with a comfortable mess tent where Stephano's passion for Italian cooking manifests itself in the appetizing shape of home-made focaccia, fresh pasta and salads dressed with the finest Tuscan olive oil.

Unlike the rest of Laikipia, Mugie had been blessed with rain, drawing an abundance of game to its green plains. Herds of eland thronged every horizon. Jackson's hartebeest – unique to Laikipia – pranced away from our Land-Rover with their curious dressage gait, and all around us were the beautiful dry-country animals of northern Kenya: reticulated giraffe, beisa oryx and pin-striped Grevy's zebras. A kilometre from camp we found the Mugie lion pride slumped around the carcass of an eland. The assortment of lionesses and cubs was watched over by two majestic pride males, which stared at us with baleful eyes as if warning us to keep our distance.

Next day I flew to Borana to meet Michael and Nikki Dyer on their 14,000ha ranch at the southern end of Laikipia, whose far-ranging horizons are dominated by the snaggle-toothed summit of Mount Kenya. The Dyers belong to a dynasty of settlers founded in the 1920s by Will Powys, a soldier of the Great War, and they still live in a kind of barbaric splendour like the marcher lords of medieval England, in a high-roofed hall with huge dogs sprawled in front of a blazing log fire. Near by, they have built an idyllic lodge, an oasis of green in a desert of thorns. Sometimes elephants come to drink from the swimming pool. But as Michael Dyer says, 'It's no use us sitting here in comfort when there is poverty and land degradation on the other side of the fence. We have to get these people on board. Only then will there be a real future for us and for them and for wildlife.'

That is why the Dyers are currently helping their Laikipiak Masai neighbours to invest in wildlife tourism as an alternative to their traditional way of life, with its almost total dependence on cattle. To see what they were doing we drove through the bone-dry cedar forests of the Mukogodo Hills to Lekurruki, where a new community-run safari lodge is springing up with support from the Dyers. This year, with herdsmen losing up to 90 per cent of their livestock to the worst drought in living memory, it makes more sense than ever.

The man generally credited with pioneering the move to tourism is Ian Craig, a third-generation farmer sitting on 22,000ha of rolling savannah at Lewa Downs, near Nanyuki. It was Craig, a restless, quietly spoken Kenyan citizen with a lifelong passion for the bush, who led the way by transforming his ranch into the Lewa Wildlife Conservancy. In 1983 Kenya's first rhino sanctuary was created here. Today, Lewa has 26 black rhinos and 32 white rhinos, watched over by a small army of SAS-trained security patrols.

Outside Lewa it is a different story. 'Between us and the Ethiopian border there is just one wild rhino left,' Craig told me. 'Poachers have killed the rest.' Would his rhinos also be poached if they were left unprotected, I asked him? 'For sure,' he says.

'Land use is the key,' he says. 'We worked our hearts out in the cattle business but we were just going nowhere.' Now tourists pay good money to see Lewa's wildlife, not only rhinos but the rest of the 'big five' – elephant, buffalo, lion and leopard – plus one-fifth of the world's Grevy's zebras. Convincing Laikipia's farmers that living with big game could be more profitable than ranching was not easy. 'At first they were aghast,' one of Craig's friends told me. 'It was almost heresy – like listening to someone swearing in church. But in the end the economic arguments were unassailable.'

KENYA – BACK FROM THE DEAD

We drove slowly through Tsavo, the red dust pluming in our wake as we scanned the surrounding bush for movement. Somewhere out in that grey-green sea of thorny thickets were the *shifta*, Somali bandits and ivory poachers. The *shifta* were dangerous, armed with automatic weapons, and we didn't want to run into them.

This was Tsavo in 1988, when parts of Kenya's greatest animal stronghold were considered too dangerous for tourists and placed off-limits as soldiers, police and anti-poaching patrols engaged the ivory gangs in bloody skirmishes that left dead and wounded on both sides. But I went anyway, to report for the *Sunday Times* on the poaching war that was turning Tsavo into an elephants' graveyard of rotting corpses and bleached bones.

Inevitably, it was the vultures that gave the game away. Dozens of them, hunched in the leafless trees like obscene fruit. As we drew closer, the dry, pure air of Tsavo was poisoned by the gut-churning stench of death. There were six carcasses: an entire family, machine-gunned on its way to water. All had been small elephants and they had fallen where the poachers had surprised them. One had col-lapsed in a kneeling position, as it lay now, its huge ears still spread as in life, a grotesque parody of an elephant with its trunk chopped off and its tusks hacked out. I could see the holes where the poach-ers' bullets had struck. The elephants had been dead only two weeks, but a fortnight in the sun had reduced them to shrunken tents of red hide, splashed with vulture droppings and hollowed by hyenas.

As we drove away a wind blew over the plains, trailing a curtain of rain between us and the Sagala Hills, as if God were trying to cover up the sight of what man had done to His most majestic creation. Yet even then, amid the butchery, it was impossible not to be aware of the splendour of this harsh land long used to death – the very name Tsavo is a Wakamba word for slaughter – and it was profoundly reas-suring to discover that despite everything its immense vistas were still vibrantly alive. The air held that wonderful smell of air after rain.

Golden pipits – a Tsavo speciality – fluttered up from beneath our wheels, and a troop of oryx, horns glinting in the morning light, cantered off as if they were running for the sheer joy of being alive. Beauty there was, and wildness and freedom undiminished, but also a bitter sense of tragedy and heartbreak beyond bearing that clung to Tsavo's hills and plains like the taint of an old kill; and the threat of violence remained as strong as ever. A week later the same gang murdered another six elephants, but this time their luck ran out. As they made for their hideout in the Kulalu Hills they were spotted from the air by the park's head warden. Within 20 minutes his anti-poaching patrols were deployed, and in the shoot-out that followed two poachers were killed and another three captured.

Tsavo is the largest national park in East Africa, an arid wilderness the size of Wales, much of it buried in thick commiphora bush with only an occasional river or distant range of shattered hills to break the infinity of the plains. Ironically it was set aside for wildlife only because its sun-stricken thirstlands were of little use for anything else, and its sheer size – although a nightmare to patrol – is ultimately its greatest strength. Despite years of slaughter by ivory poachers, Tsavo still holds out the best long-term hope for the survival of a greater number of animals than almost any other park in Africa – not only elephants, but also lions, leopards, buffaloes, giraffes, zebras, antelopes and gazelles.

What other park could have survived the terrible five-year drought that began in 1970 and killed 9,000 elephants? But in 1988 it seemed as if the poachers were going to finish the herds for good. This was the year when Tsavo should have been celebrating its 40th anniversary as Kenya's finest elephant sanctuary. Instead, the elephants were fleeing from the most savage poaching onslaught in the country's history.

Yet when I returned exactly a year later in November 1989, the fortunes of the African elephant and its greatest Kenyan stronghold had both undergone a miraculous transformation. In Nairobi in July, President Moi had publicly torched a great pile of tusks worth £2 million in a courageous gesture affirming his country's right to protect its remaining elephants. Then, in October, at the CITES (Convention on International Trade in Endangered Species) meeting in Lausanne, the world voted for an end to ivory trading – at least until 1992.

For Tsavo the road to recovery had begun in April 1989, when Dr Richard Leakey was appointed as Kenya's Director of Wildlife and Conservation Management. Out in their dozens went the corrupt rangers and wildlife officials who had connived and colluded with the ivory traders, to be replaced by men of integrity whom Leakey could rely upon to take the poachers on. One of his first acts was to rid Tsavo of the *shifta* gangs, who were hunted down without mercy.

'A year ago we were losing elephants at the rate of two a day,' said Leakey, a thick-set man in his mid-forties whose warm smile and easy manner belied a steely determination to succeed. 'Now our daily patrols aren't even finding poacher tracks entering the park.'

It was good to be back, driving down the red-dirt roads of a land I had come to love as deeply as my own, and this time with no fear of a poacher's bullet smashing into the windscreen. For months the brick-red earth had lain cracked and blistered as Tsavo endured one of its periodic droughts. Every day the sun had glittered on a million cruel thorns, on the quartz pebbles of dried-up rivers and on the bleached bones of old lion kills.

Now thunder rumbled among the hills. The rains had come like an expiation, washing away the past and replenishing the gasping plains, transforming the ashen Nyika scrub into a leafy paradise. Acacias blossomed, cloying the air with honeyed scent. New grasses put out tender shoots and white anthericum lilies sprang up overnight, rushing to complete their brief cycle of flowering and fruiting before the dry season returned.

The rain had refilled the waterholes, and all the way to Voi the plains were alive with the movements of kongoni and Thomson's gazelles. Zebras grazed on the new green grass, buffaloes rose dark and glistening from their mud wallows, and a leopard that had been sunning itself in the road streaked for cover as we approached.

We reached Voi Lodge as the sun was dropping behind the hills. A solitary impala stood by the road, staring intently into a brush-choked gully where guinea fowl were cackling in alarm. I could see no lurking predator, but later, in the small hours, I awoke to the thrilling sound of a lion, and wondered if it was a descendant of the legendary man-eaters of Tsavo whose reign of terror had delayed the building of the Uganda railway a hundred years ago.

Voi Lodge clings to the side of a granite ridge, with a swimming pool built among the rocks and half of Tsavo at its feet. At night, genets emerge to forage in the floodlit garden, and at daybreak the colonies of little swifts that nest under the lodge rafters rush out like an arrow storm to greet the sun.

When the day had grown warmer I sat on the terrace with a cold beer, watching the fat African clouds sailing up over the rim of the earth. High above me, a coal-black Verreaux's eagle hung crook-winged in the breeze. Below and beyond lay nothing but bush, threaded with game trails, dotted with anthills and the flat crowns of acacia trees – the sprawling emptiness of the plains as they must appear to the endlessly circling vultures.

Next day I rejoined Herbie Paul, the veteran big-game fisherman I had met in Malindi (*see* page 158) and who had invited me to stay at his safari camp on the banks of the Galana River. 'This country is so big you often have to drive a long way to find the game,' he said as we cruised across the plains near the Aruba Dam, 'but I can show you a wilder, far more exciting park than the standard minibus safari ever sees.'

He was right. Near by his sharp eyes picked out two lionesses with pale grey coats, hidden deep in a thicket. Tsavo lions are not at all like the big, relaxed cats of the Masai Mara. Uneasy at our presence, they whirled to face us, ears flattened and canines exposed in nervous snarls that warned us to keep our distance.

We drove on, heading slowly for the Galana. 'This is hard country,' said Herbie, staring at the desolation of stony plains and broken tree stumps that stretched away in all directions. 'It's good for nothing but elephants. I love it,' he added with quiet satisfaction.

Later there were more lions, herds of buffalo, a mother cheetah with a single cub, and what seemed like all the wintering swallows of Europe swooping and twittering over the river. And, best of all, a small family group of red Tsavo elephants, led by a ragged-eared matriarch with long, thin tusks who was quite happy to let us drive by slowly within a few metres of her as she rubbed her backside against a large acacia. Here was proof positive that Tsavo's elephants had come back from the dead. Now, if the ivory ban could be maintained, Tsavo might yet become what it was always meant to be: a haven for people and elephants together.

Back in camp, showered and filled with contentment at what I had witnessed of Tsavo's rebirth, I watched the sun go down and the pelicans coming in to roost in the trees across the river. Out in midstream a hippo surfaced, then submerged with a luxurious sigh. When night fell with its customary tropical swiftness and the first scops owl began to chirrup under the stars, Herbie's Waliangulu tracker cut two firesticks – a softwood base and a hardwood spinner – which he twirled between his palms until smoke arose from the dried elephant dung he used for tinder. It was a scene as old as Tsavo itself. Out in the darkness the air shivered to the rumble of lions, but we were safe in our circle of warmth as the sparks flew upwards into the vast African night.

KENYA – ELSA'S KOPJE

A mother leopard and her two cubs live on Elsa's Kopje in Meru National Park. At night you may hear the gruff, wood-sawing rasp of her mate as he patrols his rocky territory, and sometimes in the stillness that comes just before dawn, the roar of lions from the plains below, like an echo of Elsa herself, as if her ghost still haunts this wild land where she and George and Joy Adamson lived the legend of *Born Free*.

George Adamson was born in India in 1906 but grew up in Kenya, where he enjoyed a colourful career as an ivory hunter, beeswax trader and gold prospector before finding his true vocation as a game warden in 1938. Then came the two events that would transform his life: in 1944 he married Joy Bally, a volatile Austrian divorcee with a talent for painting; and in 1956, after shooting a stock-raiding lioness, he found himself with three orphaned cubs on his hands. The smallest was a female. The Adamsons called her Elsa.

So began the extraordinary story of *Born Free*, the moving tale of a lioness who was raised by the Adamsons and returned to the wilds of Meru National Park, where she bore a litter of cubs before dying of tick fever in 1961. By then, Joy Adamson's book, published the previous year, had become a bestseller, and was followed in 1964 by the *Born Free* film, starring Virginia McKenna as Joy Adamson and Bill Travers, Virginia's husband, as George.

Elsa's story brought international acclaim for Joy, but led George down a different road. By the time filming was over, the Adamsons had more or less separated for good. Joy's hot temper and promiscuous nature had earned her the nickname 'the man-eater of Meru', and George, preferring the company of lions to that of his wife, set up camp at the foot of Elsa's Kopje, taking with him three of the two dozen tame lions used in the film. These, like Elsa before them, he later released into the park. Joy, meanwhile, built her own camp a few kilometres away before moving on to

Shaba Game Reserve, where she was stabbed to death by her cook in 1980. In August 1989, George Adamson was gunned down by Somali bandits.

Today, many of Meru's wild lions are the descendants of George's original man-made pride, and the red, rocky hilltop where George sat with his lions and his pipe and his nightly sundowner of White Horse whisky is now the site of one of Kenya's most exclusive safari lodges. It is called Elsa's Kopje – *kopje* being an old Afrikaans word for the granite outcrops that dominate the surrounding plains.

'I searched for five years to find the right site for a lodge,' said Stefano Cheli, the Italian-born owner of Elsa's Kopje. 'I looked all over Kenya. I even went down to the Serengeti in Tanzania, but this was the best. Nowhere else is half as wild and remote and beautiful as Meru.'

It is hard to disagree. From the veranda of my cottage, perched on the *kopje*'s granite boulders, I looked out across a sea of bush. On one side rose the blue Nyambeni Mountains, rolling away towards Mount Kenya. Far away in the other direction, as if on the outermost rim of the world, I could just make out the hills of Kora, where I had stayed with George Adamson and his lions in 1982 on an assignment for the *Sunday Times Magazine*. In between, there was nothing but the immense emptiness of the old Northern Frontier District running up to Ethiopia. Down below, giraffe were moving slowly through the lion-coloured grass between the scattered combretum trees that give Meru's plains the look of a vast, neglected orchard. And from all around came the cries of birds, the clucking of hornbills, the squeal of parrots, the sad-sounding descant of emerald-spotted doves.

Elsa's Kopje has been designed for the top end of Kenya's tourist industry. Not for Stefano Cheli the old, 120-bed lodges built for the minibus safaris of the past three decades. Instead, there are just eight luxuriously comfortable guest cottages, each with its own butler. The roofs are thatched with local reed and the stone walls framed with driftwood logs hauled out of the Tana River, blending so naturally into the rocky hillsides that they are scarcely visible from the plains below. Inside are split-level floors and ethnic rugs, sunken baths and king-size beds draped in mosquito nets. In some rooms the living rock provides a natural wall. Others have albizia trees growing through them, with mottled trunks as smooth as marble, and two of the cottages are so secluded that you can reach them only by means of a rope suspension bridge. At the very edge of the *kopje* is a swimming pool and, overlooking the pool, dining-tables set with glass and silver, where Cheli's Italian origins are reflected in the way his chefs have been taught the arts of preparing delicious fresh pasta and home-made ice-cream.

Elsa's Kopje opened in early June 1999 with a party. Virginia McKenna, who had flown in as the guest of honour, launched the lodge by smashing a bottle of champagne on the rocks. Richard Leakey, the charismatic former head of the Kenya Wildlife Service, came to join in the celebrations with Mark Jenkins, Meru's new park warden. Later, after a campfire had been lit on top of the *kopje*, the African night echoed to Cheli's robust rendition of 'Nessum Dorma'.

'The importance of Elsa and her story as told in *Born Free* is that it has changed for ever the way people will think about lions,' said McKenna. I asked her how she felt about returning to a place with so many memories. 'Very strange at first,' she said, 'but then I felt quite wonderful quite quickly. I think it felt strange because there is nobody left. George and Joy and Elsa, and Bill my husband are all gone. I first came here with Joy in 1965 when I finished filming *Born Free*. We climbed the rock, swam in the Ura River and visted Elsa's grave. Now, 34 years have passed and the only one left is me.'

Everyone, it seemed, had been touched in some way by the Adamson saga, even Richard Leakey. As the new Kenya Wildlife Service supremo in 1989, he had been faced with the unenviable task of winding up George Adamson's lion project in the adjoining Kora Reserve. 'The trouble was, his programme of releasing lions into the wild simply wasn't sustainable,' he said. 'But it was an awkward situation because George had become a symbol and closing him down was going to get us into a lot of trouble. Then he was murdered and I had to fly up to Kora and bring his body back to Nairobi. It was one of my first official duties as head of KWS, and a very sad one. In scientific terms his lion project achieved very little, but his work in raising the profile of Africa and the big cats has guaranteed him a place at conservation's high table.'

It was Leakey, then at the end of his second stint as director of KWS after an absence of three years, who had just appointed Mark Jenkins as Meru's new warden. Mark is the son of Peter Jenkins, one of East Africa's legendary old-time game wardens who, with David Sheldrick in Tsavo and Billy Woodley in the Aberdares forests, fought to save Kenya's parks from the poaching holocaust that came close to wiping out the country's black rhino and elephant herds.

Elsa died before Mark Jenkins was born, but as a child growing up in Meru where his father was the park's first warden, he, too, had been caught up in the Adamson story. When he was three years old, one of George's lions grabbed him by the arm and tried to drag him out of his father's Land-Rover. He still has the scars, but remembers nothing except lying in hospital next to a girl who had been savaged by a dog. 'She was in a much worse state than I was.' Surprisingly, perhaps, the incident has not prejudiced his views of lions or of George Adamson. 'I met him at Kora when I was older. The last time I saw him was after Joy's murder when he came to Meru to scatter her ashes on the grave of Pippa, her cheetah.'

But no one who was present at the opening of Elsa's Kopje could have had such poignant memories of those *Born Free* years as Virginia McKenna. The day after the party, I went with her and Jenkins to visit Elsa's grave – a stone-paved mound beneath an old acacia tree on the banks of the Ura. Joy had placed a plaque there, inscribed in Old German, which translates as:

> *The wind, the wind, the heavenly child,*
> *softly going over the stone,*
> *It strokes and kisses the lonesome night*
> *In which a deep secret lies bewitched.*
> Elsa – January 1956–January 1961

On the way back, we stopped to climb Elsa's Rock, a spectacular whaleback of rust-red granite looming over the surrounding bush. From its bald summit stretches a 360-degree view of wildest Africa, an endless panorama of grey commiphora thickets, bottle-shaped baobabs, green doum-palms and, in the distance, the shark's-fin shapes of bony mountains receding over the horizon.

'Until I came to work on *Born Free*, I had no idea how it would change my life,' said McKenna. 'But Africa does that to you. And coming back, looking out at a scene which has not changed since George was here, is quite wonderful.'

Mark had brought a breakfast hamper of sandwiches and hard-boiled eggs and we sat on the sun-warmed rock, drinking coffee while Virginia recalled how it was at the foot of this *kopje* that Elsa's cubs were born and how, soon after, Elsa had led them proudly across the river and introduced them to Joy and George.

'When Elsa went off into the wild,' she said, 'George would climb this rock and fire his rifle, and she would come back to see them. Not always straight away. It might be two hours later, or even the next day. But she would always turn up. And when you think that by then she was a wild lion with her own family it was truly extraordinary that she should have returned at all, and it was a measure of her trust in Joy and George that she brought her cubs for them to see.'

Working on *Born Free* was the first time Virginia had been close to lions. 'The first ones we used were circus lions. Bill and I used to work with them for two hours every day before filming started. We would walk with them on the plains and allow them to let off steam. It was an unbelievable experience. But then I had an accident. One of the lions – Boy – jumped on me and broke my ankle. It wasn't his fault. We had been stalking some gazelle together and he just got excited. When I returned from hospital, he was the first lion I saw. He put his head through the window to greet me, and as soon as I saw him I knew everything was fine.'

The experience with Boy taught her to respect wild animals. Like George, she could no longer bear to think of a lion that was not free, and she came to believe, as he did, that one should not dominate animals. 'Rather, one should share what experiences you can share with them. I have also come to realize that you cannot breed the wildness out of them, not even if you try for generations.'

And like others before her, McKenna also discovered that Joy Adamson could be as unpredictable as any lion. 'When I spent some time with her after we had finished filming *Born Free*, I have to say she was absolutely wonderful,' said McKenna. 'I loved her. I really did. But then she fell out with Bill and things were never really the same again. When we came back again in 1968 to make another film [*An Elephant called Slowly*], we tried to make up, but it was as if she had just decided to cut us out of her life.'

It was Joy Adamson's tragedy that her restless spirit could not find the kind of peace that George had discovered. 'She had such incredible talents,' said McKenna. 'Not only her writing and painting but the extraordinary experience of Elsa which made her unique in the world. She lived in a country she loved and yet she was never at peace. Instead she was a soul in torment, worrying that people were against her, as if they were trying to take something away from her instead of admiring her for what she was.'

George Adamson was different. 'He was a totally non-judgemental person who lived what he believed in. He was utterly unchanged by his fame and loved his lions above everything, and we remained the best of friends until the day he died.'

George Adamson's violent death at the hands of Somali bandits is symptomatic of the lawlessness that has beset Kenya for the past two decades. During that time, poaching for ivory and rhino horn – often with the collusion of park rangers and government officials – brought Meru to total collapse.

'In my father's day, Meru was considered to be the finest park in East Africa,' said Jenkins. 'When he arrived here in 1968 it had more than 3,000 elephant. But then poaching became big business and the *shifta* – the Somali bandit gangs – swept down from the north with their AK47s. In 1979, my dad was moved from the park for five months, and in that time 85 per cent of Meru's black rhinos were killed.'

Things came to a head in 1989 when two French tourists were shot dead by poachers. Shortly after, Meru's six white rhinos – the only ones in Kenya – were killed. Overnight, Meru became a no-go area for tourists. Its only lodge, Meru Mulika, was burned down and the park ground to a halt. For a while, after the Kenya Wildlife Service took over the running of the parks from the old, corrupt wildlife department, things looked more hopeful for Meru. Led by Leakey, the newly recruited KWS rangers took on the bandits and drove them back into Somalia. But then Leakey was forced out of his job. Without his dynamic presence the KWS slid into bankruptcy and Meru's infrastructure collapsed once more.

Now Meru's star is rising again. Leakey has moved on but has left the KWS in the hands of Nehemiah Rotich, a capable new supremo whose armed patrols keep a close watch on Meru. Access has been improved in the form of a new bridge across the Tana River at Adamson's Falls, and Jenkins has come home to run the park.

'I always wanted to do this job, to follow in my dad's footsteps,' he said. 'It's a way of life, the only one I know. But there is much to be done. Since I was last here in 1991, the poachers have had a field day. Still, we've just completed a game count and found 306 elephant, so things are looking up.'

With the opening of Elsa's Kopje, Meru looks set to regain its place among East Africa's top wildlife strongholds. This is the real *Born Free* legacy: 870sq km of pristine bush, as wild as it was when the Adamsons were here. Today, of course, you can fly there in less than an hour from Nairobi (the lodge has its own airstrip), but its greatest luxury is knowing that whenever you set out on a game drive you can have the entire park to yourself. Game is still scarce, but a restocking programme is already under way. All the major predators – lion, leopard and cheetah – are present, together with large herds of buffalo, hippo, waterbuck, eland, and the beautiful dry-country animals of northern Kenya: the rare Grevy's zebra with its big, bat ears and pin-striped coat; and the reticulated giraffe, whose ox-blood hide is meshed with a crazy-paving pattern of fine white lines.

On my last day at the lodge, just before leaving to fly back to Nairobi, I opened the visitors' book and read what Virginia McKenna had written on the opening page. 'If George Adamson was standing where I am now, his heart would be as joyous as mine. Meru is still wild and beautiful as I remember it 34 years ago and this wonderful Elsa's Kopje has kept the simplicity and atmosphere that is the essence of a true camp. I lift my glass to the spirit of Elsa, to join George and all the people who have created this perfect haven.'

KENYA – RECLAIMING THE LAST FRONTEIR

At Namunyak, on the edge of the Mathews Mountains, where thorn scrub and semi-desert reach out to infinity, Kenya's Northern Frontier Province is enduring its worst drought in living memory. In the bone-dry sand rivers, which flow only during the rains, Samburu herdsmen with pierced earlobes and leaf-bladed spears have dug wells 10m deep to find water, filling cans which they pass up in a human chain, chanting as they work.

These singing wells, as they are known, are all that keep the Samburus' scrawny cows and goats alive. Yet already some herders have lost 90 per cent of their stock and no rain is due for at least two months. A sensible time, then, for these proud, warlike pastoralists to take a hard look at their traditional way of life. After all, even in the longest drought, the wildlife – elephant, lion, oryx, gerenuk – has evolved strategies for survival. If the Samburu are to survive, they may have to do the same.

Already some have taken the plunge, diversifying into tourism to relieve their dependency on livestock grazing. At Namunyak, deep in the *bundu* – that evocative Swahili word for the bush – a new safari lodge has sprung up. Helped into being by the descendants of the European settlers who pioneered their way to wealth on the nearby ranches of Lewa Downs and the Laikipia Plateau, it is itself a pioneer, breaking new ground on the frontiers of wildlife conservation.

Sarara Lodge is run by the Namunyak Wildlife Conservation Trust, which represents the local Samburu community and gives them a 50 per cent stake in the business. It opened only in 1988, with help from the Kenya Wildlife Service and the Lewa Wildlife Conservancy, in an area once notorious for banditry. Today there are observation posts on the surrounding hilltops. This is Neighbourhood Watch, Kenyan style, with teams of heavily armed rangers operating round-the-clock patrols to safeguard the Samburu, their guests and the wildlife. As yet the animals are still shy, but already leopard and elephant come to drink at the waterhole and poaching has almost been eliminated.

It is the same story at Il Ngwesi Lodge, 70km to the south. Like Sarara, Il Ngwesi is an African ark, built of dead trees knocked down by elephants; a ship of the desert, cast upon a rocky hill at the foot of the Laikipia Plateau. This is Masai country, a land of resounding distance, measured by the stark shapes of granite hills and inselbergs that rise like tombstones from the plains. When I arrived I was greeted by a posse of Laikipiak Masai warriors, wrapped in blood-red *shukas*, who offered me cold fruit juice before showing me to my room.

When Il Ngwesi opened in 1996 it became the first lodge in Africa to be 100 per cent owned and run by the local community. Until then its Masai owners had used their 16,000ha group ranch exclusively as grazing land. Now it is managed primarily as a wildlife resource, bringing in £1 million a year which the community could never have earned without tourism.

Il Ngwesi's four guest rooms are more like private tree-houses, built on stilts beneath high thatched roofs. All have king-size four-poster beds, solar panels for hot showers under the stars, and what James Ole Kinyaga, the lodge manager, calls 'a loo with a view'. There are no doors or windows; everything is open to the wind, yet privacy is absolute. There is also a spring-fed swimming pool, a main dining area with stunning views, and a hide overlooking a waterhole to which a leopard has become a regular visitor.

In the evening I spoke to Simon Ole Kinyaga, the local Masai chief, who was dressed in European clothes but still carried his ceremonial *rungu* – a wooden club with a beadwork handle. We talked of the visit he had made to London to collect the British Airways Tourism for Tomorrow Award, which Il Ngwesi had won in 1997. What had impressed him most in London, I asked him? 'The streets,' he said. 'So clean. No rubbish. Not at all like Nairobi.'

In the Masai language, Il Ngwesi means 'the Wildlife People', and wildlife is certainly what you get when you stay here. After dinner (buttered corn-on-the-cob followed by roast leg of lamb and assorted vegetables), I sat on the veranda, listening to the rumble of lions on the plains. Whenever I awoke during the night I heard them roaring, sometimes close, sometimes distant – the most thrilling sound in Africa – and at first light, while enjoying my early morning tea, I watched as a lioness and her two small cubs emerged from the bush to drink at the waterhole. But don't expect game drives. Instead, you track animals on foot, ride a camel along the Ngare Ndare sand river or, uniquely, go honey-hunting with the Masai, following the honey-guide, a little bird that leads humans to wild bees' nests for a share of the spoils.

Slowly, after years of lawlessness, Kenya's last frontier is being reclaimed for tourism. Using Sarara and Il Ngwesi as stepping stones, it is now possible to plan a whole new safari circuit through northern Kenya, taking in Elsa's Kopje lodge in Meru National Park, where George and Joy Adamson once roamed with Elsa, their *Born Free* lioness (*see* page 123).

If remoteness is what you are seeking, then the Desert Rose Retreat is the place to be, an enchanted eyrie perched halfway up Mount Nyiru, the most sacred mountain in Samburuland, near the southern end of Lake Turkana. It took Emma Chen and Yoav, her ex-kibbutznik tank commander husband, a year just to build the road up the mountain, and another seven years to get the lodge ready. To get there involves a daunting, day-long drive from Nairobi. But imagine the joy of arriving in this blissful oasis of emerald lawns and mountain streams in time for tea and chocolate cake, in the shade of tall forest trees, with a swimming pool beside you and sweeping views over the Elbarta Plains 600m below. Each of the half-dozen rooms has been lovingly designed, using local granite, polished cedar and olive wood. One room even has a wooden bath in which you can lie and watch Verreaux's eagles sailing overhead.

But to find the loneliest, most secluded hideout in Kenya you must head for Kitich Camp in the Mathews Range, beyond the Samburu National Reserve. Parts of these mountains, whose highest peaks nudge 2,000m, have never been fully explored. In the forests, among the pencil cedars and lofty podocarpus trees that clothe every mountain slope and ravine, squat cycads grow, like giant ferns, creating a Jurassic Park backdrop for the forest animals: elephant, buffalo and leopard. At least 200 kinds of birds have been recorded here, and species new to science are still waiting to be discovered. The track to Kitich – road is too good a word – is strewn with elephant dung. The journey from Wamba takes less than two hours, but even for a Land-Rover it is something of an endurance test, plunging in and out of steep-sided sand rivers before climbing into the secret valley in which the camp is hidden.

Kitich – a Samburu word meaning 'Happiness' – is a comfortable, old-style safari camp with six green canvas tents, all with bucket showers and long-drop loos, on the banks of the seasonal Ngeng River. There is no swimming pool, but Giuli Bertolli, the Italian owner, will happily lead you to a natural pool in the forest. Every lodge has its own early morning sounds. At Sarara it was the insane clucking of hornbills and the shrill 'inshallah, inshallah' cries of crested francolins. At Kitich it was the drumming of woodpeckers in the tall forest trees and the harsh cries of Hartlaub's turacos – exotic green birds with crimson wings – that flew in for their daily feast of scraps.

As at Il Ngwesi, Kitich has no game drives. But with an armed ranger riding shotgun on the back seat, Signor Bertolli drove me through the forests to a high pass between two peaks. Elephants were feeding in a clearing across the valley, and far below I could see the desert reaching all the way to Ethiopia.

Back at Kitich, the lamps were lit, the campfire glowing. Dinner was an elegant affair, with roast lamb served on soapstone plates and candlelight glittering on goblets of finest Chianti. But this was Africa. Across the river, a dead goat dangled from a tree. It was bait for a leopard I never saw, although waking in the small hours I heard a bushbuck's gruff bark of alarm. In the morning the bait was gone.

TANZANIA – THE SERENGETI

All the way from Arusha, the land was dry. Beyond the banana groves of Mto-wa-Mbu, where the road toils up the Great Rift Valley wall, clouds of dust boiled in our wake and drifted away to where pelicans were slowly turning in the hot air thermals over Lake Manyara. But an hour later, entering the montane forests of the Ngorongoro highlands, the air grew cooler and we drove on between huge, mossy trees and banks of brilliant yellow canary bush.

At the summit, arriving at Ngorongoro's crater rim, we broke our journey to look down into the vast sunken caldera 600m below. Was it only six months ago that I had watched the lions of Ngorongoro hunting zebra in the yellow grass? Now the grass was green again and from everywhere came the gleam of water.

There was no time to descend the giant amphitheatre, but there would be predators enough where we were heading and, with mounting anticipation, we drove on. Soon we were passing Lemagrut, its rounded slopes as green as Sussex, riven with dark gullies of juniper forest. And then, descending towards Olduvai, came the moment that never fails to lift my heart – the first glimpse of Tanzania's Serengeti National Park, a sunlit ocean of grass and cloud shadows rolling away to the ends of the earth.

Now only one question filled my mind. Where was the migration? Every year, in January and February, the Serengeti wildebeest gather in their tens of thousands to drop their calves on these short grass plains. What draws them here is an unusually fertile soil, the result of fine ash spewed out by the long-dead volcanoes. For half the year the land is dust, forsaken by all living things except a few kori bustards and Grant's gazelles, and underlaid by a limestone crust that few roots can penetrate. But when it rains these barren plains produce a lush carpet of succulent grasses, attracting the heaviest concentration of grazing animals on earth. At this time you can expect to see more than a million wildebeest, half a million gazelles and 200,000 zebras, together with their attendant predators: the lion, cheetah and spotted hyena. Together with the massed herds, these hunters give *Siringet* – the great Empty Space of the Masai – its constant sense of impending drama.

Yet in Africa, nothing is certain. The grass rains of November had failed. Without grass, without water, the wildebeest would soon be forced to move on. And in a park the size of Holland, even a million wildebeest can be hard to find.

I need not have worried. Despite the drought the herds had come south as expected, and were encamped on the plains from Ndutu to the Gol Mountains and all the way down to Olduvai. There, in the miraculous way of the wildebeest, they had been holding back the moment of birth until the rains began. Now it was mid-February and at last the skies had opened. All day long the rain-bird, the red-chested cuckoo, cried, 'It will rain, it will rain,' in the acacia woodlands of Ndutu. And every afternoon, sudden, violent storms trailed across the greening plains. This was the moment the herds had been waiting for since their time of conception during the full moon of May. The day we arrived we saw only two newborn wildebeest, but within a week, like a pent-up flood that could be contained no longer, the plains were alive with pale, gangling calves.

Our first camp was set up not where the migration had gathered but north of the Simba Kopjes in the centre of the park, among the grass meadows and graceful fever trees of the Seronera valley, where we arrived just in time for a buffet lunch. Later, lying in my tent until the summons for the afternoon game drive, I listened to the hypnotic bird calls of the African bush – barbet, coucal, wood dove and tinker bird – until I fell asleep.

There is a saying: someone who has been to Africa and stayed in a lodge has been on holiday, but only someone who has stayed in a tent has been on safari. And it is true. Living under canvas brings you closer to the sights and sounds of the bush without ever seriously increasing the risk of adrenalin-inducing encounters – although one night we did have a leopard walking through the camp kitchen.

Nor is camping a denial of life's luxuries. Your lavatory may be of the long-drop kind, but all other essential comforts – hot showers, cold drinks, same-day laundry – are provided. Furthermore, you sleep in a proper bed, with a hot-water bottle when nights are chilly, to be woken by early morning tea or coffee brought to your tent.

And you are treated to huge breakfasts and four-course suppers conjured up from a bed of hot ashes by the *mpishi*, or camp cook. But best of all is the sense of privacy and the gift of silence, broken at night only by the whooping of hyenas and the groaning of lions.

The Seronera valley is renowned for its large lion prides, and sure enough it was here we found the Loop Road pride, 17-strong, a mixture of adult lionesses and their half-grown cubs, heading for the shade after a fruitless dawn hunt on the plains. Later we came across another 20 lions – the Seronera River pride, with one old, grey female and a scruffy, sub-adult male, both sporting radio collars fitted by scientists from the nearby research institute. The Serengeti lion project has been running since George Schaller, the American biologist, began his study here in 1966. Approximately 2,000 lions roam the Serengeti–Mara ecosystem, making this the finest place on earth for observing these magnificent carnivores.

Sharing the valley is another top predator, whose existence was our prime reason for visiting Seronera. Along the river and its brush-choked *korongos*, or seasonal watercourses, grow dense stands of wild date palms, yellow-barked acacias and shady kigelia trees favoured by leopards. Shy, solitary and largely nocturnal, the leopard is hard to find. But it is also the most beautiful of all African animals, and therefore the one every visitor to the Serengeti wants to see.

It was Ben Kelule, my Tanzanian driver, who led us to the leopard. The safari grapevine had spread the news. The elusive '*madoa-doa*' (spots) had been seen by a vehicle from Seronera Lodge earlier that morning, and we set off in pursuit straight away. To my surprise, we found it not by the river but far out on the plain. It was fast asleep, draped along the branch of an acacia, 6m above the ground. It was still early afternoon. We decided to leave the leopard and drive up to Banagi, in the northern woodlands, where a large breeding herd of elephants had been sighted.

The presence of elephants in the Serengeti was good news. Poaching in the 1980s had decimated the Serengeti elephants and driven the survivors to seek refuge across the border in the more intensively patrolled sanctuary of Kenya's Masai Mara National Reserve. But now, in 1991, two years after the world had decided to ban the ivory trade, the tuskers were beginning to return to their former haunts.

We never caught up with the Banagi elephants. We found where they had been feeding, the broken branches stripped of bark, the trampled grass, the smell of fresh dung, but the herd had marched on into the fathomless thickets.

An hour before sunset we returned to Seronera to find the leopard still in its tree. Thunder rumbled across the plain. A storm was brewing. In the silence a solitary dove pleaded with Africa to 'work-harder, work-harder', and still the leopard slept. The sun passed down. The storm drew nearer. At last the leopard awoke, stood, stretched luxuriously, digging its claws into the bark, then slid headfirst down the trunk in a single fluid movement. There it paused, sniffing intently at the base of the tree, peed against it to leave its own pungent calling card, and then walked out into the oncoming rain, with the white tip of its tail raised like a flag above the waving grass-heads. It then vanished, melting away into the dusk.

After three nights at Seronera we struck camp and moved to a new site overlooking Lake Masek, near Ndutu. Here we were back in the midst of the wildebeest and set out early next morning to witness the spectacle from the Gol Kopjes. On the way, passing close to the park's southern entrance at Naabi Hill, we found a solitary male lion resting in the shade of a lone thorn tree. The tree's twisted trunk formed a natural arch, beneath which the old lion lay, his huge forepaws clutching a dead gazelle. As we watched he began to feed, rasping away the white belly fur with his tongue before biting into the flesh.

This lion was a nomad, an old warrior cast out from his pride, living by robbery and intimidation. We later learned from another driver that he had earlier stolen the dead gazelle, having chased away the two Naabi Hill lionesses that had killed it. His broad muzzle bore the scars of many battles. Maybe 12 times in his life he had witnessed the annual arrival of the great migration on the short-grass plains. Now his race was almost run. He had lost all his lower incisors and one of his bottom canines, so that when he ate, crunching noisily through bone and gristle, he had to lie his head on one side in order to bring his powerful carnassials to bear. But he was still a splendid specimen, with a black mane falling like a rug around his shoulders.

The Gol Kopjes have always been my favourite part of the Serengeti. Here the plains are littered with enigmatic granite outcrops, or *kopjes* – an African Dartmoor expanded to infinity, its every skyline pricked by the horned silhouettes of antelope and gazelle. Islands in the grass, the *kopjes* themselves have a life of their own.

Each one is a citadel, haunted by Cape rooks and barn owls, a watchtower for cheetahs, a refuge where lionesses can give birth to their cubs in the mouths of caves, where red and blue agama lizards bask on the hot rocks and lanner falcons hang in the updraughts.

In this wild, lovely country you feel you could drive for ever and never have enough of it. The land has a swell to it, a slow rise and fall like the sea, and each new fold held a fresh surprise: a carpet of vultures on a kill, a female cheetah and her cubs, a herd of eland running from some real or imagined danger. There were birds, too, in numbers beyond counting, including many European migrants. White storks born on the church towers of central Spain walked among the massed cohorts of zebras, snapping up termites. Caspian plovers from the Russian steppes flew past in tight formation. Montagu's harriers sailed overhead, and most poignant of all for an Englishman far from home, a rush of swallows sped over the grass, making the long trek back to Britain.

Where fresh rain had fallen, drifts of white cycnium flowers had sprung up overnight. Near by, I saw a wildebeest calf stagger to its feet within minutes of being born; half an hour later it was galloping to keep up with its mother. From now on, I thought, its existence would be a race for life. And at that moment, as if to make the point, a hyena came slouching by with the hindquarters of a Grant's gazelle dangling from its jaws. In the Serengeti, life and death go hand in hand.

Many of the young wildebeest we saw being born on these plains would not survive. Some would fall prey to lion and cheetah. Others would be drowned or crushed in the mad stampede across the Grumeti and Mara rivers when the herds trekked north to Kenya in the dry season. But the rest would march on, an invincible army moving in long columns that might take three days and nights before the last stragglers passed over the horizon.

In his novel *The Roots of Heaven*, Romain Gary saw the African elephant as a giant symbol of liberty, but for me the wildebeest migration is a far more potent metaphor. To watch that living mass of freedom swarming over the plains, to live under canvas in the sun and the wind, and to wake at dawn to the song of the lion is to breathe the air of a vanishing freedom and hope that whatever happens to this poor, proud and beautiful continent, Serengeti shall never die.

ZIMBABWE – THE MATOBO HILLS

The Matabele call it Malindidzumu – the Place of Spirits. To Cecil John Rhodes, the founder of Rhodesia, whose body still lies buried on its barren summit, it was 'the World's View'. Both names are valid. At Rhodes's grave, high in Zimbabwe's Matobo Hills, you are standing on the roof of a tumbledown landscape that was cast in granite 2,000 million years ago. In every direction, weather-stained pinnacles and rock castles stretch to the horizon. It is as if God had gathered up all the odd lumps of granite left over when the world was complete, and scattered them over 3,000sq km of Matabeleland. The best of it, some 500sq km in all, is preserved as a national park and has been nominated as a World Heritage Site, placing the Matobos in the same league as the Grand Canyon and the Great Barrier Reef.

Many of these extraordinary hills are nothing but colossal whalebacks of rock. Others resemble the ruins of lost cities, with boulders balanced precariously on top of each other, like children's bricks. One shove, you feel, could send the whole lot crashing. This is the place where Lord Baden-Powell, as an army colonel, had the inspiration to found the Boy Scout movement. The whole Matobos area, with its sacred caves and prehistoric rock paintings, has a far greater significance, though. These strange, brooding hills are a holy place, still held in awe by the Matebele people (now also known as the Ndebele). Mzilikazi, their first leader, is buried here. Mzilikazi fled across the Limpopo River in 1822 to escape from King Shaka Zulu, who called this place of granite domes Matobo – a Matabele word meaning 'Bald Heads'.

The British fought and died here 100 years ago in a series of bloody skirmishes with King Lobengula's warriors. Lobengula, who was Mzilikazi's son, had made a treaty with Rhodes. Too late, he discovered that Rhodes and his settler cronies had been economical with the truth. By 1873, the British flag was flying over Bulawayo, the Matabele capital, and Lobengula's army retreated into the Matobos where they hid in caves, waging guerrilla war until their king's death in 1894. On the same lonely summit as Rhodes's grave stands a mausoleum dedicated to Major Allan Wilson and his Shangani Patrol – the 32 'brave men' who went off after Lobengula in 1893. They had set off in hot pursuit across the Shangani River, but suddenly found themselves up against 30,000 angry warriors. Cut off by rising floods, they were unable to retreat and fought to the last man.

Now the Matobos are at peace again, with nothing but the cry of a black eagle or the hacksaw cough of a wandering leopard to disturb the silence of Lobengula's granite kingdom. Leopards are common here. The Matobos are said to hold a greater concentration than anywhere else in Africa, although they are seldom seen. Among the tumbled rocks and tangled thickets are a million places where a leopard might hide. The closest I came to seeing one was finding the fresh tracks of a big male near the Matobo Hills Lodge.

Nor should you expect to see lion, elephant or buffalo. Although Matobo is now a national park, it is not big-game country. Even so, it's a wonderful place for sable antelope, kudu, impala, tsessebe, and fleet-footed klipspringers clattering on tiptoe over the rocks. More recently the place was turned into an IPZ (Intensive Protection Zone) for the endangered rhinoceros. Here, far from the Zambian poachers who steal across the Zambezi, Zimbabwe's rhinos will make their last stand. And here, for three unforgettable days in July 1994, I shared these hills with the rhinos and klipspringers and the ghosts of Lobengula's warriors, exploring the park with Ian Mac-Donald, who runs the comfortable Matobo Hills Lodge and has known the area all his life.

The rains had ended in early January – a month earlier than normal – and would not return until November. The bush was parched, the grass yellow. The days were hot, the sky a cloudless blue. But the nights were as sharp as a driven nail, bringing five degrees of frost by dawn.

MacDonald introduced me to an extraordinary local character called the Lizard Man, a former park ranger who can be found, most days, near Rhodes's grave. Now in his late sixties, he learned long ago how to summon lizards by whistling. One minute there is not a reptile to be seen. The next minute, lizards are scuttling over the hot rocks towards him from every direction. The Lizard Man wanted to know where I came from. 'England,' I said. He shook my hand. 'How is the Queen?' he asked. They had met on a royal visit to Zimbabwe.'Tell her good morning from me,' he said.

The following day, MacDonald promised to show me some of the cave paintings for which the park is renowned. We scrambled over piles of boulders to reach an overhanging cliff whose smooth granite surface had been used as a canvas by the long-vanished San bushmen. Here, captured in red-ochre pigment, was a whole cavalcade of running animals: a warthog, zebras, the horned head of a tsessebe, a man spearing a scrub hare, and a big cat – perhaps a leopard – attacking a hunter. The pictures looked so fresh, as if the unknown artist had only just left. It was the strangest sensation. I sat on the ledge they had sat on, warmed by the same sun on my back, listening to the same, timeless sounds of the African bush: the purring of doves, the cackle of guinea fowl. Ten thousand years had passed and nothing had changed.

For a long time I stared at the painted frieze. When I turned around there were more animals, but these were real, a herd of sable with high, curving horns, moving through the golden grass in the valley below. Above the cliff lay a cave, its upper chamber lit by a long shaft of light from somewhere even higher. On the floor stood a row of rough, red-clay bins, each big enough to hide a man. Empty now, except for the dried droppings of bats, wild cats and porcupines, they had stored Matabele grain when Lobengula's warriors hid out in the hills a century ago. Who knows – maybe the great king himself had sought shelter here? It was an impressive spot. But MacDonald knew of an even better one, he said, a much bigger cave with many wonderful paintings in the Tongwe Wilderness Area.

We set off early next day, leaving our Land-Rover at the Tonghwana Dam and continuing on foot. Lost in a lonely world of granite, we scrambled over boulders as big as bungalows, following a dry watercourse. In the rainy season it would be impassable, a raging torrent. On we climbed, past the dead grey husks of the resurrection bush, which bursts into life when the rains return. At one point, MacDonald picked up a lump of slag from a primitive smelter where Iron Age smiths had forged tools and weapons, maybe 1,000 years ago.

Farther on, he pointed out a black eagle's eyrie on a dizzy cliff ledge. The black eagle is one of Africa's most spectacular birds of prey and the Matobos are its greatest stronghold, where there are more than 50 breeding pairs. 'Some of these nest sites have been occupied for centuries,' said MacDonald. 'I wouldn't be surprised if they were here when the smiths were still making their iron weapons.' Later, we saw the eagles themselves. A pair of them, whose twin shadows sailed along the lip of the crags high above us. They were hunting for dassies – squat, furry mammals that look like guinea pigs and live in crevices among the rocks. We watched them until they drifted out of sight. Then we began to climb.

Underfoot, the rough granite felt wonderfully secure, yet I could see where the rock had peeled and cracked under the endless cycle of sun and frost. 'When the sun is hot the whole mountain expands,' said MacDonald. 'At night, when it cools, it contracts and cracks.' From the wind-blown summits of the lofty whalebacks we looked down into a succession of secret valleys, each thick with yellow grass, the haunt of sable antelope and rhino.

At last we reached our destination: a great hollow in the side of the cliff, like one-half of an inverted dome, a Sistine Chapel of Stone Age art, covered with the now familiar outlines of matchstick men with bows and arrows pursuing giraffe, zebra, kudu and eland, each one as vivid as the day it was painted. As we left the cave, we passed the track of a large snake leading down into a dark crevice. 'It's very fresh,' said MacDonald. 'Must have gone in as we approached. Probably a mamba,' he added casually. 'There are plenty in these hills. The locals would tell you it's the guardian of the cave.'

By the time we got back to the lodge it was dark, and the African sky was hung with stars. This was the night when the planet Jupiter was about to be struck by a giant comet. When the predicted time approached I went outside, lay on my back and stared up into deep space through my binoculars. There was Jupiter, bigger than the surrounding stars. The air was so clear that for the first time in my life I could even see its moons. Was it my imagination, or did the planet really grow brighter when the comet struck? I cannot say. What I do know is that, with uncanny precision, at the very moment of impact, all the jackals of the Matobos began to cry, their keening voices rising and falling in the cold night air.

NAMIBIA – JOURNEY TO THE COAST OF THE DEAD

There was no road to Purros, only the ruts of old tyre tracks disappearing westward into the mountains and deserts of the Kaoko Veld, or Kaokoland. Purros itself was nothing but a scattering of shacks and mud huts belonging to the Himba, pastoralists who dress in skins and roam the ochre hills with their goats and cattle.

As we lurched down the dried-up bed of the Gomatum River, a tributary of the Hoarusib, the sky turned black and thunder rumbled in the hills. 'Is it going to rain?' I asked. Sitting at the wheel of his Toyota Land Cruiser, my companion, the photographer David Coulson, shook his head. 'Not in the desert,' he said. Even as he spoke, the first fat spots began to fall. Moments later we were in the midst of a ferocious tropical storm – and it was precisely then that fate decided we should have a puncture. There was nothing for it but to leap out into the lashing rain and change the wheel. In seconds we were soaked to the skin. When at last the wheel was fixed I took off my boots and poured the water out. It was an odd way to begin what turned out to be one of the hottest weeks of my life in one of the driest, emptiest and most inaccessible places on earth.

Namibia is the last great wilderness in southern Africa. Imagine a country four times the size of Britain with fewer than 1.2 million people. Much of the land is desert. Some of its rivers do not run for years. In some places no rain has fallen for close on a century. To explore such harsh terrain requires local expertise. That was why we were heading to Purros to meet Louw and Amy Schoeman, who were going to take us to the Skeleton Coast.

The Skeleton Coast National Park is a strip of desert up to 40km wide, running for some 500km from the Cunene River on the Angolan border down to the Ugab River near Cape Cross. In 1971, when the park was proclaimed, the northern sector was set aside as a wilderness area where only limited tourism would be allowed. In 1977 it was Louw Schoeman, a lawyer and one-time diamond prospector turned tour operator, who was awarded the concession to operate fly-in safaris there. 'Never underestimate the desert,' he says. 'It isn't hostile but it can be dangerous – even deadly if you don't know it. But I've been coming here for 30 years and it's just like moving around in my own living-room. I love it. In my opinion it's one of the most beautiful places on earth.'

From Purros we followed Schoeman across country, traversing immense gravel plains with no sign of life except for a few springbok and ostrich on the furthest horizons, until we came at sunset to his camp on the Khumib River. The river had flowed a month earlier after heavy rains up-country, but now it was bone-dry again. The mess tent was set up under the spreading branches of an ancient omumborumbonga, or leadwood, the holy tree of the Herero people. At supper-time, shy, spotted genets emerged from its branches to wait for scraps. When I went to bed I was sure I could smell the sea on the night breeze, although the coast was a good 12km away, and when I awoke I could hear the roar of the Atlantic surf.

'We're paranoid about vehicle tracks up here,' says Louw as we set out through the dune-fields towards the sea. 'The desert is easy to scar and slow to heal. I can show you tracks made in 1943 to rescue survivors from the wreck of the *Dunedin Star*. They look as if they were made only last week. And there are other places where tyre tracks will last for centuries.'

We drive on through barchan dunes – wandering sandhills wind-driven across the desert floor at the rate of as much as a kilometre a year. At first glance they seem utterly devoid of life, yet every slope bears a scribble of prints – the signatures of lizards, sidewinders and fog beetles. In places the sands are stained a rich maroon, as if someone had emptied a giant vat of claret down the slopes. Louw hands me a magnifying glass and, on hands and knees, I discover each polished grain of sand is a miniature gemstone. I am kneeling on a bed of garnets.

The secret of driving in dune-fields is to let down the tyres until they are like squashy balloons. Then, with the vehicle in four-wheel drive, you put your foot down and float through the soft sand with a sensation akin to skiing in powder snow. As we sail up over the final crest there is the glorious sight of the Atlantic, with green and white rollers crashing on an empty shore.

The beach is knee-deep in spume – an extraordinary phenomenon produced by the rich blooms of plankton that thrive in the cold Benguela Current. Whipped by the surf to the consistency of shaving cream, it lies in thick, quivering fields, slowly breaking up in the wind to roll away like tumbleweed. Up and down the coast as far as the eye can see, the sands are littered with the flotsam of centuries: a tangle of ships' masts, planks and spars, with here and there the bleached skeleton of a great whale, killed by the American whaling fleets a hundred years ago. Kelp gulls watch at a distance, and ghost crabs dance away on tiptoe over the sands, but ours are the only footprints.

The next day we flew over the Skeleton Coast on our way north to Cunene, where Schoeman has another camp, looking across the river into Angola. We flew low over a colony of Cape fur seals and narrowly missed a flock of rare Damara terns, which rose from the water in front of us. Had we hit them they would have had the effect of a ground-to-air missile, and I began to understand how he had acquired his nickname: Low-Flying Schoeman.

At last we came to the wide brown mouth of the Cunene and followed it inland across a scene of utter desolation. To the south lay nothing but salt pans, a terrifying emptiness reaching away into the dunes and mountain ranges of Kaokoland. To the north rose the sun-scorched rocks of Angola. 'Amazing to think that most of this country we've been flying over has never had a human foot on it,' Schoeman yelled above the engine's roar. 'Not even a Bushman.'

It seemed impossible that there could be any safe place to land in this burnt and broken country, but eventually a strip appeared on a wide plain and we stepped out into the gasping heat of late afternoon. A vehicle was waiting to take us to Louw's camp. The recent rains had raised a brief flush of grass from the red sand, but already it was withering in the heat. To the south a range of nameless hills raised their granite heads. Rock kestrels whistled among the crags and larks flew up as we drove along the stony ridges.

By the time we reached camp the sun was setting. Shadows seeped out of the ground like smoke, filling the hollows of the hills above the gorge in which the river hissed and swirled in spate. There was a tiny swimming pool among the rocks (the river itself was full of crocodiles), and it was bliss to cool off and then sit with a cold beer and watch the lightning flickering in the Angolan mountains. 'You don't come here to see animals,' said Schoeman. 'You come for the remoteness, the ruggedness. Mass tourism has no place here, but a few people will pay for the privilege of coming to such a wild area, and they need the kind of guidance we can provide. It's not a good place to get stuck in.'

Next morning we launched an inflatable boat powered by two giant outboard engines, and set off upstream, bumping over the racing brown current in which whirlpools spun and sinister upwellings gurgled under our bows. After a kilometre or so the gorge began to narrow and the water became even more turbulent, tumbling towards us in a series of roaring rapids. We clung on as the boat bucked and turned beneath our feet. Ahead rose towering granite walls, closing in like the gates of hell. Somehow we squeezed through and surged on between a chaos of sunless cliffs that had collapsed like a stack of giant dominoes, until at last our way was blocked by an enormous cataract and we could go no further.

Returning downstream was more enjoyable. Goliath herons flapped out of the reedbeds, and brilliant green and yellow bee-eaters sat on the swaying branches of the winterthorn trees above luxuriant tangles of morning glory flowers.

After breakfast we left the Cunene to fly back to the Khumib. Once more that savage northern landscape unfolded beneath our wings, the sands a smouldering Martian red, the soda pans blinding, the mountains flayed by wind and sun. I was glad I had seen the Cunene, but relieved to escape from its brooding hostility.

At the Khumib we made our farewells to the Schoemans and set off south down the Skeleton Coast. After an hour or so we came to the mouth of the Hoarusib. There had been more storms inland and the river was running. We waded across it to see if it was too deep to drive. The water was flowing strongly and rising as we watched, in sudden surges that spread out across the sand. It was now or never. Slowly we nosed into the flood and drove across it obliquely with the water lapping at the doors.

It was now late afternoon. Down on the shore, bathed in the golden Atlantic light, springbok were feeding. It seemed incongruous to find them beside the sea, but sometimes, said Coulson, desert-dwelling elephants followed the sand rivers down to the coast, leaving their giant footprints along the beach. And from time to time a desert lion would come wandering out of Damaraland to scavenge for seal carcasses in the surf.

Our destination was the ranger station at Möwe Bay, where we were to stay with Rod Braby, principal nature conservation officer for the Skeleton Coast National Park, and Sigi, his wife. With its bleached driftwood shacks and small gardens heaped with fishing nets, whalebones, elephant skulls and other flotsam, the bleak little settlement was like the setting for a Steinbeck novel. Yet despite its remoteness it seemed to attract a succession of the most remarkable and gifted people. One of the shacks was the home of Des and Jen Bartlett, who had lived and worked in the Namibian parks for 14 years. Over a breakfast of tea and kippers they explained how they had been using microlight aircraft to shoot the first film of desert-dwelling elephants migrating through the dunes.

Later we were to meet Garth Owen-Smith, the tall, bearded desert veteran who has done more than anyone to protect these elephants, and his colleague Rudi Loutit, who has been fighting to save the last of Namibia's desert rhinos. Loutit's latest project involved de-horning the rhinos to deny the poachers the prize they sought. 'At first people said the rhinos would be killed by lions if we removed their horns. But we went ahead and did it because we've got to get these wonderful animals into the next century, and it's been a great success.'

Beside the Atlantic I felt oddly at home. Alone with my thoughts I sat on the beach as a fog bank came rolling in, heavy with the smell of kelp. The damp sea mist clung to my bare legs but I was not cold. I walked for miles, relieved to be out of the desert heat, listening to the gulls, beachcombing for agate pebbles among the jackal prints and sea-urchin shells. It was hard to believe I was still in Africa, yet I knew that less than 8km away the sky would be a burning blue and the sand too hot to stand on.

We left the Skeleton Coast National Park at its southern end below the Ugab River. A ranger opened the gates, which are adorned with black painted skulls and crossbones, and we followed the Atlantic down to Swakopmund, a clean, cool oasis of palm trees and old-fashioned buildings still dreaming of the Kaiser's Germany. Swakopmund was a brief interlude of hot baths, clean sheets and air-conditioned rooms. Then we were off into the desert again, following the bone-dry Huasib River into the Namib-Naukluft National Park.

This was the true Namib – 'The Place Where There is Nothing' – a sunstruck wilderness of gravel plains above which mirages of distant mountaintops appeared as rocky islands in a trembling sea of blue. High rolling dunes marched south with us down to the western horizon, like the Sussex Downs painted red. Further south, at Sossusvlei, these dunes reach a height of 300m, the highest in the world. There was no water anywere, but there were trees beside the Huasib riverbed – giant winterthorns from whose broad parasols of shade had fallen large seedpods with furry shells as soft as moleskin.

Here we camped, at a place called Homeb, and in the late afternoon we crossed the riverbed and climbed up out of the valley to watch the sun descend behind the dunes. We came to a stony plateau where wind-blasted pebbles of clear white and yellow crystal glittered in the sand like fallen stars. Nothing grew here save a few sparse grey tufts of grass that creaked and hissed in the wind – yet scatterings of old, dry spoor showed that gemsbok and zebra had passed this way.

Back in camp, night came swiftly. A full moon rose, and in the clear air every detail of its cratered surface was visible through my binoculars. We barbecued the steaks we had bought in Swakopmund and ate them with potatoes and onions wrapped in foil and baked in the embers, washed down with beers from the coolbox. Later, stretched out in my sleeping bag, I lay on my back looking up at the brightest stars in Africa. The Bushmen, who believe the stars to be hunters in the heavens, say they can hear them in the deep silence of the desert. But I heard only the sepulchral hoot of an owl downriver and the jackals keening in the dunes.

Above Homeb the course of the river cuts through a range of cindery hills into the desolate Huasib canyonlands. This is where two Germans, Hermann Korn and Henno Martin, with their dog Otto, hid for nearly three years to avoid internment by the South Africans during World War II. Henno told their story in a book, *The Sheltering Desert*, in which he graphically described their solitary lives, shooting game and searching for water in the bottom of the canyons.

We visited one of their hideouts, the place they called Carp Cliff, high above the Kuiseb Canyon. Here they built a shelter under the overhanging rimrock, living like neolithic man on whatever game they could catch. The walls were still there, as was the stone slab table. Mountain zebra had come this way not long ago. We found fresh spoor at the foot of the cliff and I remembered Henno Martin's account of how he and Hermann would shoot zebra and gemsbok, turn the meat into biltong, make the blood into sausages, and sometimes enjoy a nostalgic feast of gemsbok liver, dumplings and sauerkraut.

Distance lends these far-reaching barrenlands the surreal perspective of a painting by Salvador Dalí, with the unearthly shark's-fin shapes of mountain ranges thrusting over the horizon. Here, in the pitiless heat of the Namib, the earth's rocks are being tested to destruction, blowtorched by the sun, sand-blasted by the searing winds and broken down into fissured gullies and ravines in which the eye cries out for a green tree or a pool of water.

All my life I have loved wilderness and wild places, but the Namib's unrelenting hostility defeated me. In its furnace heat I found my spirit wilting like a dying flower. Only in the last golden hour before sunset, and again in the first cool hour of dawn, does the desert relent, allowing deep shadows to soften its harsh contours, transforming it into a silent world of unearthly beauty.

On the way back to Swakopmund, driving through the burnt-out badlands and labyrinthine canyons of the Swakop River, we came to a stony valley upon whose slopes grew hundreds of *Welwitschia mirabilis*, one of the world's oldest and weirdest plants. Some of these living botanical fossils are said to be 1,500 years old, yet in their entire lifetime they produce only two leaves, which may reach a length of up to 3m and split into long leathery green fronds. They lie in the sun like something out of John Wyndham's *Day of the Triffids*, as if waiting to grab you by the ankle, suck out your juices and discard you like an empty paper bag.

Next day we drove down into the South African enclave of Walvis Bay to meet Ernst Karlowa, the Skeleton Coast Park's first warden. Now in his seventies he lives quietly in a Walvis Bay suburb.

'Until 1960 the coast and its hinterland was still an impenetrable wilderness,' he said. 'In Afrikaans we call it the Seekus van die Dood, "Sea Coast of the Dead". I spent three years alone up there. Sometimes it felt like solitary confinement, the wind howling and the camp moaning and creaking like a ship at sea. I'd never do it again. It's a hard land, and yet after a while it takes hold of you and it's hard to let go.'

In 1974, patrolling by Land-Rover in the dunes near False Cape Fria, Karlowa made an exciting discovery. 'At first I thought it was an old wooden pulley lying among some ship's timbers. I picked it up and found myself staring into this mysterious enigmatic face. It set me back on my heels, I can tell you.' What Karlowa had found was a carved wooden ship's figurehead, almost certainly from a 16th-century galleon, possibly Spanish but probably Portuguese, one of hundreds of nameless ships cast up on the Sea Coast of the Dead. One of Africa's most moving relics, it lies now in the small museum of the ranger post at Möwe Bay, gathering dust in a desert shack.

Afterwards a pilot friend of David Coulson's volunteered to take us for one last look at the Skeleton Coast before I returned to

England the next day. We flew down the coast to Sandwich Bay, an immense shallow lagoon of islands, sandbars and salt flats haunted by fleets of pelicans and flamingos. Where the surf creamed against the outermost edges of the sandbanks, colonies of Cape fur seals had hauled themselves out of the water to lie in dense, brown packs, staring at the jackals that patrolled the shore, waiting to feed on the sick and the dead.

Further south again we flew over the wreck of the *Eagle*, a 19th-century barque with her ribs and spars sticking out of the sand. We made a low pass along the beach, the yellow dunes towering above us to landward, the green waves breaking beneath our wheels, then rose until we could see the endless emptiness of the coast reaching all the way to the Orange River over the horizon.

By the time we turned for home the flowing summits of the dunes had already begun to glow in the evening light. From the air the Namib and its giant dunescapes appeared as lifeless as the moon. Then came a sight to lift the heart, as out of the shadows a group of gemsbok came galloping, their horns held high, like lances, hoofs kicking up puffs of sand as they pounded up the smooth incline and cantered away into the setting sun.

SEA TIME

THE CARIBBEAN – ALL I ASK IS A TALL SHIP

Spread-eagled in the widows' nets under the *Star Clipper*'s giant 14m-long bowsprit, I hung suspended between sea and sky. Below, through the mesh, I watched a school of dolphins joyfully bow-riding within centimetres of our prow as it sliced through the blue waters. On either side, flying fish skittered over the waves like silver skimming pebbles, and above, into a faultless Caribbean sky, rose a cloud of canvas taller than Nelson's Column. Such are the pleasures of cruising in the West Indies. But this was no ordinary cruise ship. I was one passenger among a full complement of 170 – a congenial mix of Brits, Germans and Americans, mostly couples ranging in age from twenties to eighties – enjoying what the travel trade calls 'soft adventure', sailing on one of the tallest of the world's tall ships.

The *Star Clipper* and her sister ship, *Star Flyer*, are full-blown, four-masted staysail barquentines. Built in Belgium in the early 1990s, they were the first ships of their kind to be constructed for almost a century. They are both true clippers, greyhounds of the sea, the latest of a long line of proud ships whose names – *Sea Witch*, *Ariel*, *Cutty Sark*, *Storm King* – were written on the wind.

With 3,300sq m of canvas aloft, her square sails set to catch every last breath of the north-east trade winds, the *Star Clipper* can fly over the waves at a top speed of 17 knots – 110m of sheer poetry, from her 50-tonne keel to the top of her 65m-tall mainmast. Together, she and her sister ship offer an authentic seafaring experience. True, they also have 12-cylinder diesel engines, but mostly they work with wind and waves. 'Remember,' said Captain Gerhard Lickfett, her German skipper, in his welcome speech, 'This is not a cruise. It is a voyage.'

The great 19th-century clippers were created out of the need for faster ships and smaller crews, to maximize the owners' profits whenever they set out from London or New York, bound for the Pacific, eager to be the first around Cape Horn and return home laden with China tea or Chilean saltpetre. Everything about them, from their flared bows to their graceful hulls, was built for speed. Even their name evolved from the way they flew over the water, clipping through the waves with their sharp steel bows. Inevitably, with the coming of steamships, the clippers sailed into history, but many lamented their passing. The poet John Masefield, writing at the time when the watch was being changed from sail to steam, knew the magic they could exert on men's imaginations. 'All I ask is a tall ship,' he wrote. 'The wheel's kick and the wind's song and a white sail shaking.'

Now, in these more environmentally conscious times, the sails are shaking again, for ships like the *Star Clipper* live closer to the natural world, leave no pollution, and teach respect for the sea and its uncompromising ways. Besides, who could not fall in love at first sight with the *Star Clipper*? And who better to be the master of her soul than Captain Lickfett, the last man in the German Merchant Navy to be trained on a working square-rigger. Dressed in immaculate tropical whites, with his lean good looks and thousand-mile stare, Captain Lickfett and the *Star Clipper* are a perfect marriage.

Born in Gdansk in 1937, Lickfett escaped from wartime Germany just ahead of the Russians, travelling by horse and cart with his mother and six siblings to find safety in a Danish refugee camp. But the day that truly changed his life came 10 years later when he saw the four-masted barque *Pamir* heading down the English Channel under full sail. Within weeks he had signed on as a deck boy aboard her sister ship, the *Passat*, and sailed from Hamburg to Rio. 'They worked me hard,' he said, 'but I loved to sail such a ship.'

Later, he spent 30 years sailing the world on cargo ships until, when he was 50, he decided to leave motor vessels and go back to sailing ships. By then, all the old German sea captains were gone, leaving Lickfett as the only one who had learned the ropes on a working square-rigger. Now, tall and lean with saturnine features, he is a cultured man of many enthusiasms, who learned to speak English between dances at the Hammersmith Palais in London. A Nelson scholar, in love with the sea, he can still steer by the stars even though his ship's bridge is crammed with every high-tech navigational gizmo known to science.

In summer the *Star Clipper* roams the Mediterranean, cruising from Cannes around Corsica and Sardinia and along the Ligurian coast. But in September, when the days grow shorter, she heads out into the Atlantic. 'There we sail south until the butter melts,' said Captain Lickfett, 'then go west with the trade winds to the Caribbean for the winter.'

And that was where I had joined her, in Bridgetown, Barbados, and it was from there, with Captain Lickfett at the helm, that we set sail for Tobago. One of the pleasures of sailing aboard the *Star Clipper* is her ability to steal into small ports and quiet anchorages which bigger cruise ships cannot reach. The end of that first day found us near Charlotteville in Man-o'-War Bay, a natural harbour sheltered by steep hills covered in rainforest.

Some passengers chose to go scuba-diving off the reefs, where manta rays – known locally as Tobago taxis – glide like flying carpets through the clear depths. Others disappeared to laze under the coconut palms. But I went ashore to visit the Tobago Forest Reserve, the oldest preserved rainforest in the western hemisphere, a green cathedral of giant trees and lianas as thick as the *Star Clipper*'s hawsers. The forest, I learned – parrots, hummingbirds and all – has been protected since 1765.

Every day found us at a new island. Rum shacks, reggae, dreadlocks, cricket – all the Caribbean clichés were here. But there were also green hills where nutmegs ripened like crimson conkers and bananas hung cheek by jowl with cocoa pods. In Grenada we put into St George's harbour on Labour Day to find the whole of the Carenage, the town's curving waterfront, lined with marching trade-union bands playing 'Onward Christian Soldiers'. Cruising north through the Grenadines, we passed a group of rocks known as London Bridge. Then came a fleet of islands whose names I had never heard: Caille Island, Ronde Island, the Sisters, Les Tantes, and Diamond Island rising from the waves like the summit of a drowned mountain.

By now I had begun to make sense out of the bewildering cat's cradle of shrouds, backstays, halyards and downhauls. I learned the names of all 16 sails, from the flying jib to the jigger staysail. I was taught how to brace the yards and how to tack and sail close-hauled. No doubt the old Cape Horners, those hard-driving bucko sea captains from the days of iron men and wooden ships, would have howled with derision at the *Star Clipper*'s electrically operated winches and capstans. But how they would have envied her ability to hoist all sail with only six crew on deck.

As for her luxuries – her two swimming pools, fine food, chilled wines and smooth-as-silk service – they would have popped a rivet.

Below decks, everything was polished teak and burnished brass. My air-conditioned cabin was equipped with TV and hairdryer and a loo that flushed at the press of a button – a different world from the old bucket-and-chuck-it days on the China run.

Star Clipper may look like a dream of the past but she belongs to the age of space travel. Her state-of-the-art ballast system can slow the ship's roll by two seconds – 'the difference between a glass of wine spilling over your table or staying still,' as one ship's officer put it. Not that there was a great deal of rolling in the Caribbean, and nothing remotely like the conditions we saw one morning when we were treated to the screening of a black and white movie, filmed in 1924 aboard the German four-masted barque, *Peking*. It showed her rounding Cape Horn in 150kph winds and 25m-high seas, her sails in tatters, her crew aloft, her leeside rails driven under. We, who had met nothing stronger than a force-four breeze as we sipped our tropical fruit punches, could only gasp in awe and admiration.

Even so, our own deck crew was made of the right stuff. None more so than Pirate William, the bosun, a sinewy St Lucian who always wore Raybans and a bright bandanna around his head. He first went to sea when he was nine. 'It's the best place to be,' he said. 'On land it's all corruption, crime and pollution. Me, I just like to chase the horizon.' Once, on an inter-island trip, he had spent 12 hours in the sea when his tiny one-man boat had sunk. Miraculously he survived, picked up by a passing yacht. 'All my papers were soaked,' said Pirate William. 'My passport too. Only my prayer book stayed dry. I guess somebody up there just didn't want me to die.'

Midweek found us at anchor off Carriacou, whose name means 'the Island Surrounded by Reefs', to be put ashore on a sandy cay shaded by a dozen coconut palms. Here, voluntary castaways for the day, we sunbathed, snorkelled and feasted on a magnificent barbecue of spare ribs and spicy chicken.

On the voyage to Bequia we passed a pod of pilot whales, among them a mother and calf, moving steadily north and seemingly unconcerned by our close presence. 'Blows, mon, blows!', the cry of the old-time whalers, is still heard in these waters, where Bequia men continue to hunt pilot whales. Nowadays, though, the catch is strictly limited by the International Whaling Commission to a maximum of two whales a year.

Bequia was my favourite Caribbean landfall, a small island where life seemed sweet. Nobody hurried. Everybody smiled and said hello. In Port Elizabeth the bleached wooden houses reflect the West Indian love of colour: sky-blue, lime-green and coral-pink were everywhere. Even the local church was painted blue and white, its windows left wide open to let in the breeze. Strolling under the palms at the harbour's edge, I stopped to watch a barefoot boy sailing a toy boat he had made from a coconut shell, with green leaves for sails. The Bequians were great boat-builders in the past, making island schooners like the *Friendship Rose*, which still sails regularly to Mustique, just two hours away.

That evening, eating curried shrimp on the veranda of the Gingerbread Restaurant, listening to a string band playing a strange blend of Scottish and American folk songs with a calypso beat, I began to understand why the older hands among the crew loved this island so much. But for me, even the most exciting shore excursions took second place to the voyage itself. Ashore the air was hot and sultry; at sea the trade winds brought relief. Besides, what landbound joys could compare with cruising on a tall ship under full sail? That was when I was happiest, standing on the scrubbed teak deck, feeling the *Star Clipper* rise and fall under me as she rode the rolling swell.

Too soon it was time to leave St Lucia, our final port of call. As always aboard the *Star Clipper*, this manoeuvre was accompanied by the Vangelis theme music from the Columbus film, *1492*, broadcast over the ship's loudspeakers. Somehow it transformed each departure into a *coup de théâtre*, in which every passenger had a walk-on part, watched by the envious crowds onshore. Its refrain haunts me still, and whenever I hear it I remember that last farewell.

I remember Pirate William crying, 'Sail stations,' summoning the crew on deck, bells ringing, commands being yelled and the capstan grumbling as the anchor chain is hauled in, link after dripping link, and the sails are set. Slowly the ship's head swings round, away from the roofs of Soufrière, past the twin green steeples of the Pitons. Then, gracefully, silently, she heads out into the boundless ocean, the most beautiful object men have made for close on a hundred years.

KENYA – GIANTS AT THE END OF THE LINE

We put to sea with the early morning breeze at our backs. It blew steadily across the water, carrying the mingled scents of grass and mango trees and warm, wet earth: the smell of Africa. In Kenya they call this land breeze the *umande*, and look upon it as a sign of good fishing. By the time we reached the blue waters beyond the reefs where the big fish roam, the wind would go round and the *kaskazi* would set in. This north-east monsoon once brought the dhows of Arabia drifting like leaves down to Mombasa and Malindi to trade cargoes of salt fish, dried shark, chests and carpets for coffee, charcoal, ivory and simsim (sesame) oil.

Today the traditional ocean-going dhows, the *booms* and *sambuks* from Dubai and Khorramshahr, are only a memory, but the Malindi fishermen still set sail in their local craft: *ngalawas* with crude outriggers, and the larger, more graceful *jahazis* with their lateen sails and painted hulls. Like us they were heading for the banks and deeps beyond the reefs, but there the similarity ended.

Our boat, *Tina*, was a different breed, a 10m Striker, built in Holland and powered by twin diesel 180hp Ford Sabre engines that could push her through the water at 20 knots. Her flying bridge and the outriggers sprouting like long, white whiskers from her superstructure immediately marked her for what she was. And so too did the fighting chair in the stern, where the angler would sit, feet braced against the transom and the butt of his rod anchored in a metal socket, to pit skill and strength against the giant billfish of the Indian Ocean.

Every November when the *kaskazi* begins to blow, the billfish arrive in the 200km of fishing grounds that extend down the Kenyan coast from Malindi to Shimoni. Here they stay, feeding and fattening on the huge numbers of smaller fish – bonito, garfish, Malindi herring – until the south-westerly monsoon sets in during early March and they drift away to spawn, nobody knows where, on their immense and mysterious migrations. Billfish are nomads, powerful and streamlined, built for wandering the wide oceans. There are five species – swordfish, sailfish, black marlin, and blue and striped marlin – each one carrying the distinctive bony beak that is used not to impale its prey but rather to club it to death with a sideways swipe of the head.

Biggest is the black marlin – the Black Prince of gamefish – which can weigh well over 500kg and hits the bait like a charging buffalo. But at Malindi the most sought-after quarry are the sailfish, which gather in large numbers off the mouth of the Sabaki River. Apart from Costa Rica, the waters here are the best in the world for this species. In 1989, the year before my visit, Malindi boats landed 2,451 sailfish, with *Tina* averaging two every trip.

Sailfish hunt in packs up to 20 strong, and swim at 65kph. Everything about them is designed for speed. Even their pelvic fins fold away into a slit in the belly to reduce drag through the water, and they grow to an impressive size, though not as big as marlins – the Kenyan record stands at 66kg. But what brings the big-game aficionados to Malindi is not the sailfish's weight; it is its spectacular beauty, all violet and shining silver, the peacock-blue spots shimmering on its great dorsal sail as it leaps for its life at the end of the line.

Yet for all the numbers of billfish caught, they remain an enigma. 'We still don't know their migratory patterns,' says *Tina*'s owner, Herbie Paul. 'Some think they migrate in huge circles as far as the Seychelles, but we know only that they come here to feed. Then for eight months of the year they simply vanish.'

The Pauls, Herbie and Angus, father and son, are the best big-game fishermen on the Kenyan coast. In 1986 they caught 16 sailfish between them in a single morning. Herbie, now in his fourth year as president of the Malindi Sea Fishing Club, was born in Rostock, Germany, and came to Kenya when he was only six months old. As a young man he worked for a time with the local dhow fishermen, netting sharks for food. Later he tried his hand at sisal farming, but his love for the sea was too strong and he returned to Malindi as a charter skipper, taking clients out after billfish. Now, given another 10 years, Herbie Paul might easily pass as the unforgettable marlin fisherman whom Hemingway described in the opening page of his masterpiece, *The Old Man and the Sea*: 'Everything about him was old except for his eyes and they were cheerful and undefeated.'

Marlin were always Herbie's favourite quarry. A lot of people ask him to take them shark fishing but he is very reluctant. 'I like sharks,' he says. 'They've been around a long time. They're the old-est living things in the sea. I like their efficiency and the way they move and everything about them except their mouths.' Nowadays he is even losing the taste for billfishing and prefers to let Angus run the boat. 'Big-game fishing is like hunting,' he told me. 'After a while you just don't want to kill any more.'

Angus is different. A lean, brown, laid-back version of his father, he still has a young man's hunger for the thrill of the hunt, the chance of hooking yet another record fish. 'No one on this coast has yet landed a 1,000lb marlin on rod and line,' he says, 'but they're out there.'

Now, dressed in ragged shorts, T-shirt and yachting cap, he lounged barefoot at the wheel, chatting in Swahili to his crew. Mahomed, the captain, has been with the Pauls for 10 years. Like Saidi the deckhand, he is a Muslim, a Bajuni from the island of Lamu, and both men are expert at baiting the wicked 5cm hooks. The best bait, Angus explained, was fresh Malindi herring or a strip cut from the golden belly of a dorado, the dolphin fish, lashed to the hook and trolled astern with a garish assortment of artificial jigs and lures.

Although I was the only client, we fished with seven stubby glass-fibre rods, each with its metal butt sunk in a socket in the gun-whales. To avoid a tangle, the two outermost lines are held up and away from the boat by the outriggers with the aid of sheaves and tackles and spring-loaded clips. If a fish should strike, the clip releases and the pull of the line comes directly on the rod tip in the normal way.

By now we were off Mambrui, trolling at 6 knots and rolling like a pig in the uncomfortable swell. Here the silt-laden Sabaki River, swollen with the November rains, had disgorged an enormous bulge of jade-green water extending for 8km out to sea. It was here, following the distinctive line where the green flood met the unsul-lied blue of the true ocean, that the sailfish loved to feed.

Beyond Mambrui the coast was quite deserted – nothing but sandhills rolling away towards Somalia. As the day grew hotter the rising air drew huge cloud castles into the sky. To the west the coral-sand beaches of Malindi and Watamu were dazzling in the sun, but inland I could see veils of rain trailing away towards the distant ele-phant country of the Tsavo National Park. Ahead of us, clouds of terns were hovering, thick as mosquitoes over a lake. '*Ndege mingi*,' cried Said eagerly. 'Many birds.' The terns were a good sign. They hunt the fry driven to the surface by garfish and bonito, which in turn are pursued by the bigger predators, the sailfish and tuna, wahoo, dorado, and the lean and silver kingfish with its razor teeth.

As we drew closer the water began to seethe with whitebait and the terns fell upon them in a frenzy. Now we could see schools of bonito feeding, their polished backs rolling like barrels as they tore through the frantic shoals. Without warning, a reel began to scream and, before I knew it, Saidi was shoving me into the fighting chair and handing me the rod. With the butt end firmly anchored in the socket between my knees, I began pumping in the fish – up with the rod, then lean forward and reel in. I had no idea what was on the other end of the line, but it felt as heavy as a horse, and already my forearms ached with the strain.

Minutes later, deep down but drawing closer, a dark shape appeared, a gleaming bronze ingot, thickset and curving. The rod shook as the fish tugged and twisted with all its strength, but in vain. Said was so quick with the gaff. In a single swift movement it was driven home and the fish hauled over the transom to thump its life away on the teak deck. First blood: a yellowfin tuna, built like a bullet.

But there was no time to admire its iridescent mackerel colours. Already Angus was yelling from the wheelhouse and pointing astern to where a giant blue fin was slicing through our wake. 'Sail!' Again there came the unnerving scream of the reel, the same frantic rush to get into the chair and take the strain. This time the fish dived deep, stripping line in a long, steady plunge. Then suddenly there was no pressure at all.

Had I lost him? I reeled in hard, felt the rod shiver and looked up to see him rising from the water with his huge dorsal fin erect. For a moment, it seemed, he hung suspended in mid-air – all 2m or more of him shining purple and silver in the sun – then he re-entered the water cleanly, like a porpoise, his powerful crescent-moon tail going under and the line running out once more.

At last, after an eternity of heaving and winding, he began to tire. I looked down into the water and saw the sun's rays lancing through the cobalt depths, and a huge brown shadow coming slow-ly to the surface. When he was close enough, Mahomed leaned over the side and grabbed him by his bony bill, then clubbed him over the head and laid him out full length across the deck.

We fished on into the early afternoon, with the hot sun shining and the terns screaming and dark thunderheads blossoming along the eastern horizon. From time to time the voices of other charter skippers came over the radio, distorted by static as they chatted to each other like fighter pilots. *'Tina, Tina, Tina.* How's it going? Over.' One boat had just missed a big sailfish, which had jumped and thrown the hook. Another had just caught a good tunny in the Boiling Pot, a favourite fishing spot off Watamu, where underwater banks cause a violent upwelling of conflicting currents.

But there were no more big fish for us. Only a burnished green-gold dorado covered in blue spots as if it had just been splashed with ink, and a 4kg kingfish with bulldog jaws. We passed a turtle, its polished brown carapace as big as a bathtub, drifting serenely with the current. Sometimes, said Angus, you might see manta rays gliding through the deep on 3m wings, or a whale shark, a gentle giant bigger than our boat.

As we headed in through a *mlango* – literally a gateway in the reef – we ran out a red pennant of triumph, the traditional signal of a Malindi boat with a sailfish on board (blue for a marlin, yellow for a shark), but I was now filled with remorse for the magnificent fish I had killed. I stared at its leathery corpse in the scuppers. How swiftly its quicksilver colours had faded. The dull disc of its cold fish eye, so fierce and glittering in life, stared back at me reproachfully in death. I had not enjoyed the manner of its dying and I wondered afterwards if I was the only fisherman that day who was hoping not to make another strike. Not so much a triumph, but more an act of murder in which the fish's very size seemed to compound the crime. Killing a sailfish was far worse than catching a mackerel.

'Don't worry,' said Angus, as if reading my thoughts. 'Not an ounce will be wasted. The sailfish is smoked and sold to the resort hotels along the coast. It's a great Kenyan delicacy. And the rest of the catch goes to the locals.'

In Malindi the catch was dumped in a wooden handcart and hauled off to be weighed, hung up on a gantry and displayed like the victims on a gamekeeper's gibbet. My sailfish weighed nearly 30kg – not a bad fish, but no record-breaker. I didn't want a photograph but I badly needed a beer and wandered off to meet Herbie Paul in the Malindi Sea Fishing Club bar.

The clubhouse lies right on the seafront beneath a barn-like roof of casuarina poles covered with *makuti* thatch. Inside, fans stirred the soupy air that blows straight in from the sea. Herbie pointed to the mounted head of a black marlin, a 375kg monster caught by *Tina* in 1980. The talk turned to other homeric struggles with big fish of the past – including the 289kg mako shark hooked off Shimoni in 1964, which had lunged across the transom in a deliberate attempt to reach the man in the fighting chair, a true-life forerunner of *Jaws*. It was a tale fit for Hemingway, who fished at Malindi and in the Pemba Channel in 1954, and who has now given his name to a luxury hotel just down the coast at Watamu. Already it has a big reputation for blue-water billfishing. Within four months of opening in the late 1980s, one of the hotel boats, *Ol Jogi*, achieved the grand slam, one of the rarest events in gamefishing, by catching a sailfish and all three species of marlin in a single day.

Gary Cullen, who presides over Hemingways, showed me one of his most prized possessions, a faded copy of *A Farewell to Arms* signed by the author for his old fishing chum, Colonel 'Benji' Horton. But the game has changed a lot since then, he said. 'In Hemingway's day it was a proper battle. You had to sit there and slug it out with the fish. Now we throw the boat backwards at the fish while you reel, reel, reel.'

Cullen himself was a professional tournament golfer on the major European circuit until he packed it in to become a fisherman like his father, Anthony Cullen, whose book, *Crash Strike*, is a classic of East African big-game fishing. 'Golf is great,' said Gary, 'but whenever the marlin were running I'm afraid I'd just duck out and head for Kenya. Billfish are so royal, so powerful and dignified and yet so vulnerable. They captivate me. In fact I don't much like catching them myself any more, although I love taking people fishing. Even then I find myself hoping that the fish will get away, especially if the client doesn't deserve it.'

Sadly for Kenya, and for the rest of the world, the days of these giant ocean wanderers are numbered. Japanese fishermen with longlines and 'wall-of-death' nets are moving in. They first appeared inside Kenyan territorial waters in 1977 and were back again the year before my visit. 'They can follow the fish with electronic gadgets,' says Cullen. 'They can stalk a shoal for days. One Japanese longliner with 5,000 hooks strung out through miles of ocean can take in a single night what Kenya's entire sport-fishing fleet takes in a year. It's the elephant story all over again. Billfish are vanishing and nobody's listening.'

Later I went again to the seafront at Malindi as the sun was dipping behind the Arab houses of the Old Town. The monsoon breeze had died and the local inshore fishing dhows lay at rest in the shallows with their sails furled. An odd, dark shape on the sand caught my eye. It was the huge severed head of a giant marlin the fishermen had caught in their nets that day. The carcass had gone to market and the head had been left on the beach for the tide to take away. Now it stood in the swiftly falling dusk with its bill pointing at the African sky while the sea turned to gold and then blood-red: a cenotaph for a doomed race.

SCOTLAND – THE HEBRIDES

'Minke whale, starboard bow!' The cry came from the crow's-nest, 15m above the wooden deck of the *Marguerite Explorer* as she rolled in the swell. The whale surfaced again, a huge, dark head, like a slab of basalt, then the polished back and small dorsal fin rolled forward as if fixed to a slowly rotating wheel, to disappear beneath the waves. Whale-watching is one of eco-tourism's most popular ventures, and nowadays people fly halfway around the world to meet these majestic leviathans. But my close encounters took place within 100km of Glasgow.

The *Marguerite Explorer* is a born-again Danish trawler, launched in 1934 and rebuilt in 1989 by Christopher Swann, her British owner-skipper. From stern to bowsprit she measures 25m, weighs 74 tonnes and is everything a good sea boat should be: solid and reassuring, but also with wonderful flowing curves.

Swann, known to everyone as Swanny, is a latter-day Captain Ahab, but instead of hunting whales with a harpoon he carries nothing deadlier than a pair of binoculars. Impervious to wind and rain, he stands at the wheel clad in just shirt and trousers, a silk scarf knotted around his throat and a weather-stained leather jacket over his shoulders. He has spent most of his adult life at sea, including a stint in the Royal Navy learning to be a diver. Then, in the mid-1980s, after sailing on square-riggers, he fell in love with the *Marguerite Explorer*. 'I found her in Holland,' he says. 'She was just a fishing boat then. I'd looked at hundreds of boats. Most of them were either too big or rotten. But *Marguerite* was as solid as an ox and had very pretty lines.

'I had already decided to base myself in the Hebrides. I'd sailed there before and I had read all of Gavin Maxwell's books, so I knew how rich the wildlife was.

'The Hebrides are an undiscovered paradise,' declares Swanny, 'and they're on our doorstep. All you have to do is jump on a train to Oban.'

He is right, as I discovered on a week's cruise from Oban in June 1994. All around us, out of its magical seascapes, rose islands and mountains, now soft and furred with rain, now sunlit, luminous and sharp. For much of the time I was cold and wet, but I would not have missed it for the world. In the long Hebridean summer evenings the daylight lingered close to midnight, and whenever the sun did appear, transforming the water from gun-metal-grey to an Aegean blue, we sailed among seas that sparkled. Here in the far north the Atlantic air is never still and the shifting light adds a heightened sense of drama to everything it touches.

The first night found us at anchor in Loch Spelve, on the coast of Mull. The wind had died but the midsummer evening went on and on until, wrapped in an eerie half-light that was neither night or day, we slept under cloud-capped hills. The Gaelic names of Mull's sombre summits set my scalp tingling: Creach Beinn (Plunder Mountain), Sgurr Dearg (Hill of the Red Deer) and Dun da Gaoithe (Hill of the Two Winds). When morning came we went ashore. Red stags watched us like Apache scouts from a distant skyline. Bluebells grew among the bracken, and across the loch a cuckoo called, its voice clearly audible from a kilometre away.

Mull is golden eagle country. The previous evening we had sailed past an eyrie on a cliff ledge, a pile of sticks the size of a sofa, with two chicks peering over the rim. Now we saw one of the adults, a huge, dark shape aloft, like a flying door, sailing over the hills in search of prey. Later we also saw a pair of sea eagles. Absent from Scotland for half a century, these splendid birds are now staging a comeback after their reintroduction from Norway. In Gaelic they have a wonderful name, which translates as 'the eagle of the sunlit eye'. But all I could see were their flat wings and white tails as they soared above the boat.

The following day we had rounded Ardnamurchan Point before breakfast and were bearing away for the island of Coll. Our eyes were peeled for the tell-tale clouds of gulls and gannets that feed on fish driven to the surface by whales and dolphins. Suddenly, out of nowhere, a school of common dolphins came rollicking towards us to ride our bow-waves, leaping and plunging with such obvious enjoyment that everyone on board whooped and yelled like children. All whale and dolphin sightings on the *Marguerite Explorer* are passed to Evans the Whale, better known in scientific circles as Dr Peter Evans, a distinguished cetacean expert from Oxford University's zoology department, who has been gathering data for the Sea Watch Foundation.

[165]

Sadly, it was too early for me to witness the highlight of Swanny's Hebridean year. That would come later in the summer with the arrival of the orcas, or killer whales, 8-tonne sea monsters with sleek pied skins and dorsal fins like dinghy sails. One year he followed a group of orcas for 14 hours. 'I really get fired up on them,' he says.

One orca in particular he sees every summer. This particular animal is easily recognized by the distinctive notch in his dorsal fin. Swanny calls him John Coe. 'When I first saw him, I was reading a story about an African slave who was given his freedom in the Bahamas. He became a turtle fisherman, a free spirit roaming the Gulf of Mexico. His name was John Coe and it seemed just right for a wild orca.'

We anchored for the night in Loch Eatharna, in sight of Arinagour, Coll's only village, but were away again before mid-morning. Shearwaters boomeranged past us, drawing sweet curves over the waves as we put on all sail in the force-five wind and flew between the blue hills of the sea, heading for the Treshnish Isles. On Lunga, largest of the Treshnish group, we lay among soft clumps of sea pinks, practically rubbing noses with the thousands of puffins that nest in burrows on the clifftops.

Next morning we motored north past the island of Eigg, its green slopes crowned by a mighty dorsal fin of rock called the Sgurr, and anchored in Loch Scresort on the island of Rum. Here there are midges by the million. Sometimes they are so bad, one islander told me, that he regularly woke himself up at night in order to dig his garden in the small hours, when they were less bothersome. 'Aye,' he sighed with an air of resignation, 'kill a midge and a million will come to its funeral.' But the island also has a colony of Manx shearwaters, 100,000 strong, that come ashore during the brief Hebridean summer nights to their mountaintop burrows on the slopes of Hallival, filling the sky with unearthly moaning cries.

From Rum we sailed over the sea to Skye, to Loch Scavaig at the foot of the Cuillin Hills. The pilot book calls Scavaig the most dramatic anchorage in Europe and I would not disagree. It was as if we had come to rest in the drowned nave of an immense and roofless cathedral whose broken walls echoed to the constant hiss of falling water. Above us, the Cuillins crowded in, as dark as treachery, with snow still lying in the highest corries and cloud trailing across their jagged ridges.

We left the haunted hills of Skye on what Scots call a 'dreich' day, but the fine rain served only to intensify the beauty of a world painted in a hundred shades of grey. Oystercatchers piped us on our way and Atlantic seals with Roman noses and mottled salt-and-pepper coats stared at us with soft brown eyes from rocks polished smooth by the last ice age. There was no wind. All morning we motored on through an oily calm until we came once more to the area Swanny calls Cetacean City, so frequent are the whale sightings. Sure enough, the familiar cry rang out again. 'Minke whale!' And there they were, mother and calf, surfacing at regular four-minute intervals as they fed unhurriedly no more than 30m from the boat.

The minke may be the smallest of the great whales but it still grows to a length of 9m and a weight of 7 tonnes. Watching these slow, harmless creatures, I reflected that these were the same species the Japanese and Norwegian whale butchers would love to get their flensing hooks into.

For a week I had followed the whale's path, living beyond reach of telephone, in a world without TV or traffic fumes, among lonely islands inhabited by otters, deer and eagles. Now the voyage was over I could not bear the thought of leaving. How I would miss the evenings of wine and poetry, jokes and banter that bound everyone aboard into a close-knit fellowship of the sea. For a week the *Marguerite Explorer*'s snug saloon had been the centre of my world, a haven of warmth and comfort filled by delicious smells from the galley, where Pauline Yeld, alias 'Powerful', the talented ship's cook, rustled up miraculous feasts of salmon and venison. In the visitors' book, someone had written: 'I hope the boat breaks down before we reach Oban.' I knew exactly how they felt.

MEXICO – GREY WHALES OF THE BAJA

We left the mother-ship anchored far out in the middle of the lagoon. Now, alone in our flimsy aluminium skiff, we drifted with the current in a silent world of sea and sky towards the spot where the whale was feeding.

Its movements were slow and leisurely. Every so often it would raise a massive pectoral flipper and roll on its side to shovel its blunt snout into the shallow seabed, scooping up giant mouthfuls of mud, which it then expelled through the baleen plates in its jaws. These bony fringes combed the mud, trapping the assorted titbits – small crabs, shrimp, anchovies and eel-grass – that sustained its 28-tonne bulk through the Mexican winter.

Suddenly, while still more than a boat's length away, it turned and began to swim unhurriedly towards us. At once the skiff driver eased back the throttle until the outboard motor was barely idling. Huddled in our Mae West jackets, we held our breath and watched in disbelief as the whale slid directly beneath our stern. It was so close that I could count the barnacles on its mottled back. One flip of its 3m-wide tail would have sent us spinning to kingdom come, but it glided serenely on its way, leaving us whooping and gasping at the closeness of our encounter. Afterwards, we measured the depth with an oar and calculated that the whale had passed beneath us in less than 2.5m of water.

The grey whales of Baja California belong to another age. Theirs is a weightless world of tides and currents, awash with sounds and sonic visions we can never know. Only occasionally, as when their myopic 10cm eyes perceive our distorted images through the waves, do their lives and ours collide. Their evolution was completed aeons ago. Long before mankind first walked the earth, the grey whales were roaming the Arctic and Pacific seaways, fearing nothing except the orca and the great white shark. That is, until the coming of the whale-hunters.

It was in the middle of the 19th century that, sailing down the west coast of Baja California, a masthead lookout on board a whaling ship spotted what appeared to be the spouts of whales rising from the desert. What Charles Melville Scammon and his crew had stumbled on was a vast lagoon hidden from the sea by rolling dunes, its entrance obscured by foaming surf – the secret breeding ground of the grey whales.

Within a few years, most of the whales had been massacred. Scammon's Lagoon was abandoned as a breeding site, and Scammon himself must have looked into his soul and wondered what he had done. 'The mammoth bones of the California Grey lie bleaching on the shores of those silvery waters, and are scattered along the broken coasts, from Siberia to the Gulf of California,' he wrote in 1875; 'and ere long it may be questioned whether this mammal will not be numbered among the extinct species of the Pacific.'

Yet somehow the species survived. By the 1970s the world was running against the endless slaughter of the great whales, and in 1972 the hunting of the greys was banned by the US Marine Mammals Protection Act. That same year Mexico made Scammon's Lagoon (now also called Laguna Ojo de Liebre) the world's first whale sanctuary, and in 1988 the Mexican government extended its protection to the nearby Laguna San Ignacio by including it in a huge, all-embracing national park, the Biósfera El Vizcaíno, containing the best of the Baja's pristine coast.

Ironically, after so many decades of slaughter, these splendid animals are now worth far more alive than dead. The reason is whale-watching, an American craze that has become an industry with a turnover exceeding US$100 million. Protection for the grey whale has brought about a dramatic recovery. With a population now nudging 20,000, their presence every winter off the Pacific coast has become the basis of a Californian tourist gold-rush attracting 250,000 visitors a year.

The whales' migratory route takes them along the American Pacific seaboard, from the Baja to the Bering Sea and back – a 17,700km round trip, the longest migration of any living mammal. They remain in the north for several months, feeding and fattening in the high Arctic summer. Only when the days grow shorter and the pack ice crackles in the shivering bays do the whales begin their homeward journey back to the breeding lagoons of the Baja, where they begin to gather at the end of January.

The capital of America's West Coast whale-watching fraternity is San Diego, the Californian seaport city best placed for cruises down Mexico way. It was there in the winter of 1990 that I joined *Searcher*, a 30m luxury sport-fishing craft that makes regular trips to the grey whale sanctuary of San Ignacio, some 800km to the south.

My fellow passengers were the kind of mixed bunch that you could meet only in America. Among them were two psychiatrists, a poet, a neurosurgeon, a Mississippi river-boat pilot, and Vera, aged 82 from Texas. Vera was one of those indomitable American ladies you find in the most outlandish places. Small, silver-haired and utterly fearless, she had watched tigers in Nepal and gorillas in Rwanda. Now she had come to see the whales of San Ignacio 'before the old rocking chair gets me'.

John Kipling, *Searcher*'s resident naturalist, was a veteran of 40 previous expeditions to the Baja and a self-confessed whale-freak. 'I sometimes feel I have a debt to them,' he said. 'Despite everything mankind has done to them, they are so trusting that nursing mothers will bring their calves to see the boats.' Kipling was down in the Baja when the whale-watching phenomenon began, back in 1976. 'There was this young male whale, maybe three years old. Somebody called him George. He was definitely curious. We jumped in a skiff and got close enough to touch him. It was such a strange feeling. He was so surprisingly warm and soft and rubbery. That night, two more whales came visiting. It was as if the word had got around.'

The voyage south was broken by visits to a succession of desert islands. On Todos Santos, harbour seals with liquid eyes watched us land on a beach of shells the size of fists. The air smelled of kelp, guano and California sagebrush. Cormorants perched on dizzy stacks above the Pacific swell, and everywhere, colonies of western gulls, looking like our own British lesser black-backs, were pairing off for the coming breeding season.

On San Benitos the ospreys were already sitting tight on clifftop nests the size of armchairs, and century plants bloomed yellow on the hillsides. Just once in their long lives these tall succulents produce a triumphant crown of golden flowers, and then they die – but not before providing a feast of nectar for ravens and hummingbirds. In winter San Benitos is home to thousands of elephant seals. The adult males arrive in December, and soon every pebbly cove has its yowling, honking colony of mothers, calves and bachelor bulls, ruled by a dominant bull or beachmaster – 2 tonnes of ponderous muscle and blubber culminating in an extraordinary proboscis. With necks raised and heads flung back, the rival bulls face each other like sumo wrestlers, their cavernous threats echoing above the booming rollers.

Already, on our way, we had spotted the far-off plumes of spouting whales. Like us, many were heading for Laguna San Ignacio, winter home to some 300 grey whales. The entrance is a sailor's nightmare of pounding surf and treacherous shoals, but once inside, its waters flatten and spread out, spilling inland for 25km towards the sombre volcanic peaks of the Santa Clara mountains.

The lagoon is a magical place of tidal channels, shining sandbanks, mudflats and mangrove creeks, an oasis of marine life in the midst of the Mexican desert. Here live not only the grey whales but also dolphins and sea lions, pelicans, ospreys and a host of shorebirds. Jaegers and peregrines patrol the skies, and coyotes roam the desert shores. We anchored in midstream as Ed 'Mitch' Mitchell prepared supper. Apart from Kipling and Art Taylor, *Searcher*'s owner-skipper, Mitch was the most important crew member. From his spotless galley emerged mountains of good all-American food: steaks and salads, ice-cream and blueberry pie, and enormous breakfasts with hash browns and muffins and eggs over-easy.

The breeze died, the tide slackened, the lagoon became a burnished mirror. But out in the surf where the sun was setting, a 15m whale breached six times in succession, flinging its huge body halfway clear of the water and then falling back in a crash of spray. And as we watched, we could hear the luxurious sighs of other whales as they surfaced, and could see their white spouts rising and falling in the windless air. Sometimes they would raise their tail flukes when they submerged – signalling a deep dive – after which they might stay down for several minutes. At other times they surfaced with a lazy rolling surge, exposing their black, knuckled backs as they slid under again. Then, from the depths would arise a string of smooth whirlpools – the whale's 'footprints' – each upwelling representing a single flap of the broad tail.

Next morning I went beachcombing along the edge of the lagoon. The desert air was cold and clean, but the sun was shining and I walked for miles, barefoot in the creaming tide, putting up flocks of plovers and sanderlings along the water's edge. An osprey flew overhead, clutching a fish in its talons, and a solitary coyote trotted away into the sandhills. On that lonely shore, among the empty shells and smooth driftwood, the soft mats of dried eel-grass and the bleached bones of long-dead whales, his and mine were the only footprints.

Back on board there was much jubilation. One of the six-man skiffs had gone out with Greg, a laid-back Californian crewman, and had actually managed to touch a whale. They were ecstatic. Even the laconic Greg was grinning under his sombrero. 'I told everybody to be calm and have positive thoughts and the whale would let us get real close,' said Greg, 'and he did.'

At dusk the moon rose ripe and orange over the Vizcaíno desert. It was the time of the spring tides, and the water ran past our bows like a river, pulling the anchor chain until it was as taut as an iron bar. The whales had been late arriving this year. The winter had been milder and they had stayed longer in the Bering Sea, but now more were coming in with every tide.

For three days we stayed in that enchanted anchorage, and all the time the whales grew increasingly more tolerant, regularly allowing us within a skiff's length. When they spouted, a fine spray drifted over us, misting the lenses of my binoculars. When they 'spy-hopped', standing on their tails with their barnacled heads raised clear of the water as if to get a better look at us, it was impossible not to feel one's senses reaching out to them.

Who, watching those strange, monolithic snouts rising so trust-ingly into the air, could fail to be moved profoundly, knowing how cruelly we have persecuted these huge, innocent creatures down the centuries? The voyage, begun in a spirit of adventure and curiosity, had ended as a kind of pilgrimage. Like penitents seeking absolu-tion from the sins of our fathers, we had sought and found forgive-ness among the leviathans of San Ignacio.

DISTANT
HORIZONS

INDIA – THE TIGERS OF KANHA

Dawn in the Deccan. Dew dripping off the leaves of the sal trees and a mist hanging over the wild meadows of Kanha. Later, the day will fill with drowsy golden warmth, but in January these Indian winter mornings are always cold.

The meadows are alive with ghostly drifting shapes. Chital – the beautiful spotted deer of India – are moving through the mist, their velvet antlers backlit by the rising sun. Doves are cooing in the trees. The deer are feeding. It is hard to imagine a more peaceful scene. Then a peacock begins to yowl at the edge of the forest. Suddenly, tension crackles. The chital are nervous. Heads up, they shrill their unease – and from somewhere deep in the forest booms a cavernous roar. The Kanha Meadows tiger is on the prowl.

Kanha is probably the finest place in the world to watch wild tigers. This national park the size of Surrey is set in the heart of Mother India, in the hills of Madhya Pradesh between Nagpur and Jabalpur. The Sunderbans – those sinister Bengal delta-lands, with their mangroves and man-eaters, may hold more tigers – and the tigers of Ranthambhor in Rajasthan may be less camera-shy, but Kanha is wild India as it used to be, the land of Kipling's *Jungle Book* and the home of Shere Khan, Kipling's tiger. Kipling never set foot in Kanha, but his imagination was fired by tales of the local forest officers. Today, if you want to look for the descendants of Shere Khan, you set out in the old way as befits the lord of the jungle, 3m above the ground on the back of an elephant.

Kanha has always been good tiger country. The British Raj bagged it as its own exclusive hunting ground until 1933, when 249sq km of the Banjar valley were set aside as a wildlife sanctuary, but it was not until 1955 that Kanha's future was assured. Ironically the catalyst was a trigger-happy sportsman who was given permission to shoot 30 tigers. The massacre caused such an outcry that Kanha was made a national park. By this time the tiger was in retreat throughout India. At the turn of the last century about 40,000 tigers roamed the Indian subcontinent; by 1972 fewer than 2,000 survived. Today, thanks to the various efforts of India's Project Tiger and worldwide publicity of the big cats' plight, Kanha remains one of their major strongholds.

In Kanha I stayed, appropriately, at Kipling Camp, only a tiger's roar from the edge of the park. The year was 1988 and the camp was run by Bob Wright, a retired British Army major, and Belinda, his daughter, who was also a distinguished wildlife film-maker. Accommodation was fairly basic: a dozen bungalows, beamed and barn-like, with lime-washed mud walls and ceilings of thin crooked sticks under bare tiles. The beds were traditional rope-netted charpoys overlaid with cotton mattresses, sheets and duvets, and at night chital grazed outside the windows. The year before my stay, one was killed by a tiger only 3m from the room in which I slept. In the airy communal dining room, excellent food (steaks, curries, pancakes cooked in rum and orange) was rustled up with consumate skill by Nabi, a nut-brown Jeeves who was also the camp factotum, assisted by a trio of jolly English girls.

It was still dark at 5.30 when Nabi brought my early morning tea and a bucket of hot water for washing. Then it was on with three sweaters and out into the bone-clenching chill in the back of an open Land-Rover for game-viewing and a picnic breakfast. Every morning we looked for the fresh pug marks that blossomed overnight along the roads where dust lay thick as pollen, but although twice I heard the resounding 'aaounnh' of a lovelorn tiger, the big cats stayed frustratingly out of sight. It seemed that my only chance of seeing a tiger would be from the back of an elephant. Fortunately, I found myself perched behind the best tiger-tracker in India.

Sabir, a thin man in his early thirties, had been working with elephants for most of his life. A mahout like his father before him, he came to Kanha in 1975, bringing with him his lordly tusker, Shivaji. Now Shivaji was in his prime. He was the pride of the park and, despite his size, the gentlest of juggernauts. If, while riding through the forest, a branch should knock your hat off, Shivaji would, with impeccable manners, retrieve it with the tip of his trunk and courteously hand it back to you.

Shivaji had been afraid of tigers until Sabir trained him to overcome his fear. Now the pair were inseparable. It was an extraordinary partnership – the 60kg mahout and his devoted 4-tonne companion. Together they had taken out all kinds of VIPs, including the

Duke of Edinburgh. Now here I was, seated on the duke's elephant, waiting for an introduction to the lord of the jungle. If anyone could find me a tiger it was Sabir and Shivaji.

We set off at a steady pace, lurching and swaying through the yellow light of mid-afternoon. Heat lapped around us, the leaves hung limp, but once inside the sal forest all was shade and coolness. Swinging his trunk and sawn-off tusks, Shivaji bulldozed a path through the towering bamboos and we broke out again briefly into bright sunlight, where monsoon rains had carved a deep stony nullah. Now its bed was choked with tall grass whose tasselled tops brushed my legs – perfect tiger country.

Shivaji surged on, sloshing belly-deep down a long pool, and then came to a halt at Sabir's quiet command. Perched cross-legged on his elephant's neck, Sabir leaned down and pointed with his stick. There in the mud were the fresh paw marks of a large tiger. I hoped they belonged to Lungri, the huge male that Sabir had been following for the past nine years and whose photograph adorned the bar at Kipling Camp. His name meant 'the Lame One', recalling a time when he was involved in a fight with another tiger and suffered an injury that caused him to limp for several months afterwards.

The tracks led up a narrow gully and we followed, threading between the dense bamboos whose overhanging leaves rustled past us and all around us. Here, whispered Sabir, the tiger had sat down briefly before moving off again up the hillside. We were getting closer. Somewhere ahead the high-pitched alarm call of a chital broke the silence. We stopped and listened. Again it called, and again, more urgently. 'Tiger near,' hissed Sabir, and urged Shivaji forward, drumming with his bare heels on the giant grey head.

And suddenly there was the tiger: the ultimate carnivore, 200kg of molten copper moving like flame between the bamboos. It was not Lungri, but he was still a magnificent animal, 3m long and a true descendant of Shere Khan. He stared at us with stunning indifference and continued to pad unhurriedly up the hill while we followed as best we could, smashing through the bamboo in showers of falling twigs and leaves, gripped with a wild exhilaration at being so close.

We kept him in sight for maybe 15 minutes. Then he eluded us. He didn't give us the slip; he just vanished, melting into the jungle as if the ground had swallowed him up. It was a superb demonstration – both of Sabir's abilities as a tracker and of the elusive nature of the king of cats.

Compared to the teeming African plains, India is another world, a different experience. It cannot compete with the sheer abundance of game to be found in parks like the Serengeti. Kanha, it is true, is full of animals: elegant blackbuck and barasingha, leopards, sloth bears, wild boar, hunting dogs, grey langur monkeys and many more. But they are shy and elusive, and the cover is so thick that you could drive past a tiger lying a few metres off the track and never know it was there.

Yet even without any animals the park is a joy to explore, with its wide-spreading banyan trees, its tall grass meadows and deep ravines. I loved our early morning picnic drives, the jackals keening in the cold and the air filled with fresh jungle smells. Once we surprised a leopard slipping soundlessly back to its lair in a tumble of rocks. But the tiger is always the main prize, and its powerful presence is everywhere.

There are times when Kanha looks and feels a bit like Windsor Great Park, with its groves and glades and grazing deer. Outwardly it is all so peaceful and benign – the cooing doves, the parkland trees pressing their cool shadows on the grass. But Kanha's tranquillity is an illusion, a cruel mask behind which lurks the age-old spectre of the tiger.

Down in the nullahs, in the lank grass where the great cats have trodden narrow tunnels, we came across a charnel house of bones and the half-eaten leg of a barasingha hind. This was the haunt of the Kanha Meadows tigress. And once again it was the tell-tale sounds of the jungle that betrayed her. From 200m away we heard the sharp 'ka-ko-ka' of the langur monkeys and in this way we found her, sleek, regal and incredibly beautiful.

For the next half-hour we followed her. Sometimes we could see only her distinctive black and white ears. At other times she was merely a movement of waving grass-heads. Once, she allowed us to come within 4m of her. With my legs dangling over the edge of the elephant's howdah, it was interesting to speculate what might have happened had she taken a sudden dislike to us, but I need not have worried. She simply rose to her feet and padded on, then bounded effortlessly across a stream and disappeared into the forest on the other side. And I knew then what I knew even before I went to Kanha: that I would not have traded that vision of a tiger for all the Taj Mahals in India.

AUSTRALIA – KAKADU DREAMTIME

Out on the Kakadu floodplains, where the noonday temperature never falls below 30°C, a dingo stands over a dead wallaby. Flocks of birds – kites, magpie geese, lumbering jabiru storks – wheel over the billabongs and paperbark swamps. When the monsoon comes in November, all this low country will be underwater until the knock-'em-down storms of April signal the end of the wet season. At the moment the plains are dry and the mud has cracks a metre deep.

Few people outside Australia had heard of Kakadu National Park before *Crocodile Dundee* was filmed there. But ever since the actor Paul Hogan came striding out of this spectacular wilderness with his hat-band full of crocodile teeth, the place has been overrun with visitors. In 1985 it welcomed 100,000 tourists. Three years later the figure had more than doubled, and even in Darwin, almost 200km away, the crocodile is now firmly embedded in the local culture. Smart city hotels invite their guests to 'crocktail hours' and local eateries advertise everything from 'croc-burgers' to 'croc schnitzel'. In Kakadu itself there are even plans to build a new motel in the shape of a monster croc, with its main entrance framed by a set of gently smiling jaws. And while no one is actually offering *Crocodile Dundee* tours of the park, the local guides have become every bit as laconic as 'Hoges' himself. They delight in pointing out where Mick Dundee stood on Ubirr (Obiri Rock) or where he put the evil eye on the buffalo.

The result is that tourism is booming in the Northern Territory as never before. That may be good news in Darwin, the territory's capital, but in Kakadu itself it has become a big headache for the park authorities and a cause of disquiet among the 290 Aboriginal people whose land this is, and for whom its sun-scorched emptiness has a spiritual importance beyond Western understanding.

If the Australian Outback has a heart then it is surely here in Kakadu, in the Top End of Down Under, between the Wildman

River and Arnhem Land escarpments, among the fathomless forests of ghost gums and pandanus palms, the glittering bill-abongs, lotus lilies, goose marshes and great sandstone cliffs that glow furnace-red in the setting sun. Every day the visitors pour in from Darwin by air-conditioned coach, protected from the stunning heat and the ever-present flies. In a couple of days at Kakadu you can visit the dramatic gorge at Jim Jim Falls, admire the Aboriginal rock paintings at Nourlangie and drift by flat-bottomed boat between fleets of water-lilies, where crocodiles lurk beneath the surface. Brumbies – descendants of the horses brought here in the 1920s by Yorky Bill, the buffalo hunter – graze on the shimmering plains.

You can even go on a walkabout safari and learn how the Aborigines live off the land, spearing mud-crabs, netting barramundi and cooking them in paperbark parcels on a bed of hot stones. But at the end of it you realize you have barely scratched the surface of this immense and mysterious country.

Kakadu National Park is bigger than Israel. It is 20,000sq km of wallabies and bandicoots, giant saltwater crocodiles, frilled lizards, king brown snakes, pelicans, kookaburras and noisy gangs of cockatoos. It is also the repository of the finest Aboriginal rock-art sites on the continent. The galleries at Nourlangie and Obiri Rock – some are almost 100m long – rival anything the prehistoric caves of Lascaux can offer, with paintings dating back 20,000 years. Here, picked out in red oxide and white pipe clay, are vivid images of spirits, hunters and the wild creatures that still inhabit Kakadu's timeless landscapes. So precious are they that in 1981 a third of the park was declared a World Heritage Site by Unesco, putting it in the same league as the Pyramids and the Grand Canyon.

With Terry Reece, one of Kakadu's tourist guides, I paused in the shade of an overhanging cliff covered in paintings of birds and fish and weird, stick-thin warriors – the 'mini-spirits' so revered by the Aborigines. 'Whenever I come to Nourlangie it rings primal bells,' said Reece. 'It's one of the cathedrals of the first Australians.'

And it's true. Wandering among these huge stone canvasses it is impossible not to sense their strange power. Cliffs and canyons they may be, wild and open to the sky, but Obiri and Nourlangie are no less sacred than Canterbury or Rheims.

For the Gagadju elders, Kakadu's traditional owners, this is still the land of the Dreamtime, where the Ancestral Beings in animal and human forms rose from the earth to create the world. When their work was done they returned to their birthplaces: rivers, bill-abongs, rocks and caves that remain sacred to this day. That is why the land means so much to Australia's Aborigines. They remain tied to it by the spirits of their ancestors, a bond that not even death can break. The belief is that when they die they return to the 'dream-ings', and re-enter the sites from which their spirits originally sprang. To use an Aboriginal expression, they 'go back in'.

Given the nature of this hallowed ground and its universal recog-nition, it might be assumed that Kakadu would be protected for ever. But all the time, waiting under the ground like the fearsome Rainbow Serpent of Aboriginal mythology, lie powerful forces that could cause untold damage to the park's fragile Dreamtime land-scapes and make a mockery of its World Heritage status. For Kakadu, the world's biggest national park, is sitting on the world's richest uranium deposits. The uranium was discovered in 1969 – thousands upon thousands of tonnes of it. And not only uranium, but also gold and platinum, enough to wipe out Australia's nation-al debt overnight.

The discovery of so much wealth should have been a cause for national jubilation. Instead, it has presented Australians with an agonizing dilemma: are they morally justified in mining a national park of worldwide importance for economic gain? It is a question that divides Australia into two camps – the dreamers and the prag-matists – with the powerful mining lobby set against the country's growing ranks of 'greenies'. And it has still not been resolved.

Conservationists argue that the park's integrity has been com-promised, its wildlife threatened by the spectre of pollution and its future jeopardized by fears of further mining within the precious wetlands. But so far, the Ranger Mine at Jabiru has caused no seri-ous pollution problems, and has literally paved the way for a bitu-minous road from Darwin – something for which Kakadu's visitors should be eternally grateful.

As for Kakadu's Aboriginal owners, most take a fairly relaxed view about the miners and the tourist hordes. 'They're okay so long as we can live our traditional lives in peace,' said Mick Alderson of the local Morrenbor clan. Alderson is that rare bird, an Aboriginal tour operator who shows visitors around his ancestral lands, the wild goose marshes of the Bamurru Djadjam. In his father's day, he told me, his people were paid with flour and sugar. Now, royalties from uranium mining and tourist dollars have given them a new sense of power, pride and security.

Nevertheless, more visitors mean new roads, more lodges, cabins, campgrounds and litter, leading to fears that parts of Kakadu could become little more than camping slums. 'There's no doubt that we need tourism,' said Dan Gillespie, assistant director of Australia's National Parks and Wildlife Service in Darwin. 'But it has really stretched our resources. One of these days we're going to have to look down the barrel at it and see how we can limit potential damage to sensitive sites.'

There is no doubt that the *Crocodile Dundee* bandwagon has speeded up the process of change in Kakadu. The first time Paul Hogan went there it cost him nothing to shoot the film. But when he went back to film *Crocodile Dundee II*, the park's traditional landowners put the bite on 'Hoges' and demanded a $200,000 location fee. And if the film's producers didn't like it, said Big Bill Neitje, the senior traditional owner, 'they could roll their swags'.

Now even the crocodiles are biting back – so much so that the 'saltie' of the northern coasts and rivers has replaced the shark as public enemy number one in Australian mythology. And with good reason. Growing up to 5m long and armed with jaws capable of exerting a pressure of 3,500kg to the square centimetre, a full-grown saltie is an awesome creature.

Humans are easy meat for these ancient predators. 'To them it's just like picking a bloody apple off a tree,' said my guide on a croc-watching cruise on the Yellow Waters billabong. Even as he spoke, a corrugated snout broke the surface, as sinister as a U-boat, regarded us with an unblinking, gold-flecked eye, then sank without a ripple. 'They move fast, too,' said the guide. 'The safest way to watch crocs on land is to take a mate who can't run as fast as you.'

In the old days, when a 3m crocodile skin was worth US$1,000, the salties were wary. 'One false move and they'd be off like a bride's nightie,' says Tom Winter, a former hunter and Mick Dundee lookalike who was now running tourist safaris into Kakadu and neighbouring Arnhem Land. 'Now they are protected and they've lost their fear of man.'

Yet despite the warnings posted throughout the park, people still get killed. At Cahill's Crossing on the East Alligator River they will tell you about the local man taken by a 4.5m saltie while trying to wade across the causeway. No wonder an organization called SCRAM (Saltwater Crocodile Removal Action Movement) had sprung up in Darwin to campaign for a return to shooting.

But for now the big crocs still cruise among the lily-pads. The paintings still glow in the caves of Nourlangie and the people of the Gagadju remain hunter-gatherers like their fathers, even if nowadays they own rifles and Toyota Land Cruisers. For them, Kakadu is still a land of plenty, filled with all kinds of 'bush tucker', from honey ants to billy goat plums. Everything in its place, just as it was in Australia's age of innocence when the Dreamtime Ancestors sang the world into being.

MOROCCO – THE LAND WHERE SPRING IS BORN

For sun-starved Europeans, Morocco is the land where spring is born. South of the Atlas Mountains it comes as early as January, when the first warm breath from the Sahara coaxes the almond orchards into flower. By March, temperatures exceed 20°C and the season is in full flood, flowing north with the migrating swallows as they pour across the Strait of Gibraltar.

No wonder southern Morocco is becoming a chic destination, both for winter-sunshine seekers and the film industry. Yet it was not so long ago that Ouarzazate – the Crossroads of the Desert – was a French Foreign Legion outpost guarding the caravan routes that once brought slaves and gold across the Sahara to Marrakech. Even in the early 1970s there were only two hotels in Ouarzazate. Now there are at least 15, including the swanky Le Berbere Palace, and the town has become North Africa's Hollywood, with an average of five films a year played out against a desert backdrop of stony steppes and coppery mountains.

It was from Ouarzazate that I set out into what, until half a century ago, was still known as the Bled es Siba – the Lawless Land. With Said, my English-speaking guide, we drove south, heading for Zagora across treeless plains still flushed with green despite three months of drought. Once in a while we would pass distant flocks of sheep backlit by the sun, and solitary shepherds, cowled like monks in long woollen djellabas, and then nothing but mountains, remote and mysterious, leached of all substance by the hot desert air.

We stopped briefly at Agdz, a town short on vowels but offering a good line in mint tea, before entering the Drâa valley. Fed by the snows of the High Atlas, the Drâa is Morocco's longest river but seldom runs its full course to the Atlantic. Most years, Said told me, it falters and dies in the desert somewhere beyond Tamegroute. But in the 124km between Agdz and Zagora it forms a linear oasis of date palms watched over by brooding kasbahs with ochre walls and towers. Built improbably of *pisé* – mud stiffened with palm fibre – these sun-dried citadels of clay rank among the great glories of North Africa.

Along the roadsides, children held up baskets of dates, and although it was still only mid-March, the barley stood knee-high in the palmeries, shot through with scarlet poppies. To wander through these oases is to experience an Arab dream of heaven on earth. On all sides the cloistered palms close in, like the pillars of a mosque, creating green aisles of light and shade in which the only sounds are of bees and birdsong and trickling water.

In Zagora we passed a sign that said 'Timbuktu – 52 days by camel'. This dusty little town was once a port of the desert, the last chance to stock up before hitting the Sahara. Eating here was not expensive. At the modest little Hotel La Fibule a pool-side lunch (salad, a tagine of lamb and prunes, followed by oranges dusted with cinnamon) cost less than £6.

The late King Hassan II of Morocco once likened his country to a tree with its roots deep down in Africa and its leaves reaching up into the heady air of Europe. But south of the Atlas there is no doubting which continent you are in. The barren landscapes are an exact reprint of Namibia, and as we drove back to Ouarzazate with the evening light falling across immense vistas of empty steppe and shadowy mountains, I felt the freedom that always comes with Africa's boundless horizons.

Yet the magic of Morocco goes much deeper. This is a country still lost in a reverie of the Middle Ages, where old and new live side by side: medieval kasbahs sporting satellite dishes; a man dressed in a traditional djellaba and state-of-the-art Raybans, riding on a donkey; whole villages still lit by candles and oil lamps. It is as if you could drive out of present-day London and find people living in Warwickshire just as they did in Shakespeare's time.

At Skoura, in the Dadès valley, I strolled across a dried-up riverbed to visit the Kasbah of Ameridhl, a desert Chatsworth built of mud and featured on every 50-dirham Moroccan banknote. Inside was a *riad*, or courtyard, with a well and a fig tree, in whose shade I was invited to wash my hands and remove my shoes and sit on a rug, to drink mint tea and eat bread dipped in olive oil. This was, of course, something put on for tourists, but conducted with such innate courtesy and warmth that it made the whole place come alive.

The road to Tinerhir through the Dadès valley – the so-called 'Valley of 1,000 Kasbahs' – has to be one of the great drives of the world. To the north you can see the snows of the High Atlas. To the south loom the unforgiving ranges of the Jebel Sahro, where it took the full military might of France to defeat 1,000 warriors of the Ait 'Atta tribe in the 1930s. And in between is an endless procession of feathery date palms and red ramparts, in which even the rose-water factory at El Kelaâ-des Mgouna is disguised as a kasbah.

West of Ouarzazate the semi-desert and cindery mountains give way to austere valleys sown with saffron, and as we drew closer to Taroudannt we entered a more fertile countryside. With its orchards and olive groves it might have been somewhere in Extremadura had it not been for the extraordinary spectacle of Morocco's tree-climbing goats, tempted aloft by the yellow fruit of the argan trees, which grow nowhere else except here and in Mexico.

The Gazelle d'Or Hotel, where I spent my first day in Taroudannt, is for the seriously rich and is possibly the most expensive tourist oasis in North Africa. But a night here followed by an alfresco breakfast on the veranda of your private cottage (pancakes soaked in honey, oranges fresh from the gardens) is one of the 10 best things you can do in Morocco. If you can't afford the Gazelle d'Or, it is certainly worth splashing out on the Palais Salam, a four-star hotel built seamlessly into Taroudannt's 16th-century city walls. Here I lived like a sultan in a tiled suite, with my own private rooftop balcony, where I lay on a sunbed until the evening sky filled with circling storks and the summons to prayer echoed across the flat roofs of the medina.

Later, eating under the stars, I heard for the first time the searing voices of the Gnaoua, a musical sect whose trance-inducing rhythms, beaten out with iron castanets and a long-necked lute, are famous throughout Morocco. Their dress is Arab-style, with long white djellabas, but their black faces and chanting voices belong to forgotten homelands beyond the Sahara, from where their ancestors came in chains in the long ago. Led by a gnomish, capering man in a red cloak and tasselled cap, they sang and danced with unrestrained joy, weaving a spell of Africa out of the soft desert air.

Within the walls of Taroudannt lies the mother of all street markets, a warren of souks selling everything from fruit and spices to water jugs fashioned out of car tyres. A guide is essential, if only to help you to find the Antiquaire Haut Atlas at 36 Souk Smara, with its hoard of Berber silver, and the Ali Baba carpet shop, whose customers range from President Chirac to the Rolling Stones.

At Taroudannt we turned north towards Marrakech, zigzagging into the High Atlas over the Tizi n' Test Pass, a tarmac tightrope suspended midway between the sky and the yawning void 2,000m below. On the way down we passed the mud houses of the Berber mountain tribes, clinging like swallows' nests to the crags. Three hours after leaving Taroudannt I was checking in at the Résidence de la Roseraie, an idyllic haven in the Val d'Ouirgane, 1,000m above the heat of Marrakech.

La Roseraie is the mountain equivalent of a desert oasis. It is surrounded by 25ha of terraced fields and orchards, and in springtime, when the nightingales are singing and the air is heavy with the scent of roses, its gardens are among the loveliest in the world. Near by there are mountain cascades and Berber villages to explore, but it is hard to tear yourself away. Instead, I sat by the pool under a flowering quince listening to a cuckoo calling across the valley and wished I could have stayed for a week.

And so to Marrakech, the Red City, still encircled by its 12th-century ramparts, and the art-deco elegance of La Mamounia Hotel, where Winston Churchill came to paint. He stayed in room 300 – now the Churchill Suite – at the end of a corridor hung with black and white photos of the old man with his Homburg hat and his big cigar. Outside, the beautiful people were lazing on sunbeds around a pool, while a jazz band played under the palms, like a scene from *The Great Gatsby*. But the heart and soul of Marrakech is out in the souks of the old medina, and above all in the great square of the Djemaa el Fna, the Place of the Dead.

Sunset is the time to be here, drinking mint tea on the terrace of a rooftop café while the sun behind the Koutoubia Minaret turns as red as a Berber rug. As the crowd gathers in the square below, pigeons wheel overhead and smoke rises from scores of food stalls. Here, for about £3 per head, you can sit on plain wooden benches and rub shoulders with the Marrakechis as they tuck into lamb brochettes, spicy merguez sausages, calves' feet and tagines of chicken served up with couscous, chickpeas or bread and olives.

But the main attraction for this seething ant-heap of humanity is the street entertainers – the acrobats and fire-eaters, scribes and soothsayers, storytellers, snake-charmers, water-sellers, musicians, hawkers and hustlers to be found here every night of the year. Backpackers and tourist coach parties mingle with Berber tribesmen and over everything hangs the smells of dust and spices and sizzling meat, the reed wailing of the snake-charmers' pipes and the steady clip-clop of horse-drawn calèches. It is pure street theatre – a perfect Moroccan grand finale – and it costs no more than a pocketful of change.

BRAZIL – THE PANTANAL

Early morning dew on the grass, and groves of acuri palms casting long shadows. The big horizons remind me of Africa, but the sounds are unfamiliar. That ringing 'aaark' is the cry of a toucan with a beak like a traffic cone. Those raucous voices belong to a pair of hyacinth macaws – an endangered species with yellow-rimmed, coat-button eyes, whose strongold is the Pantanal.

The Pantanal is the world's biggest floodplain. You could fit the whole of Britain into it and still have room to spare. It lies in the Brazilian outback, on the borders of Bolivia, and is so flat that its main river, the Paraguay, drops only 30cm in 1,300km. The result is dramatic. When the flood waters build up in the rainy season, the rivers are overwhelmed and the land goes under. Then the dry season returns and the floods recede, leaving behind a lush mosaic of swamplands, bayous and park-like savannahs. Throw in a couple of elephants and it could be Botswana's Okavango Delta. But the Pantanal has its own distinctive wildlife: plains alive with pampas deer; rivers heaving with piranhas; forests concealing all sorts of creatures, from collared peccaries (fierce wild pigs) to Brazilian tapirs.

For sheer numbers of animals, the Pantanal can never compete with Africa's big-game parks. Yet taken in the round, its teeming birdlife and half-submerged landscapes, lonely ranches and cloudless skies, combine to make the Pantanal unique. And it is possibly the only place on earth where you might – just might – meet a jaguar. Weighing in at anything up to 120kg, the elusive jaguar is Latin America's top predator, and the fact that it is widespread in the Pantanal makes for a spine-tingling buzz. It's a bit like visiting a haunted house – you can sense the jaguar's ghostly presence in every forest shadow.

Perhaps surprisingly, Brazil's big-cat country is also home to more than 3 million cattle. For 200 years the Pantanal has been a place where ranching and wildlife have gone hand in hand, and it's common to see enormous herds of white, humpbacked zebu cattle roaming the wild savannahs. They are watched over by the *pantaneiros*, Brazilian cowboys with Zapata moustaches and thousand-mile stares, who live on a diet of jerked beef and rice, and loll in their sheepskin-lined saddles as if they were born there.

Until 1990, the only visitors to the Pantanal were cattlemen. Now, times are changing. Eco-tourism has arrived, and the more switched-on *fazendas* (cattle ranches) have begun to cater for overseas visitors. The Refugio Ecológico Caiman is one such place, a 1920s *fazenda* with 26,000 cattle ranging over 53,000ha of plains and forests. This is where eco-tourism first took root, and today it has a main lodge, built in Spanish-colonial style, with 11 comfortable en suite rooms, as well as a couple of smaller, more exclusive lodges.

I arrive in time for a night safari in an open truck. Perched on a padded cowhide seat, I follow the spotlight as it picks out an anteater rooting around in the stockyards. Further on, we pass a creek filled with caymans – 2m-long, fish-eating alligators – whose eyes glow ruby-red in the light. The caimans are harmless, but then we find a more sinister denizen: a hairy spider that looks like a brown woolly glove, doing press-ups on a tree trunk.

Next morning I'm wide awake at first light. Forget jet lag: nobody sleeps late in the Pantanal, not with 650 different species of birds announcing their presence. The result is deafening. Noisiest is the chaco chachalaca, a weird kind of flying turkey that shouts its name from the treetops. But there are plenty of runners-up – raucous macaws, ibises with rusty, squealing voices, and the dull boom-boom of curassows.

This is a birdwatcher's heaven. There are snail-eating kites, bat-eating falcons and shockheaded kingfishers the size of chickens. Some species sound as if they belong to another planet. Can you believe the limpkin? The potoo? The striated caracara? The most striking of all is the jabiru (also known as the tuiuiu), a giant stork that is as tall as a man, with a pickaxe beak and a swollen black and crimson neck.

During the rains, temperatures soar to an unbelievable 45°C, bringing a million mosquitoes, eager to gorge themselves on gringo blood. But now it is the dry season, with zero humidity, few insects and the temperature down to a mere 35°C. Even so, by mid-morning I am grateful for the faintest breeze, the briefest patch of dappled shade, and find myself longing to cool off in the lodge pool.

After lunch comes siesta time, swaying in a hammock under the lodge's peach-coloured arches until the next activity: a three-hour horse ride, led by a brawny *pantaneiro* with a butcher's knife stuck in his waistband. Trucks and Land-Rovers are all very well, but it's only on horseback that you can really explore the Pantanal – as well as being quiet and eco-friendly, a horse allows you to wade rivers and cross swamps where a truck might sink up to its axles. Clip-clopping along at an easy pace, we soon leave the post-and-rail fences behind, and head out into the open savannah, where mustangs roam free under groves of purple-flowering piuva trees. By the time we return, it is almost evening, with a full moon rising and a giant anteater shuffling through the grass.

Come midweek, it's time to move on. The Refugio Ecológico Caiman gives a 'soft' experience of the Pantanal – civilized, organized and great for beginners – but now I want more of a challenge. A bumpy six-seater bush aeroplane takes me to the Fazenda Barra Mansa, on the banks of the Río Negro. It's a small ranch by Brazilian standards – a mere 1,200ha – but it lies in the roadless heart of the Pantanal. A visiting Italian summed up the difference between the two to perfection. 'At Caiman,' he said, 'they welcome you with a glass of fruit juice. At Barra Mansa, they meet you with a six-shooter.'

Guilherme Rondon, Barra Mansa's gun-toting owner, is a *pantaneiro* through and through. He is also one of Brazil's best-known country singers: his cattle are stamped with a guitar-shaped brand. His grandfather, who pioneered this land, once owned a chunk of Brazil bigger than many small countries, and the ranch house dates from that time. 'It took three years to build,' says Guilherme. 'Every brick came in by ox and cart.'

Like his grandfather, Guilherme is a pioneer, but his field is eco-tourism, and he started only four years before my visit, in 1997. He has gone upmarket, keeping Barra Mansa small and exclusive, with just five double rooms and a guide for every two guests. Using nothing more high-tech than a wood-fired stove, his cook bakes her own bread and conjures up delicious feasts of rice and beans, fish from the river and beef from the ranch, all washed down with jugs of fresh tropical juice and the world's greatest coffee.

Staying here undoubtedly brings you closer to the wild. In the morning, I awake to find a family of capybaras – sheep-sized rodents with guinea-pig faces – grazing under my bedroom window. To see more of the ranch, I am hoisted into the saddle of a grey stallion named Cruzeiro. We pass patches of grassland ploughed up in the night by the tusks of peccaries, skirt reedy lagoons where giant anacondas sleep and find a carcass smothered in vultures. Has the jaguar walked this way? Guilherme shrugs. 'You cannot find the jaguar,' he says. 'It is she who decides whether to show herself or not.'

We ride on, fording clear streams, splashing belly-deep through limpid bayous graced by reflections of roseate spoonbills. Swaying along on Cruzeiro's broad back, in this pulsating world of pure air and boundless freedom, I can almost envy the hard, lonely life of the *pantaneiros*.

In a world without roads, the rivers are the only highways, and they provide the greatest opportunities for wildlife-viewing. The Río Negro is especially good in this respect, a pristine waterway with nobody else around. There's a mist over the water when we pile into the launch, but the sky above is a faultless blue, and the day will not stay cool for long. For an hour or so, we zoom upriver between emerald walls of impenetrable forest, then switch off the outboard and drift soundlessly back downstream.

Of all the pleasures of the Pantanal, this is the one I like best, just sitting back and going with the flow past an endless cavalcade of creatures. It's like watching a television wildlife movie. There's everything here except David Attenborough: a butterfly sipping salt tears from a cayman's eyes; skimmers with red bills scissoring the water; a tapir standing on a bank. 'You're lucky,' a visiting wildlife photographer tells me later. 'Tapir sightings are almost as rare as jaguars. I've been here six weeks and I haven't seen one.'

We float on. Flocks of parakeets scream overhead like showers of emerald meteorites. Then suddenly, we round a bend and find ourselves surrounded by a family of giant river otters. Utterly fearless, they yowl at us through bared teeth, romping and rollicking around the boat, until they finally tire of their sport and disappear upriver.

At last we come to a bone-white beach of burning sand as soft as talc. We stop to swim in the coffee-brown water. Like all the Pantanal rivers, it is full of piranhas, but Guilherme knows where it is safe to bathe. Afterwards I wander down the beach, allowing the sun to dry my skin, and find the tracks of a large cat pressed deep into the sand. A jaguar has walked where I stand now. The prints are old, but I don't care. I bend and touch them with my outstretched palm. Contact at last.

BELIZE – BRITAIN'S LOST EMPIRE OF THE SUN

Flippers kicking against the tide, I floated above the blossoming coral heads of the Hol Chan Marine Reserve, staring down into a translucent world of blue water and drifting shadows. The sea was so clear that I could see the surface stretching away above my head for 30m in every direction, like a rippling silk sheet. Beneath it, a grouper the size of a Labrador, with fat lips and a doleful expression, hung in the slanting light as if suspended on an invisible thread.

Earlier, someone has seen a small shark. 'A nurse shark,' said Steve, the boatman who had brought me to Hol Chan from Ambergris Caye. 'They don't give you no trouble.' But I saw nothing more sinister than a barracuda, a long, silver sword-blade with wolfish jaws and murderer's eyes. All around me now, fish were moving in an endless carousel of colour. Shoals of yellow-tailed snappers rose and fell like flurries of leaves caught in slow motion. Angel-fish nosed among the corals, and a queen triggerfish, its fins glowing deep purple, came sailing over the sea grass.

No wonder Belize is known as the aquarium of the Americas. Its coastline, protected by the longest unbroken reef of living coral in the western hemisphere, is home to all kinds of sea creatures. Out beyond the breaking surf, where the coral falls away in spectacular 40m drop-offs, cruise manta rays with 3m wings. Steve had dived with them as they glided like giant bats in the dusky deeps.

Between the reef and the mainland, among the shallow banks where the bonefish and great silver tarpon roam, low-lying islands known as cays (pronounced 'keys') stretch south from Mexico's Yucatán Peninsula to the Gulf of Honduras. Until recently these sandy hideaways, with their coconut palms and clapboard houses, were known only to big-game fishermen and scuba divers. Like Belize itself, they hardly figured on the world tourist map. Now the cays are changing. Holiday flights are jetting into Belize City from Miami, and beach resorts such as the Journey's End Caribbean Club on Ambergris Caye offer air-conditioning as well as a hammock in which to loll as you sip your pina colada. Even so, one of the most popular T-shirts you can buy locally carries the slogan: 'Where the hell IS Belize?'

But for me, at the end of a week exploring Belize's reefs and rain-forests, a much bigger question remained. How could such a beau-tiful country have been overlooked for so long? Until 1981 Belize didn't even exist. Before independence it was known as British Honduras, a far-away colony founded by 17th-century buccaneers who used its cays as bases from which to attack the Spanish fleets. There is still a British military presence on Belize, but today Britain's lost empire of the sun lives in peace with its neighbours.

It is a small country, about the size of Wales, democratic, stable and thoroughly eco-friendly. As well as Hol Chan, the first marine reserve in Central America, it has the world's only jaguar reserve, in the Cockscomb Basin. It also has spectacular ruined cities, the lega-cy of the mysterious Maya, the ancient civilization that flourished until the coming of the Spaniards in the 16th century. One of the finest sites is Altun Ha, a favourite whole-day excursion from Ambergris Caye, involving a 40-minute boat-ride to the mainland.

With Rico, our speedboat skipper, at the wheel, we skimmed south around the cay. Offshore, cormorants were resting on a row of wooden posts. 'Fish traps,' said Rico. 'In November when the fish come south me uncle catch 2,000lb of fish each day in them traps. Snapper. Grunts. Jack trevallys. All kinds.'

We raced on across the bonefish flats, past mangrove islands where piratical frigate birds patrolled the skies, until the last of the cays disappeared over the eastern horizon and we entered the mouth of the Northern River. At once the mangroves closed in, an entire forest balancing on the bony fingertips of its long grey roots. The water slid by, black as Guinness. The trees above were fes-tooned with orchids and starbursts of bromeliads. No birds sang, but a pair of fish-eating bats went ghosting away upstream ahead of us.

Eventually we reached the village of Bomba, a collection of shacks where free-range chickens wandered under the palms. A clapped-out Canadian schoolbus, still wearing its original coat of yellow paint, was waiting for us. Inside, posters warned of the evils of mar-ijuana, known locally as 'Belize breeze'.

There were no other tourists at Altun Ha when we arrived. Once, its giant pyramids were covered in plaster and painted blood-red.

Now, ferns sprout from the walls and the plaster has long since crumbled, like the bones of the Maya who lived here 400 years ago. Yet even in decay it is hugely impressive, a haunted place, like the backdrop for an Indiana Jones adventure, ringed by jungle.

At Altun Ha the Maya worshipped their sun god, Kinich Ahau, in gruesome ceremonies led by their king, who repeatedly stabbed his penis with a stingray barb until he began to hallucinate and – not surprisingly – cry out to his people. And it was here in the 1950s that the skeleton of an old man was uncovered. Inside his tomb was found one of the greatest treasures of the Americas: a carved jade head with obsidian eyes, thought to represent the implacable Kinich Ahau.

Next day I flew to Chan Chich in a single-engine Cessna. Beneath us lay an unbroken canopy of rainforest, reaching deep into Guatemala. I looked down into its dense green fleece and recalled the worlds of Captain Grief, a pilot I had met the day before in San Pedro. 'Man, if a plane comes down over the rainforest, it can disappear without trace.' But we made it safely to the airstrip at Gallon Jug, a back-country farming community hacked out of the jungle near the Guatemalan border. There we were met and driven to the Chan Chich Jungle Lodge, deep in the rainforest.

Chan Chich means 'Little Bird' in Maya, and is an oasis of luxury in the middle of a private 50,000ha nature reserve. It was built within the plaza of an ancient Maya city by Barry Bowen, a US-educated, seventh-generation Belizian. In 1997, when Bowen first began clearing the site, the area was a nest of marijuana-growers, hunters and tomb-robbers. 'We chased them out,' he says. 'Now our presence ensures that the ruins, rainforest and wildlife are protected.'

Chan Chich is an idyllic spot. Lolling in a hammock on the veranda of my cabana, I watched keel-billed toucans – the national bird of Belize – flaunting their sulphur-yellow bibs in the surrounding treetops. Wild turkeys strutted across the lawns, and a black woodpecker with a punkish crest of crimson feathers drummed a tattoo on a hollow trunk.

But the whole point of coming here is to see the rainforest. Gilberto was my guide, a lithe Maya Indian aged 52, with twinkling eyes and a profound understanding of the forest and its secrets. It was Gilberto who showed me a vine which, when cut, yields half a cup of pure water, and the give-and-take tree, whose cotton pith can staunch a bleeding wound. So many trees: cedars and hogplums;

allspice and rubber trees; sapodilla trees with chewing-gum sap; and the forest giants, kapok, guam and mahogany. Walking among them, dwarfed by buttressed trunks so tall they seem to be holding up the sky, the first thing you notice is the silence. Sometimes, when a breeze passes overhead, the forest sighs, a sound like falling rain. Then the hush returns, broken only by the call of forest birds: tanagers, vireos, squealing parrots. Underfoot, endless columns of leaf-cutter ants marched along the forest trails. They were guarded by 2cm-long warrior-ants with bulldog jaws, and I understood now why Gilberto wore his trousers tucked inside his boots.

Later I went on a night drive. The air was surprisingly cool and sweet, heavy with the scent of flowering palms. Nightjars flitted in and out of our light-beams, orange eyes glowing, and a tarantula the size of my hand scuttled across the road. The spider's presence was a reminder that the rainforest is also home to a host of unpleasant denizens. Among them is the fer-de-lance, a nocturnal viper with large fangs and a deadly venom – hence its Central American name of *tres minutos*, meaning 'three-minute snake'.

I didn't particularly want to run into the fer-de-lance but I was desperately keen to see a jaguar, the great spotted cat – known here as *el tigre* – that is the king of the Central American rainforest. At Chan Chich they turn up once a month on average, but I was out of luck, although I did see an ocelot, a small cousin of the jaguar, and heard the eerie, roaring chorus of howler monkeys echoing among the trees.

A couple of nights at Chan Chich is all you need to become an ardent conservationist. In the kingdom of the jaguar, among the orchids, toucans and tropical butterflies, the message strikes vividly home. Save the rainforest? Yes indeed.

TURKEY – A LYCIAN RHAPSODY

'*Merhaba*,' beamed the boatman, waiting to ferry me to the Sultan Palas Hotel. 'Welcome to Dalyan.' With one bare foot resting lazily on the tiller, he steered us across the jade-green Dalyan River. Marsh frogs gulped among the reeds. Carp leapt from the water, their bronze scales gleaming, and squadrons of dragonflies swarmed overhead in the warm evening light.

There is nowhere else in the world like the Dalyan Delta. Imagine, if you can, an Ottoman version of the Norfolk Broads, surrounded by cotton fields and ringed by hot stony mountains. At its heart lies the Dalyan River, winding through the reedbeds from Köyçeğis Lake to reach the sea a kilometre or so beyond Dalyan village.

In this dreamy Turkish waterland there is only one way to travel: in a shallow-draught boat, with a shady blue canvas canopy to keep you cool. For thousands of years Dalyan has lived by fishing. Even its name comes from the elaborate fish traps in which, every winter, 200 tonnes of mullet are taken, along with carp, eels and sea bream. But tourism provides a more profitable catch, and the village waterfront is thronged with boats waiting to transport visitors downriver to the beach.

The deck of every boat is covered with a Turkish rug – a delightful tradition that allows you to kick off your shoes and enjoy the sensation of drifting by magic carpet between banks of oleanders and tasselled reeds, past Lycian tombs carved in the cliffs and the crouching shape of the Lion Rock, at whose base lie the 3,000-year-old ruins of Kaunos. Half an hour later you are decanted onto the curving scimitar of beach that divides the delta from the sea. Sadly, the ramshackle huddle of Cannery Row shacks that once stood here has been demolished in the name of progress – replaced by lavatories, changing rooms and beach bars selling beers and kebabs. But once you walk past the last sunbed, there is nothing but a flawless arc of sand receding into the heat haze.

In places you may find trails left by loggerhead turtles, which struggle ashore on summer nights to lay their eggs in the sand. The loggerheads, endangered creatures the size of a coffee table, are the reason for Dalyan's fame. The beach is one of their last breeding strongholds, and in the 1980s it became an environmental *cause célèbre* when German developers planned to build an 1,800-bed holiday village on it. The scheme was scuppered, thanks largely to the tireless lobbying of June Haimoff, an eccentric Englishwoman known locally as 'Kaptan June', who lives in Dalyan with her nine dogs and 12 cats. She was delighted that the Turtle Beach had been saved, she told me, but was pessimistic about the loggerheads' future. 'The pressures on them are just too great. Every year there are fewer. In time I think they will simply fade away.' Similar pressures threaten Dalyan itself. 'When I first came here in 1975 the village had just 30 boats,' said Kaptan June. 'Now they have hundreds.'

But behind the coast Turkey remains locked in a dream of the past. Women in headscarves and baggy trousers still toil in the cotton fields, hoeing and hand-weeding between the rows, and the village elders end their days as they have always done, playing backgammon under the mulberry trees. With Durmus Yeter, a local guide, I set off to explore Dalyan's sleepy hinterland, and soon we were deep in rural Turkey. Blue beehives stood among the pines and tortoises shuffled in slow motion across the roads.

Later, sipping sweet apple tea at a roadside bar, I watched milk being collected from plastic pails kept cool in the local mill stream, and wondered what would happen if Turkey gains admission to the European Union. 'It's not like England,' said Durmas. 'Here every family still keeps a cow. Every housewife makes her own yogurt and butter.'

In the village of Eski Köyçeğis we were invited to lunch at a farmhouse where we sat outside, lounging like pashas on tapestry rugs while our hosts produced endless dishes of home-baked cornbread, stuffed aubergines and salad, to be washed down with *ayran*, a refreshing cold drink of salted yogurt mixed with water.

Inland Turkey is full of surprises. One day I went hiking in the pine-scented hills. I waded up the Yuvarlak River, lying deep in its limestone gorge, and ended up eating grilled trout at a makeshift restaurant built with typical Turkish ingenuity on stilts above the water. Another time I drove to Tlos, perched dramatically on a rocky hilltop between the Taurus mountains and the coastal plains. There are places where it seems as if the whole of Turkey is one vast open-air museum, and Tlos is one of them. Its hillsides are strewn with Roman ruins, its cliffs honeycombed with Lycian tombs. Among its stones, history and legend lie inextricably mixed. I scrambled down a narrow track under the cliffs, looking for the tomb of Pegasus, the fabled winged steed ridden by Bellerophon when he killed the Chimera. Eventually I found the tomb, its marbled doorway decorated with figures carved in bas-relief: an antelope, a lion and the legendary horse itself.

All this part of Turkey was once ruled by the Lycians, who colonized the region during the second millennium BC. In turn they were conquered by Alexander the Great and later by the Romans, who found them so troublesome that they eventually restored their independence. Today the Lycians are no more; their bones are dust. But between Kalkan and Kekova their ancient sea kingdom has changed little. Long stretches of this mountainous coast are still inaccessible by road and the only way to explore them in comfort is to cruise on board a *gulet*, one of the stately, twin-masted motor ketches that ply the waters between Bodrum and Antalya. A week is ideal but, as I discovered, even a couple of days afloat will give you a taste of these wild shores.

Lying alongside the wall in Kalkan harbour, the *Cemel Efe* was one of the more handsome *gulets* on show. From her rakish bowsprit to her elegant poop deck she was 20m long, and every inch a lady. Her polished woodwork gleamed in the sun, coated in varnish as thick as barley sugar, and a Turkish flag as big as a bedspread fluttered from her stern. There seemed to be only one rule on board: no shoes on deck. So, for the next two days, I lived barefoot as we chugged at a steady 8 knots past the crocodile shapes of bony headlands and fleets of islands as stark as the Hebrides.

On our first evening we anchored in a turquoise bay just beyond the little port of Kaş, and swam under sunlit cliffs from which Lycian tombs stared like eyeless sockets. Even in early June it was warm enough to sleep on deck under the stars. By the time breakfast arrived (cheese, olives, cucumber and tomato, boiled eggs, melon, cartwheels of bread and local honey), the sun was already scorching.

A peregrine falcon sat on a crag, guarding the entrance to the fjord-like channel that divides Kekova island from the mainland. Slowly we cruised along the island's inner shore, where the ruins of a Lycian city – walls, steps and floors – lay half-submerged in the limpid waters. The island itself is deserted now, but across the roadstead lies the fishing village of Kale and its Beau Geste castle, a

Turkish flag flying from its dog-toothed battlements. We anchored near the waterfront, close enough to hear the cicadas wheezing in the morning heat, and went ashore in the dinghy.

Kalkan may have doubled in size, but Kale had not changed. Still accessible only by boat, it was just as I remembered it 10 years ago, when I had sailed by bareboat from the seaport of Fethiye. Now, as then, its balconied houses lay scattered among the rocks, a village without streets, only a labyrinth of unpaved alleys leading up to the castle. Here, as on Kekova, the past is everywhere. Temple columns have been recycled as masonry for garden walls and there are so many stone tombs that one is used as a litter bin.

Even in a land of hospitable people, the inhabitants of Kale are exceptionally welcoming. At the Friendship Tea Room I sat on a rug under a 1,500-year-old olive tree while a girl squeezed fresh orange juice into a glass. There were just 24 families in Kale, she told me in perfect English, plus a Japanese woman and a German. In winter, she said, her father travelled to Rome to sell carpets, but he always came back for the tourist season, upon which the village now depended.

Next day, woken at dawn by a chorus of cockerels, I went on deck and watched Kale come alive. As the morning sun lit the castle ramparts an old lady emerged from a cottage doorway to feed her chickens, then sat among them, staring across the water as if lost in contemplation. How hard her years must have been, I thought, wresting a living from those barren shores. But for a moment I envied her. The next morning, when I was driving back to Dalaman airport, she would still be there, dreaming beside Turkey's timeless seas.

TURKEY – CAPPADOCIA

It was 6 May – celebrated in Turkey as the first day of summer – and down in the Ilhara valley in Anatolia, local families were preparing a village barbecue. After days of indifferent weather, summer had indeed arrived, blown in on a hot dusty wind that bent the riverside poplars in whose shade cauldrons of chopped vegetables seethed on glowing charcoal fires.

The Ilhara valley lies in that extraordinary region of central Anatolia known as Cappadocia, whose weird lunar landscapes, riddled with cave-dwellings, churches and rock-cut monasteries, are like nowhere else on earth. Its heartland is a labyrinth of sculpted canyons, a magic triangle between the troglodyte towns of Ürgüp, Nevsehir and Avanos. Most visitors seldom stay more than a couple of days, which is utterly mad. I stayed a week and still found it hard to leave.

In Ürgüp, the region's best touring centre, I stayed in one of Cappadocia's famous cave houses, a small private bed-and-breakfast hotel called Esbelli House. It had eight bedrooms that were carved out of the biscuit-coloured rock in Roman times, and a terrace where I ate each morning, sipping freshly squeezed orange juice and watching the swifts as they swooped over the town's rooftops. My cave came with all mod cons – shower, telephone, even a hairdryer. Its walls were decorated with Turkish rugs and – rather incongruously – two large teddy bears from Harrods. Even when the temperature soared outside, the air inside remained blissfully cool, so much so that at night I would sometimes switch on the electric heater thoughtfully provided by Suha Ersoz, the hotel's owner.

In the mornings I would wake to the hollow clip-clop of horses' hooves, reminding me that Cappadocia was a Persian name meaning 'the Land of Beautiful Horses'. To the east I could see snow shining on the 3,916m summit of Erciyes Dagi, the House of the Gods, one of the great mythological mountains of ancient Turkey. Like Hasan Dagi in the south-west of the region, it is an extinct volcano, and together these two snowcapped giants were responsible for creating Cappadocia's unique landscape. Millions of years ago they spewed out a thick layer of volcanic ash, which later became the soft porous rock known as tufa. In time, wind and water set to work, carving deep valleys and petrified forests of lofty stone pinnacles – the so-called 'fairy chimneys' that have become Cappadocia's geological trademark.

Some of these gigantic stalagmites have acquired extraordinary shapes: a crouching vulture, a cowled monk, or a great ape balancing precariously on a dizzy spire. And nearly every valley has its pepperpot pinnacles, like grotesque fungi, with dunces' caps of more durable lava protecting the softer supporting cones beneath. Judged on landscape alone, Cappadocia would rate among the wonders of the world. But what puts it in a class of its own is the human imprint left by generations of cave-dwellers who have tunnelled like termites into every available cliff and rock steeple.

For centuries Anatolia has been swept by invaders: Phrygians, Persians, Alexander the Great, Romans, Arabs, Seljuks and Ottomans. To hide from their oppressors the locals literally went to ground. Some of Cappadocia's caves and subterranean dwellings were begun by the Hittites 3,000 years ago, but it was the Christians of Byzantium, fleeing before the Arab armies in the 7th century, who put cave-dwelling on a new level. In the Zelve valley their rock churches, oratories and monastic cells are everywhere. In their cliff dwellings you can still see the smoke-blackened kitchens with their *tandir* ovens, the mangers for their livestock, and their bolt-holes, which could be blocked by heavy circular stones in times of danger. Here, if need be, they could survive an entire summer under siege until the first winter snows drove the invaders away.

Elsewhere in the region are entire underground cities, such as the one beneath the present-day town of Derinkuyu. Although local people were aware of the tunnels beneath their town, the outside world knew nothing until the 1960s, when a German journalist literally stumbled on their secret as he fell through a hole into one of the chambers. An expedition was mounted, fired by dreams of Trojan gold. What they found instead was the subterranean city of Melegopia, an ants' nest of rooms and connecting tunnels big enough to house 10,000 people. The only light was the flicker of oil lamps, which could be extinguished if invaders entered. This gave its inhabitants a huge advantage, since they knew each rat-run blindfolded and organized various ambush points where they could welcome their enemies with a well-placed spear or a tub of boiling oil.

Today the whole place is lit by electricity for the benefit of tourists. Even so, it is no place for the claustrophobic. To venture into the bowels of this spooky Anatolian underworld, you must sometimes bend double where the roof presses in, or scuttle along passages barely wide enough for one person at a time, until eventually you reach the lowest level, eight floors down and 55m beneath the present-day bus station.

Back in the real world again and in need of fresh air, I drove to Uçhisar and climbed the castle rock that looms over the town like a rotten molar. At the top I stood among the open rock tombs of Uçhisar's Christian rulers – who wished to be buried closer to heaven – while the wind plucked at my shirt, crag martins whirled past and cloud shadows rippled over the eerie moonscape of the Göreme valley.

Tourism has hit Göreme in a big way, and its early Christian founders must be spinning in their graves at the presence of the Berlin Camping site, the Flintstone Bar and the roadside stalls peddling tourist tat. But nothing can detract from the beauty of Göreme's painted churches, each with its glowing frescos, offered up to God by Byzantine craftsmen with an unswerving belief that what they had created would last for eternity.

Sadly, their faith has been betrayed down the years, and the murals have been damaged both by vandals and the slow drip of time. Most of the churches themselves, however, have survived remarkably well. The best is the Karanlik Kilise, the Dark Church, so called because it has only one small window to let in the light. Once your eyes become accustomed to the gloom you find yourself surrounded by Apostles and archangels painted in rich antique colours, along with frescos depicting the Nativity, the Last Supper and the Crucifixion. The whole valley is now a Unesco World Heritage Site, attracting 1.5 million visitors a year.

Yet despite Cappadocia's growing popularity it is still possible to elude the crowds. One way, I discovered, is to follow the easy, two-hour trail down the Rose Valley to Cavusin. The valley is a medley of cliffs and pinnacles honeycombed with the dark mouths of cave houses and frescoed churches. A stream flows through it, bordered by slender poplars whose tall silhouettes perfectly complement the surrounding rock spires.

Deeper into the canyon, down flights of steps and through a narrow cave, I emerged into a paradise of apricot and quince orchards in full blossom. The air was spiced with the scent of watermint. Swallow-tail butterflies flipped through the sunlight and all around rang the echoing voices of hoopoes and nightingales. Mesmerized by their haunting music, I walked on as if in a dream, conscious that I was listening to the same sounds the cave-dwellers and the church-painters must have heard long ago.

Yet even this heavenly valley is upstaged by the beauty of the Ilhara Valley, where the Melendiz River flows for 14km through a deep gorge in the Anatolian plateau. I went there with a guide called Ali, driving towards the snows of Hasan Dagi across a landscape as wide as Africa. Out in the fields, men were ploughing with horses, preparing the ground for pumpkins and watermelons. 'Early May is the best time to come here,' said Ali. 'While the land is still green. Come June, everything will be parched and shrivelled.'

It was midday when we reached the valley, and the first warm winds of summer were hissing through the trees. We lunched at a restaurant on the lip of the gorge, on spicy lentil soup followed by lamb stew on a tin plate with a burner beneath it to keep it warm. From our table I could see the river 161m below, green with meltwater from the distant Melendiz mountains. 'Down there,' said Ali, 'there are 106 churches and 4,000 caves.' He had been to Ilhara many times, so often, he said, that he knew every one of the 328 steps that led to the valley bottom.

It was in this timeless valley, listening to nightingales singing among the silent churches, that I felt closest to the real Cappadocia. We followed the river through a jungle of wych-elms and wild geraniums, and entered a church through a hole in the rock to see a fresco in which a three-headed snake was devouring sinners. Outside in the sunshine, boys were fishing with home-made rods, and a pair of eagles hunted along the canyon walls. Under the red cliffs, arched over by a sky of purest blue, the light was dazzling. It glittered on the rushing river, on the gnarled old pollard willows and the trembling poplars. The 20th century had been put on hold, and London, if it existed at all, was 1,000 years away.

HOME GROUND

CORNWALL – WEST PENWITH

There is always something special about granite landscapes, whether in Brittany or Connemara, or here in West Penwith at the toe-end of Cornwall. In the Penwith Peninsula everything is granite, from the moors above to the cliffs below. It is the key to understanding the obdurate nature of these parishes, whose inhabitants still live in granite farmhouses, sail from granite harbours and worship from granite churches, as they have done for a thousand years.

Life here has always been a struggle, fishing and farming in the eye of the wind, or wresting tin and copper from deep shafts that, in places, run out for a couple of kilometres under the seabed. The narrow roads, the unyielding hedgebanks, the remoteness which comes with being an extremity – all have conspired to hold back the forces that have been relentlessly smothering the rest of England under a creeping blanket of Home Counties' culture.

This was the Cornwall that attracted generations of painters to Newlyn and St Ives, lured by the Mediterranean brilliance of the light flung up from its encircling seas. St Ives may have changed, but Penwith is timeless. Like sand in an hourglass, everything that is most Cornish about Cornwall has settled here. West Penwith is Cornwall's last stand. Even a cursory glance at the map shows this to be no ordinary corner of Britain. The Cornish language was finally snuffed out when Dolly Petreath, its last speaker, died in Mousehole in 1777, but Penwith's weird place-names – Skewjack, Crows-an-wra, Polgigga, Woon Gumpus – still resonate with its Celtic past.

The best way to enter Penwith is to leave St Ives in early evening and head out into the Celtic twilight along the B3306 road to St Just. To the late Patrick Heron, the doyen of modern Cornish painters, the B3306 was an essential part of the Penwith magic. 'A wonderful, enlarged footpath of a road,' he called it, 'slipping and squirming between the rocks and the fields, twisting and turning through the granite-walled hamlets of Porthmeor and Rosemergy with a total disregard for the needs of holiday traffic.' For years it has resisted all attempts to be straightened or widened, and long may it remain as it is: one of the most dramatic drives in Britain.

Follow it west across these last few kilometres of England and you can feel the land running out, the sea closing in. On one side are the West Penwith moors, a pagan world of standing stones and sweeps of bracken crowned by granite outcrops twice as old as the Alps. On the other, bounded by the blue Atlantic, the low light pours across the finest prehistoric landscape in Europe, a maze of small, misshapen fields, a green-gold quilt of cattle pastures held fast since the Iron Age in a web of granite hedgebanks.

In West Penwith the past is everywhere. Just west of Lamorna Cove at Boleigh – the 'Field of Blood', where, according to legend, the Saxon king Athelstan crushed the last Cornish resistance – the roadsides bristle with Celtic crosses and standing stones. And a few kilometres on, St Buryan's Church tower summons visitors to the prehistoric stone circle of Boscawen-un.

On the edge of the moors near Sancreed, I parked beside a lonely farm called Goon Vran, and walked up a narrow track to Carn Euny, the site of a farming community established 2,000 years ago. Dog violets bloomed among its granite hut circles, and stone steps led down into a fogou, a mysterious underground chamber with a roof of massive granite slabs made by the forgotten people of the moors.

Every inch of the peninsula is filled with surprises. At Madron I followed a path almost buried under a bridal veil of blackthorn blossom, to a Celtic chapel beside one of Cornwall's innumerable holy wells. Near by, its roots clenched in the shallow waters of a kingcup marsh, stood the strangest sight – a goat willow covered with votive offerings. Some visitors had tied strips of coloured cloth to its branches. Others had left handkerchiefs, scarves, necklaces, ties and shoelaces. One hopeful had even left a lottery ticket. Who said tree worship was dead in Britain?

The entire landcape, with its tumbled rocks and gnarled thorn-bushes flying in the wind, has the fey, eerie quality of an Arthur Rackham illustration. At Porthmeor I came upon a white goose asleep in the road. Near by, a girl stood kissing a horse in a field, like a scene from an Irish folk tale.

But there is also a brooding sense of sadness here, a feeling of dereliction and betrayal. 'Fish, tin and copper' was a famous Cornish toast, but no more. No one will ever see the pilchard shoals spreading like cloud shadows across the sea, bringing prosperity to the fishermen of Sennen and St Ives. As for the hard-rock men of St

Just, their day is done. The mines are closed, the deserted engine houses stand open to the sky, leaving only Geevor Museum at Pendeen, and the National Trust's wonderfully restored Levant beam engine on the cliffs below, to remind tourists of Penwith's industrial past.

At Sennen Cove I stayed at the Old Success Inn, named after one of the fishing companies that thrived on the mullet and pilchard shoals in earlier times. Now only tourism keeps the place alive. In one of Sennen's art and craft shops I spoke to a fisherman's wife who remembered the last time the mullet shoals swarmed in, a couple of decades ago. The occasion led to bitter rivalry between the Sennen fishermen and others from up-country. 'War was declared,' she said solemnly. 'They nearly killed each other.'

From the cliffs behind Sennen I looked down on the rock stack called the Irish Lady, her granite crinoline laced with spray, and across the bay to Land's End. Offshore, etched in black against a silver sea, stood the Longships lighthouse and its sinister rocks: Carn Bras, Kettle's Bottom, the Shark's Fin and the Tal-y-maen. It is a spectacular view, but it is easily upstaged by the cliff scenery higher up the Penwith coast between Cape Cornwall and Zennor Head. The wildest spot is Gurnard's Head, a gaunt, sphinx-shaped promontory exposed to the full force of the Atlantic.

In Treen Cove, in the lee of Gurnard's Head, I met Roger Crowther, a woodworker who lives in a former fisherman's cottage barely metres above the waves. So many times, he told me, dolphins play in these waters. Basking sharks cruise through the summer seas, cleaving the surface with their black angular dorsal fins, and once, back in the 1970s, he had seen a huge shoal of mullet. 'An inky shadow, solid with fish, stretching from end to end of the cove.'

Paradoxically, the wildest coast of all lies to the south of Land's End between Penberth Cove and Pordenack Point, where gulls wail endlessly above the zawns, or chasms, and the waves break with gasping force against the buttressed cliffs. In springtime the clifftops become a giant rock garden smothered in wildflowers – bluebells, alliums, primroses and violets – to be followed in early summer by foxglove spires and pink clumps of thrift. And nowhere is the coastal scenery more uplifting than at the fortress cliffs of Treryn Dinas, a granite headland overlooking white curves of sand.

Penberth Cove, now cared for by the National Trust like so much of the Cornish coast, is an archetypal fishing cove: a dozen small boats hauled up on a steep stone slipway, an old wooden capstan, a clutter of crab pots, a handful of cottages and a clear stream bubbling under a clapper bridge. The cliffs may be windswept but these seaward-running valley bottoms are almost subtropical, with their sheltered jungles of bamboos and hazel thickets.

Porthgwarra, where you can walk down to the sea through a cave, is the starting-point for a glorious section of the long-distance South West Coast Path, which leads past Gwennap Head towards Land's End. Out here, there is not a tree in sight; even the ubiquitous Cornish gorse bushes have been pruned to near ground level by the sea winds. In winter you could be blown off your feet, but in midsummer, when the sun is shining and the thrift is in flower and the sea is as blue as the Aegean, you would not wish to be anywhere else.

Around Pendower Cove the cliffs are seamed and fissured, forming fantastic sculpted shapes, like Easter Island statues. Ahead lies the wet mouth of a sea cave big enough to hide a tall ship, with Nanjizel Bay just around the corner. Another couple of kilometres would bring you to Land's End itself, where souvenir shops, exhibitions and the Last Labyrinth Theatre mark the most westerly point in England. But what you see between Porthgwarra and Pordenack is the real Land's End – the spiritual grand finale of the most exhilarating coastal walk in Britain.

DEVON – TARKA COUNTRY

'The stream flowed below a churchyard wall and by a thatched cottage where a man, a dog and a cat were sitting before a fire of elm brands on the open hearth. The wind blew the scent of the otter under the door and the cat fumed and growled, standing with fluffed back and twitching tail beside her basket of kittens.'

In the north Devon village of Georgeham the cottage still stands beside the stream, but the man who lived there and wrote those words now lies in the churchyard beneath a simple slate stone inscribed with the image of a barn owl. Henry Williamson died in 1977, but *Tarka the Otter*, his 'joyful water life and death in the Country of the Two Rivers', remains the greatest nature classic in English literature. More than any other writer since Hardy, he caught the spirit of a special corner of England and made it his own.

Williamson country lies between Exmoor and Dartmoor where two Devon rivers, the Taw and Torridge, emerge from their deep wooded valleys to meet the Atlantic in a vast estuary of saltmarsh, dunes and sandbars. Williamson knew and loved every inch of it. And even now, with a map, you can follow his footsteps through the printed pages.

Henry Williamson was born in London in 1895. In 1914 he joined the army and fought on the Western Front until, traumatically, he was sent home badly shell-shocked and suffering from dysentery. After the war he worked in London as a freelance journalist, but city life proved too much for his shattered nerves. In 1921 he climbed onto his 499cc BRS Norton motorbike and headed for a new life in north Devon.

At Georgeham he rented Skirr Cottage, a cob and thatch labourer's dwelling that had been built in the days of King John. He paid 18 pence a week and inherited a family of barn owls that nested above the ceiling. The barn owl at once became his totem, its outline picked out in paint on his cottage door. Apart from the birds, his only companions were dogs, cats and at one stage an otter cub whose mother had been shot. Williamson persuaded his cat –

already nursing a kitten – to suckle the cub, and the young otter took to following him on long walks around the countryside. But their relationship ended one evening when the animal stepped in a gin trap. By the time Williamson managed to release it, the trap had almost severed three of the otter's toes. Utterly frightened, it wriggled from his grasp and vanished.

He never saw his otter again, but the idea of *Tarka* had been born, and in 1923 he began to write. Soon afterwards he was married, a son was born and the family moved to Crowberry Cottage, just a few doors down the road from Skirr. It was here, having been laboriously revised 17 times, that *Tarka* was finished in 1927. It won him the Hawthornden Prize. 'A hundred pounds and fame,' he cried on hearing the news. He spent the money on a field at Ox's Cross, near Georgeham, where his elmboard writing hut still stands.

By the time he was 74 he had completed two sprawling sagas – the four-volume *The Flax of Dreams* and *A Chronicle of Ancient Sunlight*, an immense 15-volume canvas stretching from the turn of the last century across two world wars. It should have assured him a place among the greatest English writers of the century, but none of his later work ever achieved the lasting impact of *Tarka*.

The writer Kenneth Allsop believed Williamson was a genius. 'I think I can be objective about expressing this judgement of him,' he wrote, 'because in fact his political philosophy could hardly be more different from my personal outlook on man and society.' And yet Williamson was to die unhonoured, a loner to the end and, but for *Tarka*, almost forgotten.

How could an author praised by Arnold Bennett and T.E. Lawrence, whose works had been compared to Dickens and Tolstoy, receive so little recognition? And why are all but a handful of his books now out of print? The clue lies in Allsop's comments about his politics. Ever since the trauma of the Western Front, Williamson maintained a naive but unswerving support for the fascist beliefs espoused by Oswald Mosley. The Establishment never forgave him.

'*Tarka*'s fame irritated Henry,' said Daniel Farson, Williamson's biographer and friend for a quarter of a century, 'and yet he was also immensely proud of it.' Farson was still in his teens when they first met, and he remembered Henry in those days as 'a lean, vibrant, almost quivering man with blazing mesmeric eyes'. When I met Farson he was dividing his time between Turkey, Soho and Appledore, where he had lived for 12 years in a converted boat-builder's loft overlooking the estuary.

'They were idyllic days,' said Farson, describing the summers of the late 1940s. Yet even by 1953, as Farson's biography of Williamson records, Henry was already lamenting the changes that had overtaken Appledore. 'Paper, Wall's ice cream cartons, shrieking children. A polluted estuary; a £1 million electric coal station erected just over the water on the snipe bogs that once were. The Burrows are a tank ground now.'

Luckily, Williamson was spared the most insidious blight. For years the Torridge, where much of *Tarka* is set, was one of England's finest salmon rivers. In the 1920s, rods were taking 1,000 salmon a year and the fishery was worth £2 million. In 1984 only 26 salmon were caught and the fishery had declined in value to £84,000. Three years later, said local anglers, there were no juvenile salmon in the Torridge at all. Beneath the surface, outwardly so serene, something sinister had happened.

In 1980, when the National Water Council carried out a countrywide review of rivers, the Torridge emerged with flying colours. It was listed as Class 1a, alongside the purest Hampshire chalk streams. Five years later a similar review showed it to have suffered an environmental deterioration of 41 per cent, with long, fishless stretches reduced to Class 3 ('poor quality requiring improvement as a matter of some urgency').

What could have caused such a dramatic collapse, transforming one of Britain's loveliest rivers into one of its most shameful worst? The answer was farm pollution. Three decades of government subsidies had revolutionized West Country farming, causing livestock numbers to double. In the Torridge catchment area alone there were some 84,000 cattle and 140,000 sheep, and between them they produced the equivalent in pollution to a city the size of Sheffield – much of it entering the Torridge as farmyard slurry. There it was joined by another unwelcome agricultural by-product in the form of silage run-off, one of the most powerful of all deoxygenating pollutants. Together this unwholesome brew flowed down to the estuary, where it was enriched still further with untreated human sewage from Bideford.

Torrington District Council and the citizens of Bideford were demanding a full treatment plant to clean up their unsavoury estuary and make their beaches fit for swimming. But the powers that be had said no at that time, offering instead a new fine-screening plant. Normally such schemes rely on a long sea outfall, but Bideford, 7km from the sea, had no such opportunity. Screening would remove paper and emulsify excreta, but everything would still pour into the tideway virtually in the middle of the town.

Not surprisingly, Torrington District Council objected, the townspeople protested and there was a public inquiry. But it was all to no avail. The Department of the Environment remained unmoved. Like it or not, the citizens of Bideford were going to be fobbed off with a screening plant and the estuary would remain a pollution black spot. That was the state of play in 1987, and it was not until the creation of the National Rivers Authority at the end of the 1980s that the Torridge would be brought back from the dead.

In the 1920s Williamson could still write about the 'wild, beautiful, unexplored Atlantic seaboard; the falcons, the otters, the badgers, the salmon, the character of the people,' as if Devon were another country. It was a time when farmers in early spring would stamp out into the soft West Country dawns to plough their fields with heavy horses, when pigs were killed outside cottage doors, squealing as their blood gushed into bowls for 'bloody pie'. Across the estuary in Appledore, among the cobbled alleys and sawdust-smelling boatyards, you might still find old 'mast and yards' men who had served their sea time aboard square-rigged sailing ships. And it was not uncommon even then to see a three-masted schooner waiting for the flood tide to carry her up to Bideford with a cargo of Baltic timber.

Williamson was writing in the sunset of English rural life. In the villages the old order, shaken to its roots by the Great War, would never be the same. A land that had never moved faster than the horse was being laid open by railways and metalled roads. New bridges and viaducts brought the green and gold locomotives of the Southern Railway steaming down the valleys from Exeter, 60km away, and motor cars – a rare sight in the early 1920s – became commonplace in the lanes.

The way of life that Williamson described has been laid to rest. Yet places, echoes, ghosts remain. The setting is much the same. Only when you compare his vivid descriptions with the reality of the present is it possible to measure the changes that have overtaken, and in places overwhelmed, north Devon.

Fifteen elms stood in the churchyard when Williamson first came to Georgeham. Rooks nested in their tall canopies and barn owls emerged from the roof of Skirr Cottage to hunt among the gravestones. Now the trees are gone – victims of Dutch elm disease – and barn owls are scarcer everywhere. At the upper end of the village, the 17th-century Rock Inn now bears little resemblance to the pub of Williamson's era, when men in waistcoats and collarless shirts drank Barnstaple bitter from china mugs and sang in a haze of tobacco smoke.

Yet for Williamson's son, Richard, Georgeham was not so different from the village he remembered from his boyhood. 'There was more cow shit in the streets in those days,' he said. 'The smell of cows was everywhere. Little black cars, fewer buildings, that's what I remember. But still the same old lanes, the same stone walls. The only real change is the orange glow of the street lights from the new estate.'

On the hill above Georgeham, where four lanes meet at Ox's Cross, Williamson's elmboard writing hut still looks out across the immense sweep of Bideford Bay. The strange, Ibsenesque house he added in the 1970s has been sold out of the family, but the hut has been carefully restored by the Henry Williamson Society and remains much as he left it – his overcoat on a peg, high leather boots still on their wooden trees, all under the pines he planted more than half a century ago.

Those were the days when you could walk down to the estuary and be rowed across to Appledore for a shilling. It is all holiday coast now. Saunton and Putsborough Sands surrendered long ago to the surfers and sunbathers, and the summer lanes are choked with traffic heading for the beaches. Only Baggy Point remains untouched – a wild National Trust headland where the Atlantic bursts with thunderous force against lichen-scabbed cliffs.

To the south lies Dartmoor, where the Taw rises among desolate bogs under Hangingstone Hill. In its upper reaches the Taw is a typical Dartmoor stream, spilling over mossy boulders in a chain of amber pools. By the time it has left Belstone Cleave and slid beneath the A30 at Sticklepath it is already deep enough to hide a salmon. Downstream below King's Nympton, diesel trains rumble over iron-girdered bridges that Williamson knew in the age of steam, but here at least in the lush valley farmlands, the Taw is timeless. It remains the Gentlemen's River – so called by the old otter hunters, who knew that wherever they stopped for refreshments they would never be far from a riverside inn.

Life for Britain's otters has always been precarious. Until the Great War they were persecuted by gamekeepers and water bailiffs. Then the keepers went off to fight and the otters multiplied. Britain was never again so heavily keepered, and in the ancient, unpolluted countryside that existed between the wars, otters flourished as never before.

They continued to thrive until 1957, when their numbers suddenly plummeted. The cause was pesticides – the same persistent chemicals that were simultaneously bringing about the decline of the sparrowhawk and peregrine falcon. Eventually the more harmful poisons – Dieldrin and DDT, for example – were banned, and so, eventually, was otter hunting. In 1978 the otter was given full protection under the Conservation of Wild Creatures Act. Sadly, it came too late and was not enough to halt the slide. While birds of prey recovered well, the otter vanished from most of its former English haunts. Only in the South-West, on the Taw and Torridge river systems, had numbers increased since 1977, and even here they were still in danger.

'Practically every otter in England and Wales is full of pesticide residues,' said Don Jeffries, one of the Nature Conservancy Council's mammal experts. 'They've got Dieldrin, mercury, DDE and PCBs in their bodies, and none of these is doing the otter any good.'

Ironically, it was the otter hunters who first raised the alarm over the animal's disappearance. 'Conservationists would never have been aware that otters were in trouble if it hadn't been for the hunters getting worried over the declining numbers,' said Jeffries.

The Masters of Otter Hounds Association brought in its own voluntary ban on killing otters in the early 1970s, and legal protection finally spelt the end of otter hunting in Britain. Most hunts disbanded altogether. Others such as the Dartmoor renamed themselves as the Devon and Cornwall and re-emerged to pursue the mink that had begun to infest Britain's rivers. Many mink hunts used fox hounds, but the Devon and Cornwall still kept the real old-fashioned otter hounds, with traditional names such as Capital and Bellman, Songster and Solemn. 'Such lovely animals,' said Arlin Rickard, a former hunt master. 'Stocky and heavy-boned, with thick coats and webbed feet. As a breed they were even rarer than the otter.'

The Cheriton, which pursued Tarka on the Taw and Torridge, had already ceased hunting by 1945 and survived only as a club. But the neighbouring mink hunts were still invited to the Cheriton country, and on certain days between May and September the valleys of the Two Rivers still rang to the deep-throated belling hounds, as if haunted by Deadlock's ghost.

Nowhere in the Country of the Two Rivers is the atmosphere of Williamson's Devon richer than on the banks of the Torridge. It's an odd river, rising within 6km of the Atlantic near Hartland Point, but then, perversely, turning its back on the sea and running inland towards Dartmoor. Then once more it changes its mind and meanders east past Dippermill and Sheepwash, before looping down through high hills and hanging woods to Great Torrington and Weare Giffard, before running out into the estuary beyond Bideford.

For much of its 55km, especially in its upper reaches above Torrington, the Torridge is a secret river. Sometimes, cruising down the web of back lanes that criss-cross this corner of the county, you catch a tantalizing glimpse of it, sliding past like polished glass under bankside oaks, or running bright over stony shillets between summertime jungles of pink Himalayan balsam. But most of the time it shuns the roads, losing itself in the woods and water-meadows of a landscape unchanged since Williamson's time.

Now, as then, what the visitor sees is a time-warp countryside of herons and buttercups in which Beam Weir and Halfpenny Bridge – familiar scenes in *Tarka* – remain just as when the book was written. Even vanished landmarks have been brought back to life. Below Canal Bridge, 13 gnarled trees once stood with their roots in the river. In one was Owlery Holt – Tarka's birthplace. All are gone but 13 new trees now stand in their place, planted by the Vincent Wildlife Trust.

'For me that whole area around Weare Giffard shrieks of Tarka,' said David Cobham, the director who filmed the story in 1977 and got to know Williamson well in his last years. 'Henry even *looked* like an otter, with his bristly moustache and piercing brown eyes.'

By a strange coincidence, Cobham was filming the death of Tarka on the day Henry died. It was a glorious day in Devon on 13 August 1977, and Cobham kept on filming until early evening. The final shot, with the three bubbles rising after Deadlock is drowned and Tarka is carried away on the outgoing tide, was completed just as the light was beginning to fade. Next day Richard Williamson told him: 'I thought you should know that while you were filming Tarka's death scene yesterday, Henry died.' Cobham was stunned. 'It gave me a very prickly feeling,' he said. 'It seemed almost predestined.'

In recent years an entire local tourist industry has gathered itself around Williamson's famous otter. The Tarka Project, a Devon County Council initiative, now actively promotes sustainable tourism in the region, with a Tarka Trail – a 290km footpath – opened by Prince Charles in May 1992. Among those who advised in setting up the Tarka Trail was Trevor Beer, a local writer, and it was he who took me to Braunton Burrows, the sea of dunes that lies to the north of the estuary behind Saunton Sands. He remembers meeting Williamson there one winter. 'It was a cold day and the old man's eyes were watering.

His heavy coat was pulled about his shoulders, which were normally straight but now hunched against the winds.' Characteristically, Williamson broke off their conversation to shake his fist at a low-flying jet from RAF Chivenor.

We parked near the solitary white house on Crow Point and sat on the sea wall by Horsey Marsh as the sun burned down and moorhens hiccuped in the mace-reeds. The sands below the sea wall are still as Williamson described them, except that now, on top of the shells of razor-fish and cockles, dried seaweed thongs and bleached driftwood, our own age had added an oily flotsam of plastic bottles. Behind the highest tide-lines, the Burrows rise in a shaggy crest of marram grass. It is an extraordinary place, an English Kalahari, 1,200ha of wind-blown hills owned by the Christie Estate. The greater part is leased to the Ministry of Defence for military training, though in its turn it has leased it to English Nature as a biosphere reserve.

'One time I went down there looking for whitethroats,' said Beer, 'and commandos armed to the teeth popped up out of the dunes.' But on the whole the military and the conservationists have managed to coexist in uneasy equilibrium – exemplified by the thrush Beer watched smashing snails on an unexploded shell.

In summer the Burrows are a hot and breathless place. The sand burns underfoot. The dunes quiver in the dazzling Atlantic light. The sea wind hisses through the marram, bearing the sound of skylarks and the boom of surf breaking on Bideford Bar. But below the wind, among the mossy slacks and damp hollows, the surf is muted and the dunes are thick with flowers: wild orchids, yellow spires of evening primrose and the vivid blue of viper's bugloss.

It would be foolish to imagine that north Devon has not changed in half a century, or that rural life was better in Williamson's day. Towns and villages are bigger. Roads are busier, beaches crowded. Noise, power lines and pollution have all conspired to diminish its beauty. Yet the land of the Two Rivers remains its own place, stubborn and inward-looking. In spite of everything the magic survives – in the Burrows, in the shape of the coast, the lie of the land, its ancient geometry of fields, woods and crooked hedgebanks.

The power station that defiled Williamson's beloved snipe bogs has been demolished. The jets he hated have left RAF Chivenor. The peregrines have returned to their Atlantic eyries and, best of all, the Torridge has been reborn. Once again it has become a river fit for otters, where, long ago, a shell-shocked survivor from the trenches sought refuge with an orphaned cub in the country they made their own.

GLOUCESTERSHIRE – SLIMBRIDGE

Curlews were stalking over the roadside fields as I crossed the Sharpness–Gloucester Canal. Their hunched brown shapes were everywhere, probing with long, curved bills for worms. These level pasturelands in the Vale of Berkeley have a long tradition of good husbandry. This is the English Normandy – renowned for cider and cream and double Gloucester cheese. For centuries its fame centred around Berkeley Castle, the oldest inhabited stronghold in England, built in 1153 and still lived in by the Berkeley family. In summer, tourists flock here to admire the castle and to peer into the dismal cell where, in 1327, Edward II was put to death in so foul a manner that his screams, it is said, could be heard a kilometre away in Berkeley village.

But in winter, the greatest attraction for miles around is the Wildfowl Trust at Slimbridge. Of all the seasonal movements of wildlife that sweep the British countryside there is nothing to match the great migrations of wintering wildfowl, and nowhere better to thrill at the sight and sound of Bewick's swans, wigeon and thousands of noisy white-fronted geese than the hides and viewing towers of Slimbridge.

The trust is a non-profit-making organization that was established in 1946 by Sir Peter Scott. He started with just 9ha on the New Grounds, a 5km stretch of high salt marsh and enclosed pastureland reclaimed from the Severn Estuary in the 1600s. For centuries the area and its adjoining tidal flats had been a traditional wintering ground for geese, maintained by the Berkeley family. Now the trust owns 40ha of enclosed ponds, pens and hides, and controls a further 500ha as a wildfowl refuge. During the summer, sheep and cattle graze the refuge, but from October onwards they are withdrawn from the fields, leaving the grass for geese and wigeon.

I arrived to the clamour of Canada geese, members of a feral flock that breed on the gravel pits at Frampton, 3km upriver. Now they flew noisily overhead to join the ducks and Bewick's swans assembled on the waters of the Rushy Pen, anticipating the free handouts of grain. A notice outside the Halfway Hide announced yesterday's tally for visiting birdwatchers: 4,000 wigeon, 1,800 white-fronted geese, 224 Bewick's swans, 350 pochard, two bean geese and single sightings of pink-footed goose, peregrine, little owl, snipe and water rail.

These numbers, although impressive, were still only a fraction of the birds to be seen. Up to 40,000 common and black-headed gulls roost on the mudflats. Clouds of starlings swirl over the salt marsh, feeding in company with hundreds of lapwings, curlew, dunlin, redwing and fieldfare. And over the next few weeks, as the weather turned colder, the north-east winds would bring even more wildfowl pouring down from the Arctic, until the skies over Slimbridge become a maelstrom of circling flocks.

Beyond the slit windows of Halfway Hide, wigeon were mustered in dense congregations on the wide meadow called the Tack Piece. They are the most numerous of all the duck at Slimbridge, followed by mallard, pintail, shoveler, tufted duck, teal and pochard. The wigeon come from Iceland and Siberia, building up to a peak of around 5,000 birds in January. They are beautiful creatures – especially the drakes, with their cinnamon heads and delicate, close-grained winter plumage – and I love to hear their whistled exclamations of surprise as they come flying in through the murk of a December dusk. Now, in the cold bright sunlight, they were feeding peacefully, packed so closely together that the flock seemed to flow over the grass in a feathered tide of bobbing heads.

Where shallow flashes reflected the sky, teal swam among spikes of rushes. Others joined them, coming in fast and low like waders, disturbing a water rail that slunk deeper into cover. On the far side of the field a little owl sat on a fencepost under bare trees. Near by, a family group of four Bewick's swans were grazing. And all the time the sky was filled with the constant movement of birds: languid gulls, fast-flying pintail, echelons of swans and yodelling packs of white-fronted geese.

The white-fronts – so called because the pink bill is set off by a white mask that stops just in front of the eyes – are by far the commonest species at Slimbridge. The first groups arrive in October, having completed an epic journey of more than 3,000km from their breeding grounds in Arctic Russia. Towards Christmas their numbers build up until the flocks are 7,000 strong. They are noisy birds, constantly calling with shrill, chuckling voices. Powerful fliers, they are the most agile of all the grey geese, able to turn swiftly and slide down the sky. A skein came in now, bunching and swirling as they spilled the wind from their wings to drop steeply into the field, causing the watchers in the hide to fall silent, for nowhere else in Britain do the wary white-fronts come so close.

Afterwards I moved on to the Holden Tower, a two-storey wooden hide facing the Severn across the great salt marsh known as The Dumbles. The estuary here is about 1.5km wide and subject to fierce, racing tides that raise the river level by some 10m, drowning the mudflats and driving the birds off the saltings; but now the tide was out.

It was cold in the hide. A north wind cut like a knife through the narrow windows as I watched a female peregrine glide past, setting off a frenzy of starlings in her wake. The falcon turned and rose above the loitering river. Her sharp wings drove her swiftly back towards the tower, and I could see her huge, luminous eyes burning as she flickered past. Then she turned away once more, lifted over the sea wall and settled far out on The Dumbles, where she began to bathe.

Slowly the panic subsided. The wheeling flocks fell back to earth in languorous spirals and began to feed again, fanning out over the grass. The day was drawing to a close. Sunk between its tidal flats, the Severn lay sullen. On the far bank, beyond the silhouette of Awre church, the land rose and rolled away to the Forest of Dean, smudged with distance.

The sun was going. Willows glinted in its last rays, flaring red across the fields, but there remained one last excitement. Out of the sky rang a wild music, more fitting for a Russian forest than a Gloucestershire river valley, as a flock of Bewick's swans came in from the fields where they had been grazing. Their presence is a tribute to the work of Sir Peter Scott and the Wildfowl Trust. The first Bewick's ever to be recorded on the Severn Estuary was almost certainly decoyed from its traditional wintering grounds on the Somerset Levels by the presence of some tame North American whistling swans. That was in 1948, since when numbers have increased steadily until more than 300 swans now winter at Slimbridge for weeks on end. Like the white-fronts, they come from the tundra of Arctic Russia and are part of the 5,500-strong population that regularly overwinters in the British Isles. Some have been coming to Slimbridge for more than 20 years, and every bird can be individually recognized by its unique black and yellow bill pattern, in the same way that humans can be distinguised by their finger-prints.

They flew now in the dying light, white as snowflakes in a blue haze of downpouring dusk, coming together in long, wavering streamers. For a moment there was silence. Their beating wings gave out no sound – so different from the mute swans' singing pinions. Then again I heard their exultant chorus, falling, fading as the birds bore away to settle on Swan Lake. There they would roost secure in the foxproof pen, huddling for warmth on three small islands until dawn.

MY DORSET

I was born in suburban Surrey, in a red-brick sea of rooftops, but even before I was 10 years old I knew that one day I would live somewhere in the West Country. As a boy I thought it would be Cornwall, where my parents spent their summer holidays, but then I was side-tracked by Dorset.

It was May and I was in my early twenties. I had hitchhiked down from Surrey, on my way to West Bay to meet up with an old Royal Navy shipmate from my national service days. The hills around Beaminster were as green as only Dorset hills can be. The old-fashioned fields were full of buttercups. The apple trees were in blossom and the cuckoos were calling and I thought I had never seen anywhere so beautiful or so quintessentially English.

The years went by and I bought a tumbledown cottage in Powerstock. At first it was just a weekend retreat but later it became my permanent home. My daughter went to the village school and I fell deeper and deeper in love with Dorset. What I had stumbled on was a backwater on the way to nowhere, buried among hills too steep to plough. Chameleon country, always changing, serene in summer, withdrawn in winter, perhaps haunted, though never hostile.

As for the village itself, it was pretty but not self-consciously so. At its centre, where five lanes meet, stands the Church of St Mary, with its crooked Norman chancel arch and a gilded weathercock turning in the wind on its yellow-stone tower. The churchyard is a place of deep and ancient silence, a wild garden of sombre yews and leaning headstones. When I first lived there it was also the abode of Lazarus, a one-eyed church cat, a black-as-midnight feral tom who lived in a sepulchre and made sleep impossible with his amorous serenading. Those were the days when barn owls still drifted over the hay meadows at dusk, when cows were still driven through the lanes for milking, and the old men who sat with their pints in the Three Horseshoes or the Marquis of Lorne still spoke with such a broad Dorset burr that I could understand only one word in three.

During the week I had to go to London, where I worked as a journalist on the *Sunday Times*. But when Friday came I could hardly wait to catch the train to Dorchester and then drive westward, following the sun over the Roman road to Eggardon, the dramatic geological divide where the wide chalklands of the South Country end and the true West Country begins. And then down, down through sunken lanes awash with cow parsley and the smell of wild garlic pouring in through the car windows, down into the soft silence and folded hollows of Powerstock.

For 30 years, until I moved a couple of kilometres further down the valley, Eggardon filled my kitchen window, a billowing cloud of grassy limestone starred with grazing sheep. Eggardon is a monument to Dorset's enduring nature, a solid, reassuring presence on the eastern skyline, shutting out the world of cities. Like Karen Blixen on her farm at the foot of the Ngong Hills in Kenya, I would wake every morning and see Eggardon and think, here I am where I belong.

Upon the summit, 253m above the sea, where the wind blows and the skylarks sing among the clouds, nothing changes. 'As old as Eggardon' goes the local saying. A solitary thorn tree stands on the top, ringed by ramparts built in the Iron Age. It is said that Isaac Gulliver, an 18th-century smuggler, planted the tree as a daymark for ships beating into Lyme Bay with contraband cargoes of French silks and brandies. On a summer evening, when the sea turns to silver and the light is clear and sharp as cider and you can see as far as Dartmoor, there is no finer panaorama anywhere.

My Dorset, to be specific, is really confined to west Dorset. It has no hard and fast boundaries, only the coast between Lyme Regis and Abbotsbury, and the Devon border. Inland it runs north as far as the Beaminster tunnel. In the east it stops at Eggardon. That is the big picture. But within it hides the heartland, the magic circle, which you can pin down by sticking a compass point into Powerstock church. Within a radius of 4–6km lies the best of it, the crème de la crème in landscape terms. To get to know it you need not be streetwise but lanewise. Learn to shun the main highways, with their diesel fumes and thundering traffic, and dive down the first narrow side-road you can find. That way lies sanity.

Some of these West Country byways are more like badger trails, burrowing deep into a lushness of campion and cow parsley that brushes both sides of your car as you pass. But do not lose heart. Just let the signposts steer you deeper and deeper into the slumbering vales and rounded hills of England's soft underbelly, to quiet villages roofed with thatch, smothered in roses, built of stone like chiselled honey. Wherever you go, the past is everywhere, just under the skin of the land, visible as ripples in the turf, on Pilsdon Pen and Abbotsbury Castle, in the terraced lynchets around Uploders and in the lonely downland barrows where the Bronze Age chieftains sleep.

Rare, too, is the west Dorset village without a decent pub. In Powerstock I lived next door to the Three Horseshoes, and after a hard day's gardening I could sit in the pub's back garden under an apple tree, with a pint of local bitter (Palmers of Bridport – the only thatched brewery in Britain), and watch the sun go down over the valley. But if I really want to celebrate I'll call Arthur Watson, who owns the Riverside Restaurant in West Bay. When I first met Arthur 40 years ago he was grilling mackerel over a driftwood fire at a midnight party on Chesil Beach. Today, with Jan, his wife, he is still cooking fish, but nowadays with a style and flair that places him second only to Rick Stein.

It was West Bay that gave me my first glimpse of the Dorset coast and it was definitely a case of love at first sight. Who could resist the spectacle of those teetering yellow-sandstone cliffs overhanging the easternmost end of Chesil Beach? Or the westward view across Lyme Bay, with Golden Cap looming over the giant landslips of Black Ven and Cain's Folly?

Of all Britain's shorelines, few fling up so many surprises in so short a space. From end to end the Dorset coast is barely 130km long, yet it changes constantly: one minute a glowing curve of shingle, the next a chaos of fallen cliffs smothered with horsetails and marsh orchids. This is England's Jurassic Park, its crumbling strata stuffed full of fossils. There are ammonites the size of car tyres and the exotic remains of paddle-footed plesiosaurs and sharp-toothed ichthyosaurs, their bones returned to the sunlight after more than 150 million years. No wonder it is now a World Heritage Site, in the same league as the Grand Canyon and the Pyramids.

And even at the peak of the holiday season you can still avoid the crowds. Last year I followed a stretch of the South West Peninsula Coast Path, along Chesil Beach from West Bexington to Abbotsbury. It was high summer, with the sea-light shimmering above the hot stones, but the only sounds were the cries of terns and the rush of waves breaking on the shore.

On the eastern horizon, blue with distance, the long, bony silhouette of the Isle of Portland slides into the sea like a corpse being committed to the deep. Portland is a weird place, pitted with quarries whose incomparable limestone was shipped off to build half of London. By no stretch of the imagination can I squeeze Portland into West Dorset, but I do love to go there when the spring and autumn bird migrations are in full swing, or on a wild day when a force eight is blowing and the Race – one of the most vicious rip tides in Europe – is streaming off the end of the Bill.

But my Dorset was never just a brief summer affair. To love a place truly you must live there and know it in all its seasons. When summer is over and the last swallows have gone, you must find pleasure in damp days full of falling leaves, when the hills vanish behind grey walls of drizzle and the entire county is left as sodden as an unsqueezed sponge. This is the time for an autumn pilgrimage to Lewesdon Hill, where the beechwoods seem to glow as if lit from within, or a long walk through the roadless valleys around Loscombe and Poorton, where buzzards sail over the dying bracken and there is nothing to tell you what century you are in.

Then comes winter, when the hoar frost lingers all day under my garden hedge and foxes scream in the dead of night as if crucified by cold. In many ways it is the best time of all, a connoisseur's season of muted colours, when all Dorset becomes a watercolour wash of ghostly woods and bare horizons. The days may be short but I revel in winter walks among the leafless oaks of Powerstock Common, and the teatime ritual of drawing the curtains and lighting a fire in the inglenook. And even then, once Christmas has passed and the fieldfares have stolen the last of the holly berries, there is the sure knowledge that already, down here in England's Deep South, spring is stirring.

Soon the banks of the little Mangerton Stream at the bottom of my garden will be graced by drifts of snowdrops. Their longed-for appearance is another good reason for wanting to live in Dorset. Ours has been an age of unprecedented destruction. So much of Britain is now a wasteland, wrecked and polluted beyond recall, its farmlands emptied of wild plants and creatures, its landscapes sliced up by motorways into pockets of countryside too small to retain their former sense of distance and mystery. But somehow Dorset has fared better than anywhere else I know, and West Dorset in particular still reminds me of the vanished countryside of my childhood half a century ago. The snowdrops are part of it.

They have survived here, along with all the other wild plants and creatures that bring the West Dorset countryside to life. There are more butterflies here than in any other county – from the humble ringlet to scarcer species such as the small pearl-bordered fritillaries that frequent the riverside meadows of the Lower Kingcombe Nature Reserve.

If you are mad about wildlife, as I am, you would not wish to live anywhere else. I share my garden with great spotted woodpeckers and noctule bats. There are grass snakes in the compost heap and swallows in the carport. Badgers dig up my lawn every night and foxes are everywhere. Deer – roe, fallow and sika – all live within a kilometre or two of my home. Dormice – now also absent from much of England – nest in the unshorn hazels. Even the otter is making a comeback.

But the biggest thrill in wildlife terms has been the return of the peregrine falcon. For years they were absent from the Dorset coast, wiped out by pesticides in the 1950s. Even in the 1980s, if I wanted to watch these fabulous falcons, I had to go to Cornwall. Then, just over a decade ago, they returned to reclaim their ancestral eyries one by one, from Golden Cap to the Purbeck cliffs. A peregrine aloft is like no other bird. It carries with it a constant aura of imminent drama, and so long as it remains in the sky it possesses this extraordinary power to dominate the horizons and add another dimension to the lands it inhabits. For me there is no finer sight in nature than a peregrine cleaving the air at upwards of 300kph, and the fact that I can now watch them within a few kilometres of home is the icing on the cake.